SAIS
PAPERS

International Mediation in Theory and Practice

WESTVIEW PRESS / FOREIGN POLICY INSTITUTE
SCHOOL OF ADVANCED INTERNATIONAL STUDIES
THE JOHNS HOPKINS UNIVERSITY

SAIS PAPERS
IN INTERNATIONAL AFFAIRS

NUMBER 6

International Mediation in Theory and Practice

Saadia Touval and I. William Zartman
editors

Conflict Management Studies
SAIS

WESTVIEW PRESS / BOULDER AND LONDON
WITH THE FOREIGN POLICY INSTITUTE
SCHOOL OF ADVANCED INTERNATIONAL STUDIES
THE JOHNS HOPKINS UNIVERSITY

A Westview Press / Foreign Policy Institute Edition

Copyright © 1985 by The Johns Hopkins Foreign Policy Institute, School of Advanced International Studies (SAIS)

Published in 1985 in the United States of America by Westview Press, Inc., 5500 Central Avenue, Boulder, Colorado 80301; Frederick A. Praeger, Publisher

Library of Congress Catalog Card Number: 84-52675
ISBN: 0-8133-7008-6

Composition for this book was provided by The Work Place, Inc., Washington, D.C., for The School of Advanced International Studies (SAIS).

Printed and bound in the United States of America

10   9   8   7   6   5   4   3   2   1

The Johns Hopkins Foreign Policy Institute (FPI) was founded in 1980 and serves as the research center for the School of Advanced International Studies (SAIS) in Washington, D.C. The FPI is a meeting place for SAIS faculty members and students, as well as for government analysts, policymakers, diplomats, journalists, business leaders, and other specialists in international affairs. In addition to conducting research on various policy-related international issues, the FPI sponsors conferences, seminars, and roundtables.

The FPI's research activities are often carried on in conjunction with SAIS's regional and functional programs dealing with American foreign policy, Latin America and the Caribbean Basin, Africa, the Middle East, the Soviet Union, U.S.-Japan relations, Canada, security studies, international energy, the Far East, Europe, and international economics.

FPI publications include the *SAIS Review*, a biannual journal of foreign affairs, which is edited by SAIS students, and SAIS Papers in International Affairs, a monograph series which is copublished with Westview Press in Boulder, Colorado. For additional information regarding FPI publications, write to: Managing Editor, FPI Publications Program, School of Advanced International Studies, The Johns Hopkins University, 1740 Massachusetts Avenue, N.W. Washington, D.C. 20036.

About the Book

INTERNATIONAL MEDIATION
IN THEORY AND PRACTICE

edited by **Saadia Touval,** Tel Aviv University, and
I. William Zartman, School of Advanced International Studies (SAIS),
The Johns Hopkins University

Mediation is now almost as common as conflict in international politics, with third parties becoming increasingly reluctant to allow disputes to escalate. Bringing together the perspectives and experiences of both practitioners and scholars of mediation, this volume examines several instances of successful international mediation. By focusing on the interests and motives of all parties—disputants and mediators—it serves to illuminate how the mediation process works. This approach, in addition to providing a rich empirical base, facilitates comparative analysis and permits a more confident formulation of theoretical propositions.

CONTENTS

FOREWORD

In the midst of recurring debates over the effectiveness
and timing of U.S. mediations in a number of conflicts
throughout the world, this collection of essays constitutes a unique look at the theory and practice of international mediation. After having placed this question
within its larger theoretical framework, the editors of
this volume present several case studies with which to
evaluate the performance of nation-states and international organizations in their attempts to resolve various
conflicts. Editors and authors all assess the effectiveness of these efforts and make recommendations for the
improvement of international mediation by third parties.
        The Johns Hopkins Foreign Policy Institute of the
School of Advanced International Studies is especially
pleased to present this volume in the belief that international mediation is a vital topic that deserves and
requires further study and public debate. It is hoped
that this book will at least pave the way for additional
studies of third-party mediation--whether successful or
not--and that the principles and guidelines that shape
international mediation will come to be better understood
by the policymakers.
        Established in 1980, the Foreign Policy Institute
(FPI) is an integral part of The Johns Hopkins University
School of Advanced International Studies (SAIS). The FPI
is a research institution with a difference, thriving on
argument and reason, inquiry and scholarship. It is non-
partisan, nonideological, and free from control by any
outside sponsor. Besides its SAIS Papers series, which is
copublished with Westview Press, the FPI sponsors the
publication of the SAIS Review, the much acclaimed
student-edited journal of foreign affairs.

                                Simon Serfaty
                                Executive Director

                        ix

PREFACE

Mediation is as common in international politics as conflict inasmuch as third parties are increasingly unwilling to let conflicts continue unabated. Yet, while a considerable body of scholarship concerning conflicts has accumulated over the years, our understanding of mediation is much less advanced. Some valuable literature on international mediation does exist, contributed by both scholars and practitioners, but in view of the frequency of mediation, and its value to many actors, we ought to know more about it.

This book aims to contribute to our understanding of mediation in two ways. First, through the examination of several cases we can increase our knowledge about specific instances of conflict, about the interests and motives of the actors involved, and about the mediation processes that took place. Second, we hope that the book will also contribute to our ability to formulate better generalizations and theories on mediation. Previous studies have led to the formulation of numerous statements about the roles of mediators in negotiations, their contributions, and the factors that affect the outcome of their endeavors. These encompass the mediators' motives and interests, their qualities and resources, their tactics, the circumstances and timing for propitious intervention, and the issues in conflict and specific goals of the mediation effort. But these insights can be sharpened and made more useful to practitioners. We also assume that beyond their specific contributions to the negotiating process, mediators affect negotiations by the very fact of intervention, a fact that alters the structure of the conflict. This process has never been adequately analyzed. Finally, the mediators' involvement affects the stability

1

of the outcome of negotiations, and sets the stage for future evolution of relations among all participants. This also needs further analysis.

Our theoretical propositions can be reexamined in the light of the assembled cases, which will enable us to refine or revise hypotheses on the basis of data from a variety of political contexts. The cases were chosen to include major instances of international diplomatic mediation in recent times, as well as some of the international organizations that regularly play this role. The actors involved differed in their capabilities, their decision-making structures and processes, cultures, ideological orientations, and other characteristics. Moreover, in different cases different combinations of actors were involved. There is also much variety in the issues and circumstances of the mediations, although in all of the cases the issues included the cessation of hostilities. In most cases territorial self-determination through independence or changes in borders was at stake. In four cases one or more superpowers mediated between medium-sized states; in two others, a medium-sized state mediated conflicts between other middle-sized states or between a medium and a superpower; in several institutional cases both the mediator and the parties involved possessed similar capabilities. Actors included international organizations and nationalist anticolonial movements as well as states. In some cases there was a single mediator; in others, collective mediation was performed by a committee of states or an international body—an international political organization or a nongovernmental humanitarian organization. Some of the mediations were between states that are culturally and ideologically in sympathy with one another, while others were between actors that are culturally different and ideologically incompatible. This varied empirical basis provides an opportunity for comparative analysis, and should enable us to suggest generalizations and theoretical propositions with greater confidence.

There are many other instances of mediation which might have been included. Some have been exhaustively examined elsewhere. The most important of these—involving Israel and its Arab neighbors—is the subject of a full-length analysis by one of us, and of a collective analysis in which the other is involved. An unusual case of private mediation in the southern Sudan has been analyzed by Wai; a most insightful firsthand account of a form of domestic mediation was written by Cuomo; and the Trieste mediation has been portrayed in a collection of firsthand accounts by Campbell. For the present analysis, it seemed preferable to present some new material, inviting wherever possible a contribution by a participant in the mediation who could present firsthand insights.

A number of mediations were in full swing as the book was being prepared and therefore could not yet be given careful and informed scrutiny. The Falklands dispute, the Habib mediations in the Israeli invasion of Lebanon and in the subsequent treaty, and the various attempts to mediate settlements in the Soviet invasion of Afghanistan and in the Iraqi invasion of Iran all await their future accounts. We hope that the present analyses will provide groundwork for these studies to come. Finally, we had hoped that the present volume would include a chapter on the Cyprus mediation, an important case that has received no sound analysis. Unfortunately, our hope was not realized.

Still other cases of unsuccessful mediation might have been included. There is indeed something to be learned from failure, particularly when compared to similar but successful cases where the elements of similarity can be accurately identified. On the other hand, it is difficult to establish definitively that in cases where conflict has continued unabated, a failure in mediation is to blame. The Namibian case is included, however, both as a representative of failure (to date) and as an important event that has dominated policy in the region.

We are grateful to several sources of support for this project. The Johns Hopkins School of Advanced International Studies (SAIS) provided assistance from diverse sources: The Johns Hopkins Foreign Policy Institute, which provided assistance, conference facilities, and the opportunity to publish this book as a part of its SAIS Papers series; the Middle East Studies Program provided support for Professor Touval during his sabbatical; and the conflict management studies section of the International Relations Program provided Professor Zartman with research facilities. Tel Aviv University provided support for Professor Touval's sabbatical in Washington to work on the project.Special support for the preparation and completion of this project was given by the Charles F. Kettering Foundation, for which special appreciation is acknowledged, with thanks to Phillips Ruopp; Kettering support made possible a most useful conference on June 28 29, 1982, at which drafts were discussed. Special thanks are also due to Kristen E. Carpenter, managing editor of the SAIS Papers, whose patient and expert supervision of editorial production immeasurably improved this study. And Mary-Jane Deeb, a Ph.D. candidate in social change and development at SAIS, miraculously produced the index for this book in very short order. The following individuals, in addition to the authors, attended the conference and contributed to our understanding of the subject: Davis Bobrow, University of Maryland; Landrum Bolling, Georgetown University Institute for the Study of Diplomacy; Ambassador Ellsworth Bunker, Department of State; Yassin El-Ayouty, United Nations Secretariat;

Dean Pruitt, State University of New York; Phillips Ruopp, Kettering Foundation; Jeffrey Rubin, Tufts University; Allan Silberman, American Arbitration Association; and Peter Rodman, Georgetown University Center for Strategic and International Studies (CSIS).

Notes

1.   Saadia Touval, The Peace Brokers: Mediators in the
Arab-Israeli Conflict, 1948-1979 (Princeton: Princeton University
Press, 1982); Jeffrey Rubin, ed., Dynamics of Third-Party
Mediation: Kissinger in the Middle East (New York: Praeger, 1981).
See also John E. Mroz, Influence in Conflict: The Impact of Third
Parties on the Arab-Israeli Dispute Since 1973 (Boston: Pergamon,
1983).

2.   Dunstan Wai, The African-Arab Conflict in the Sudan
(New York: Africana, 1981).

3.   Mario Cuomo, Forest Hills Diary (New York: Vintage,
1974).

4.   John C. Campbell, ed., Successful Negotiation:
Trieste 1954 (Princeton: Princeton University Press, 1976).

INTRODUCTION: MEDIATION IN THEORY

Saadia Touval and I. William Zartman

Mediation is a form of third-party intervention in conflict for the purpose of abating or resolving that conflict through negotiation. In common with other forms of peacemaking or conflict resolution, it is an intervention that must be acceptable to the adversaries in the conflict, who cooperate diplomatically with the intervenor. Peacemaking differs from certain other forms of third-party interventions in that it does not involve the use of force and is not intended to help one of the participants win or prevail. Mediation in turn is distinguished from other forms of peacemaking by the functions the mediator performs. In addition to helping adversaries communicate (providing "good offices") and endeavoring to change their images of each other (conciliation), mediators often suggest compromises and may negotiate and bargain with adversaries in an attempt to induce them to change their stance. Mediation is distinct from arbitration, which involves judicial procedure and results in a verdict the parties have committed themselves to accept. Mediation, on the other hand, is basically a political process; there is no

I. William Zartman is professor of international politics and director of African studies at SAIS, Johns Hopkins. He is author and coauthor of a number of books and articles on mediation and negotiation. The latest, Ripe for Resolution (New York: Oxford University Press), is forthcoming.

Saadia Touval is professor of political science at Tel Aviv University. He is an Africanist and has written several articles on territorial and boundary issues as they relate to the Arab-Israeli conflict. He was Visiting Scholar in African studies at SAIS from 1982 to 1983.

advance commitment by the parties to accept the mediator's ideas.

The Motives of Mediators and Parties

Mediators aim at reducing or resolving conflict between adversaries. This peacemaking goal legitimates their intervention and may not appear to require much elaboration. However, peacemaking is often intertwined with less generous motives inspired by self-interest. These can best be described within the context of power politics.

It would be rare for governments to engage in mediation for humanitarian reasons only. In fact, in view of the considerable investment of political, moral, and material resources that mediation requires, and the risks to which mediators expose themselves, it is reasonable to assume that mediators are no less motivated by self-interest than by humanitarian impulses. To some extent, then, the mediator is a player in the plot of relations surrounding a conflict, and has some interest in the outcome (or else it would not mediate). A parallel statement can be made about the parties to the conflict. It is unlikely that they invite or accept mediation because they are interested only in peace; they probably expect the mediator's intervention to work in their favor.

From the mediator's point of view, there appear to be two kinds of interest that can be promoted through mediation. One, essentially defensive, occurs when a conflict between two actors threatens the mediator's interests. Resolving a conflict in such a case may be important to the mediator because of the conflict's effects on its relations with the parties. For example, conflict between two of the mediator's allies may weaken the alliance. Or a conflict between two states may upset a regional balance or provide opportunities for a rival power to increase its influence by intervening in the conflict. In such situations, third parties often seek to limit damage to themselves by promoting a settlement. If they see risks in direct mediation, they may appeal to an international organization or another party. Leaving the mediation to others is not without risks, however. One may lose the ability to influence developments or control events. Or, the mediation may be ineffective, particularly if carried out by an international organization. Even worse, mediation by an international organization may provide an opportunity for, or legitimate the involvement of, one's rivals. Such considerations often appear to justify direct mediation of the conflict. The interests invoked above are essentially defensive ones; mediation is used in such cases to protect the mediator's interests.

A second self-interested motive for mediation may be the desire to extend and increase one's influence. Solution of the conflict may have no direct importance to the mediator, but is only a vehicle for an interest in developing closer relations with the parties. A third party may hope to win the gratitude of one party by helping it reach somewhat better terms than it could obtain otherwise. To be sure, the mediator cannot throw its full weight behind one party without compromising its status as a mediator; the other side would withdraw its acceptance of the mediator's diplomatic intervention and cease to cooperate. Within limits, however, a mediating party may succeed in increasing its influence with one side in a conflict, particularly if its relations with the other side are closer at the outset of the mediation. The mediator may further increase its influence by making its involvement essential for any negotiations between the two adversaries, rendering each dependent upon the mediator whenever something is desired from the other. Mediators can also increase their influence by becoming guarantors for whatever agreement is reached.

It follows from the foregoing that a mediator will seldom be indifferent to the terms being negotiated. The mediator sometimes seeks peace in the abstract, but usually seeks to promote terms that are in accord with its own interests. Yet these interests usually allow for a wider range of acceptable outcomes than do the interests of the antagonists. The mediator may also have greater flexibility in bargaining through having incurred fewer commitments and invested less in the conflict than did the parties. Mediators are likely to seek terms that will increase the prospects of stability and deny their rivals opportunities for intervention. They may also wish to ensure that the terms of a settlement will enable them to continue "to have a say" in relations between the adversaries.

The political interests that may lead parties in conflict to seek or accept mediation are several. The most obvious is the expectation that a certain mediator will help one party gain a more favorable settlement than would otherwise be possible. Although the other party may have a similar assessment of consequences of the mediator's intervention, it may still agree to mediation if rejection would cause even greater harm, for example, by damaging relations with the would-be mediator. The parties may accept mediation in the hope that negotiation through an intermediary will help them reduce some of the risks that compromises entail, by protecting their image and reputation when making concessions. They may also believe that a mediator's involvement will constitute a guarantee for the eventual agreement, thus reducing the risk of violation by the adversary.

Invitation or acceptance of mediation may be related to additional power-political considerations. One or both parties may wish to gain time, or to be relieved of the dilemma of choosing between escalation and concessions. Or, one side may wish to engage the third party and enlist its support in the expectation that the negotiations will fail to produce an agreement. Another possibility (as in the case of Egypt's view of American mediation in the conflict with Israel) is that mediation will provide the occasion for improving relations with the mediator, while souring relations between the mediator and the adversary. Such power-related side effects may be an important motive for inviting or accepting mediation.

Within this context, the relationship between the mediator and the antagonistic parties is never devoid of tension. It is a relationship of continuous bargaining, and the mediator's conduct and its consequences are subject to constant scrutiny by both parties. The parties' acceptance of the mediator is not unconditional, but rather is qualified by tacitly understood conditions. These limit the respective bargaining power of the mediator and the parties.

Methods of Mediation

There are three principal methods by which mediators induce parties in conflict to agree to the concessions necessary for the reduction or resolution of the conflict. The same methods also contribute to the advancement of the mediators' self-interested goals.

One method proceeds from the very fact of the mediators' intervention in the conflict. Through the diplomatic intervention of mediation, the mediator transforms the bargaining structure from a dyad into a triangle. In a triangular relationship, the outcome of the contest may be determined by the formation of a coalition of two against one. It becomes the parties' interest to reconvert the triadic relationship back into a dyad by forming a subtle coalition with the mediator, bringing the latter in on one side without destroying its appearance of neutrality, and thereby effecting a solution that is both favorable and preferable to continued conflict. It becomes the mediator's interest to keep the parties locked in a mutual stalemate so that neither can prevail (or at least so that the one the mediator favors least cannot prevail). The parties therefore continue to look to the mediator for a way out of their joint deadlock. The triangular structure enhances the mediator's bargaining power vis-à-vis the parties because of its potential for joining one party in a coalition against the other. Although the mediator

is unlikely to do so, the possibility inevitably pro-
duces tensions between the mediator and each party. A
party may withdraw its cooperation with a mediator that
is not favorable to it by labeling the mediator a tool
or partner of the other party.

Consistent with the initial definition, if the
mediator is to mediate--that is, intervene to diminish
or resolve conflict--it must use the triangular structure to move the parties to agreement rather than creating a victory for one side. Paradoxically, this may
mean temporarily reinforcing one side to keep it in the
conflict, maintain the stalemate, and preserve the triangular relationship. Mediation as power politics means
maintenance of the mediator's role, not simply allowing
the parties to solve their own conflict by themselves;
but it also means maintenance of the parties' stalemate,
not simply allowing one party to end the conflict by
victory. A unilateral victory may not be stable because
the defeated party may seek to overthrow it at the first
occasion. It may not be fair because the defeated party
may have some important interests to be taken into
account. And it may also not be desirable from the
point of view of the mediator, which may wish to avoid
having one side emerge from a conflict with a clear and
decisive victory. Stalemate is necessary to mediation,
just as mediation is necessary to overcome stalemate.
To achieve that stalemate, the mediator must often reinforce the weaker party. This reinforcement can take the
form of tangible support during the conflict, or it can
be verbal, but it must not be unconditional. It needs
to be tied to movement toward agreement.

Another method by which mediators pursue their
dual objectives of peacemaking and protection of self-
interest is by serving as a channel of communication.
Conflict implies the breakdown of communications, so
that parties often become locked in a situation from
which they cannot extricate themselves simply because
they cannot contact each other directly. Concessions
may be required if a conflict is to be resolved, but
often these depend on the parties' ability to communicate their willingness to compromise without losing face
or appearing weak. Thus, the role of the mediator as
communicator takes a number of forms and comes into play
at various junctures in the course of discussions. The
mediator may be required to make the original contacts
and serve as a telephone wire where direct communications are broken. It may also be required to carry
proposals of concessions or word of the other's concession where conceding directly would be psychologically
or procedurally impossible. It may be required to act
as the holder of concessions or agreements where direct
agreement may be impossible. In this role, the mediator
is a passive conduit and repository. Tact, palatable

wording, and sympathetic presentation are as important as--but must not impinge on--accuracy and straightforward presentation.

A mediator may also perform a more active role. The breakdown of communications may not only impede the delivery of messages; it may also keep the parties from conceiving a solution to meet the needs of both sides. In such a situation, a formulator is needed, a third party that will be more capable of innovative thinking than the parties to the conflict. Redefining the issues in conflict, or finding a formula for its resolution or management is the key to its termination, with the parties frequently needing help in finding a solution hidden in the morass of bad relationships or in constructing a solution from the pieces of the conflict itself. The mediator as a formulator helps the two parties help themselves, by tactful, sympathetic, accurate, straightforward prodding and suggestion.

The roles of the mediator as communicator and formulator lie on a continuum ranging from passive facilitation to active formulation, often without a clear distinction between them. Yet it should be noted that both are facilitator's roles, made necessary by a breakdown in physical or psychic aspects of communication that prevents the parties from working together to find a solution to their common problem. The mediator in this role works on perceptions, doing nothing to change the nature of the problem or the circumstances of the conflict. This is "pure" mediation, in which the mediator has no interests at stake (except an interest in seeking a solution), and exercises no power (except the intangible exercise of the power to change people's minds).

In some situations, position and communication may not be enough to bring about reduction of conflict or the promotion of the mediator's self-interest. The mediator may have to use its position and other available resources to manipulate the parties into agreement, or perhaps into a particular agreement that appears to the mediator to be most stable or most favorable. The mediator as a manipulator requires leverage--resources of power, influence, and persuasion that can be brought to bear on the parties to move them to agreement. Leverage is the most elusive element of mediation: even where the need for a facilitator is glaringly apparent and the would-be mediator's interest in peace very clear, the mediator may have no ability to move the parties in the indicated direction. American mediators have complained repeatedly that the United States is unfairly charged with failure in situations in which the necessary leverage is simply not present. Yet leverage is the ticket to mediation--third parties are only accepted as mediators if they are likely to produce an agreement or help them out of a predicament, and they

can only help the parties or produce an agreement if
they have leverage.

There are many sources of leverage, beginning with
the two already discussed: the need of the parties for
help in getting out of a problem, and the position and
interest of the mediator and the parties in mediation.
One of the most important sources of leverage is found
in the ripe moment of intolerable stalemate weighing on
each party, threatening a worse outcome in the future
while offering no present way out of the deadlock. We
have seen that the mediator may even need to reinforce a
stalemate, using its own resources to add negative arguments and inducements to keep the parties from trying to
resolve the situation unilaterally. The stalemate must
be seen by both parties as unbreakable, except in the
direction of a bilateral agreement reached with the help
of the mediator. This is a tall order, which explains
why the mediator's job is so delicate.

The conceptual components of leverage are both
simple and subtle. They are carrots and sticks, used
either to make the present situation more unpleasant for
the conflicting parties (thus inducing them to come to
terms with each other under the aegis of the mediator)
or to make the future situation of mediated peace more
pleasant. Theoretically, the more ties the mediator has
with a party--the more disposable goods it possesses
that the parties value--the greater the possibility of
pressing the parties by suspending ties and withholding
value. This insight forms the basis for the effective
use of sticks (in reality, withheld carrots) in mediation. Unfortunately it is only part of the story. Suspended ties also mean reduced influence, since certain
elements of communication are thereby interrupted.
Moreover, sticks of any kind cause resentment, and the
party may decide that it can just as well do without
carrots in its diet. Finally, a too strenuous use of
sticks can cause a party to withdraw its acceptance of
mediation, and leave the mediator without a role.

The other basic tool of leverage is the carrot,
again theoretically sound when seen as the ability to
convey a future alternative that is preferable to the
present conflict. Carrots may be matters of perception,
produced by the mediator's ability to persuade the parties of a better outcome without conflict, or they may
be tangible additions to the terms of an agreement
between warring parties. But again there are obstacles.
To the perceptions, there is the limit of the mediator's
ability to convey convincingly or, in fact, to produce a
better outcome. Since the process of mediation is a
gradual one, the parties must be kept confident that
their concessions will produce counterconcessions from
the other side, in a process of moving toward an acceptable midpoint of agreement. Meanwhile, the mediator
dare not promise more than the other side can produce.

Its leverage over each party is limited by its leverage over the other. With regard to tangible inducements, there is a limit of the mediator's willingness to pay for peace in a situation where the conflict is basically not its own.

One problem that has not received as much attention as it merits is the mediator's dilemma of how to avoid eliciting concessions from one party simultaneously disinclining the other to concede. For example, assurances offered to one party by the mediator as an incentive for concessions might harden the adversary's attitude in its bargaining with the mediator. If one side's interest in a mediated settlement is the prospect that the process will strain relations between the mediator and the adversary, their rapprochement may diminish the first party's interest in an agreement.

Still another problem concerns the mediator's own compromise proposals. These may sometimes be acceptable to one party but not to the other. In such situations, the party to which the proposals were acceptable is likely to be unwilling thereafter to accept less than had been offered it by the mediator, and it will be difficult for the mediator to submit any new proposals to break the deadlock.

Requisites for Success

Scholars and practitioners alike have devoted much attention to the requisites for successful mediation. Since this subject has been treated at length elsewhere, we shall confine ourselves here to a summary of the discussion. In the concluding chapter we will have an opportunity to reexamine some of these requisites in the light of the case studies presented in this volume.

What constitutes successful mediation is of course debatable. If we took success to mean the final resolution of all conflict and the reconciliation of the parties, then there would be very few successful mediations. An alternative test of success might be a contribution toward a formal agreement promising the reduction of conflict. However, apart from the difficulty of assessing the mediator's contribution to a temporary reduction in conflict or gauging its responsibility for renewed escalation within some arbitrarily defined period of time, we are inclined to adopt as a working definition of successful mediation the conclusion of an agreement promising the reduction of conflict.

Since one of the motives for mediation is the protection or advancement of the mediator's interests, a successful exercise will result in an agreement that accords with the mediator's interests. Its terms should not provide opportunities for rival powers to gain influence, but rather should enhance the mediator's own influence.

There is wide agreement that the personal qualities of individuals are relevant to the success of mediation. Intelligence, specific knowledge and expertise in the problems at hand, imagination, persuasiveness, perseverance, commitment, tact, and drafting skills are some of the qualities that contribute to success. However, these qualities and skills are largely identical to those that are believed to be required for successful careers in business and politics generally. At this stage, it remains uncertain whether any items on the list are more important for mediation than for other roles in politics and business. Uncertainty also exists concerning the relative weight to be assigned to such personal qualities and the particular situations in which personal qualities can make the difference between success and failure.

The rank of the mediator and of his interlocutors may also be of some consequence. A mid-level official negotiating with officials of similar rank may succeed only on issues of secondary or technical importance. The higher the rank of the mediator, the more influential he is likely to be. Presumably, a high-level mediator is better able to commit his country (or organization) and its resources to the mediation effort, and will therefore be more persuasive than a mid-level official whose ability to affect such a commitment is uncertain.

Another major point in the debate over the qualities required for successful mediation is the question of impartiality, discussed by one of us in detail elsewhere. The main thrust of that discussion is that impartiality is not necessary for successful mediation. This is borne out by the success of mediators perceived to have been close to or allied with one of the parties. Witness American mediation in the Arab-Israeli conflict, Anglo-American mediation between Italy and Yugoslavia on the Trieste issue, Soviet mediation between India and Pakistan at Tashkent, and Algerian mediation between Iran and the United States on the American hostages held in Iran. As has been shown elsewhere, the acceptability of a mediator to the adversaries in a conflict is not determined by their perceptions of the mediator's general attitude and relationship with each of them. More important are considerations of the possible consequences of acceptance or rejection on the ultimate terms of an agreement and on relations with the would-be mediator. Additional side effects, both domestic and international, must also be taken into account. Neither is impartiality a necessary condition for helping adversaries to communicate. Governments generally do not lend absolute credibility to mediators (or to any other

sources or channels). Instead, information received is
interpreted in light of the assumed motives and interests of the source or the channel, and in terms of its
usefulness in furthering the recipient's own goals.

Numerous writers have commented on the importance
of the proper moment for mediation in conflict. While
some have defined the right time with reference to the
duration of the conflict, and some with reference to its
"life cycle," others have defined it with reference to
the changing fortunes and expectations of the adversaries. It seems to us that a mediator's intervention is
most propitious when a "hurting stalemate" develops.
This is a situation that is very uncomfortable to both
sides, and that appears likely to become very costly.
Such situations tend to induce policy changes, either
toward a greater investment of resources and an escalation of hostilities in the hope of tilting the scales in
one's favor, or toward deescalation and concession. A
mediator's intervention at such a moment can influence
the decision toward deescalation, concession, and compromise. Moreover, because the mediator is constrained
by his role not to exert harsh pressure on the adversaries, the pressure of circumstances can be turned to
the mediator's favor. Finally, as Frank Edmead has
pointed out, a relatively small investment of the mediator's own resources may be perceived in such situations
as an important and significant inducement to the parties to change their policies, while the same resources
offered when the parties are in a comfortable position
may not have much effect. In all respects, maintenance
of a triangular structure is often the key to success in
efforts to reduce conflict. When additional parties
intervene in support of one side or the other, it
becomes difficult for the mediator to persuade the
adversaries to make concessions or agree to compromise,
since the presence of other parties tends to stimulate
hopes that a better outcome is obtainable.

Three methods have been set forth as the inter-
changeable tools of a mediator's trade. Communication,
formulation, and manipulation are all involved in some
degree in any mediation, but their importance varies
according to the needs of the particular case. Knowing
which to emphasize is the key to mediation and the over-
arching requisite for success.

Mediation in Theory: Notes

1.   There is no single theory of mediation. However, the theoretically inclined reader may find the following of interest: Frank Edmead, "Analysis and Prediction in International Mediation," in K. Venkata Raman, ed., Dispute Settlement Through the United Nations (Dobbs Ferry, N.Y.: Oceana Publications, 1977), 247–59; Roger Fisher and William Wry, International Mediation: A Working Guide (New York: International Peace Academy, 1978); David P. Forsythe, United Nations Peacemaking: The Conciliation Commission for Palestine (Baltimore: The Johns Hopkins Press, 1972), 156–65; Elmore Jackson, Meeting of Minds (New York: McGraw-Hill, 1952); P. H. Gulliver, Disputes and Negotiations (New York: Academic Press, 1979), chap. 7; Jerome E. Podell and William M. Knapp, "The Effects of Mediation on the Perceived Firmness of the Opponent," Journal of Conflict Resolution 13 (1969): 511–20; Dean Pruitt, Negotiation Behavior (New York: Academic Press, 1981), chap. 7; K. Venkata Raman, The Ways of the Peacemaker (New York: UNITAR, 1975); Howard Raiffa, The Art and Science of Negotiation (Cambridge: Harvard University Press, 1982), chap. 15 et passim; Saadia Touval, The Peace Brokers: Mediations in the Arab-Israeli Conflict, 1948–1979 (Princeton: Princeton University Press, 1982), 3–19, 321–31; Oran R. Young, The Intermediaries (Princeton: Princeton University Press, 1967); Oran R. Young, "Intermediaries: Additional Thoughts on Third Parties," Journal of Conflict Resolution 16 (1972): 55–63; Touval, "Biased Intermediaries: Theoretical and Historical Considerations," Jerusalem Journal of International Relations 1(1975): 51–69; Jeffrey Z. Rubin, ed., Dynamics of Third Party Intervention (New York: Praeger, 1981), chap. 1.

PART I

Mediation in Practice: States

1.
THE PARTIAL NEGOTIATOR: ALGERIA AND THE U.S. HOSTAGES IN IRAN

Gary Sick

The taking of the American hostages in Iran, the prolonged confrontation between Iran and the United States that it provided, and the release of the hostages at the very moment that a new president was being inaugurated in Washington is a story so replete with improbability that it must be taken as fresh evidence that truth is stranger than fiction. The event held millions of Americans glued to their television screens for 444 days. However, the crisis also raised disturbing questions of international law, dramatized the difficulties of dealing with a revolutionary regime professing a radical Islamic ideology, and transformed the political the political and strategic relationships between the United States and the nations of the Persian Gulf.[1]

The Nature of the Conflict

The storming of the U.S. embassy in Tehran was an act of political theater intended to influence the internal struggle for control of the Iranian revolution, a struggle that vastly complicated all efforts to bring the crisis to an end. In the United States, the crisis became the backdrop to a national election and ultimately contributed to the unseating of a president. Although the participants in the drama were well aware

Gary Sick is the foreign policy program officer for the international affairs program of the Ford Foundation. He served as a National Security Council staff member for Iran under the Carter administration.

of the domestic constraints and pressures on themselves and their adversaries, neither side was ever able fully to transcend those domestic realities--even when it would have been in their own best interests to have done so.

The Iranian revolutionary leaders considered the central purpose of their political movement to be a rejection of the West generally and the United States in particular. Not only was the United States seen as the source of Iran's economic and political woes, it was portrayed as the ultimate corruptor of Iranian spiritual values--the "Great Satan." Whatever psychological appeal and political utility this slogan may have had, it meant that the Iranian leadership was effectively prevented from dealing directly with the United States, even after those in command in Tehran had concluded it was to Iran's advantage to bring the crisis to an end. As a consequence, a resolution of the dispute could be accomplished only through mediation--the positioning of a third party between the adversaries.

This essential fact was apparent to President Carter and his key advisors from the first days of the crisis. The very first U.S. initiative after the embassy seizure was to propose that two intermediaries--distinguished American citizens who had been openly sympathetic to the revolution and critical of the shah's regime--travel to Iran to discuss the release of the hostages with the Ayatollah Khomeini. The subsequent list of intermediaries included the secretary-general of the United Nations, the leaders of the Palestine Liberation Organization, religious leaders of several faiths, the heads of state and senior officials of a number of Islamic nations, numerous private individuals (often self-appointed), and the unlikely combination of Christian Bourguet, a French lawyer of the Left, and Hector Villalon, a Argentine businessman of uncertain reputation. Perhaps the only characteristic shared by all of these individuals was their inability to find a common basis for a settlement.

This account will not dwell on failures, instructive as they may be, but instead will relate the events of the final act of the drama in which the hostages finally found safe release through the mediation efforts of the government of Algeria. The story will be told from the perspective of one who observed the crisis from within the government in Washington. This account therefore enjoys the benefit of familiarity with facts and events that were not part of the public record; however, it is subject to the same limitations that apply to any participant--uncertainty about the private strategies and motivations of third parties or adversaries, and the natural tendency to interpret events from one's own perspective. Specifically, it should be emphasized that interpretations of the behavior patterns of the Iranian revolutionaries as well as of the Algerian mediation team are those of the author. In the absence of authoritative accounts by participants in Tehran and Algiers, some measure of speculation cannot be avoided.

Prologue: November 1979-September 1980

The basic facts leading up to the final negotiations between Iran and the United States through the mediation of Algeria are well known and will be sketched here only in the briefest outline.   On November 4, 1979, the American embassy in Tehran was overrun by a group of Islamic revolutionaries, and most of those present in the embassy were taken hostage. Within a day the nine-month-old revolutionary government of the Ayatollah Ruhollah Khomeini had thrown its support to the student revolutionaries, thus transforming the crisis from an isolated terrorist act into an international crisis.

The United States responded in the days that followed by imposing economic sanctions on Iran.   All Iranian assets within the reach of the U.S. government were frozen, including deposits in foreign branches of U.S. banks.   The United States also launched a diplomatic campaign against Iran in every possible international forum, seeking to bring pressure on the revolutionary leadership to release the hostages.   Suit was brought in the World Court, resulting in a preliminary judgment ordering the release of the hostages and, subsequently, a formal decision against Iran.   In late December the U.N. Security Council ordered Iran to release the hostages or face imposition of sanctions under Chapter VII of the U.N. Charter.   Iran rejected all of these pressures out of hand, while the Soviet Union vetoed the Security Council resolution in the wake of its own invasion of Iran's neighbor, Afghanistan, on December 27.

In January 1980 the United States undertook a negotiated settlement through two private intermediaries who had close relations with the newly elected president of Iran and his foreign minister. When these efforts broke down in March, President Carter imposed additional sanctions and ordered a military rescue mission.

The rescue mission failed before arriving at its objective, ending in a fiery accident at a secret desert site in which eight American military men were killed and a number of others injured.   Secretary of State Cyrus Vance resigned in protest against the decision to undertake the rescue mission, and he was replaced by former senator Edmund Muskie.

Following the failure of the rescue mission, the situation settled into a stalemate through the summer of 1980. Ayatollah Khomeini, in rejecting earlier negotiating efforts, had declared that only the Iranian Majlis (parliament) could decide the issue. The new Majlis was finally elected in May, but internal battles prevented installation of a government until early September. In the meantime, the former shah of Iran died in Cairo in late July of complications associated with cancer. The shah's entry into the United States had provided the original pretext for the attack on the embassy, and his death removed a key obstacle to a possible settlement.

On September 10, 1980, executive powers in Iran were transferred from the Revolutionary Council (the interim ruling body appointed by Khomeini) to the new government of Prime Minister Rajai. On the same day, a man known to be close to Khomeini (and related to him by marriage) contacted the German ambassador in Tehran. Sadeq Tabatabai indicated that he had met in recent days with Ahmed Khomeini, the Ayatollah's son, and Hashemi Rafsanjani, a senior cleric and Speaker of the Majlis. On the basis of their discussions, he asserted that the revolutionary government of Iran was prepared to negotiate the release of the American hostages. He asked the German ambassador to contact Washington and relay Iran's willingness to terminate the hostage crisis on the basis of three conditions: (1) the unfreezing of Iranian assets and their transfer out of the United States; (2) a binding commitment of no U.S. military or political intervention in Iranian affairs; and (3) return to Iran of the assets of the former shah and his family, or at least a U.S. commitment to that objective through court action.

In the message, Tabatabai insisted that the issue should be resolved before the first anniversary of the hostage taking, that is, November 4, 1980. This was relayed to President Carter the same day, and he directed Deputy Secretary of State Warren Christopher to meet with Tabatabai in Germany.

This was the first approach to the U.S. government from anyone within Khomeini's inner circle since the beginning of the crisis some ten months earlier. Consequently, on the American side, there was genuine concern that the approach might be a false one. Past experience provided reason to doubt that it represented Khomeini's own thinking, particularly since the Iranian demands made no mention of an apology.

Many of those concerns were laid to rest two days later. In a speech to a group of Iranian pilgrims on September 12, Khomeini delivered an unusually long, rambling speech on Islam, international affairs, and the meaning of the revolution. At the very end, in a passage that had obviously been spliced onto the body of the speech, Khomeini abruptly turned to the question of the hostage-taking and announced that "on the return of the deposed Shah's wealth and the cancellation of all the U.S. claims against Iran, a guarantee of no U.S. military and political interventions in Iran and the freeing of all our investments, the hostages will be set free."

Although the text of the speech was read over the radio by an announcer rather than by Khomeini himself, its rhetoric was unmistakably that of the Ayatollah, and not of something written by his "office." The points inserted into the speech were very similar to those that had been delivered to Washington two days earlier through the German embassy, although the speech added a fourth condition--the cancelation of all U.S. claims against Iran. There was no longer reason to doubt that this was a serious proposal, delivered with Khomeini's knowledge and acquiescence.

The next several days were spent assembling a negotiating package that Deputy Secretary Christopher could take with him to Germany. It was recognized that the "closing" of a deal in which large sums of cash or other goods were exchanged for hostages would pose some complicated and potentially very delicate questions. A number of different options were examined, including the use of third parties to hold goods and to certify the hostages' release.

Third-party Candidates

In the initial planning it was anticipated that the neutral role would be played by the Swiss, who represented U.S. interests in Iran. However, one scenario proposed that the hostages be landed temporarily in a neutral third country and held there until Iran certified that it had received its frozen assets. The country suggested in that plan was Algeria.

Algeria had played a special role during the crisis in several respects. Algeria had been chosen by Iran to represent its interests in Washington when relations were broken in April 1980. The Algerian embassy, under the direction of Ambassador Redha Malek, performed this contentious role with great skill. The U.S. ambassador in Algiers, Ulric Haynes, Jr., had established an excellent working relationship with Algerian officials and was instrumental in arranging for the archbishop of Algiers to visit the hostages inside the embassy in Tehran during the previous Christmas holidays. The Algerian ambassador in Tehran,

Abdelkarim Gharaib, was acknowledged to be one of the best-informed observers of the political scene in Tehran and one of the few ambassadors who had access to many of the key revolutionary figures. He had been among the first group of ambassadors to visit the hostages, and had continued to follow the issue closely but discreetly.

Relations between Algeria and the United States were not close, but Algeria had left the impression on several occasions that it was prepared to be helpful on a quiet basis if that assistance did not threaten its relations with Iran. Among the third countries that might be acceptable to Iran as an intermediate stopping point for the hostages, Algeria was the obvious first choice.

Act I: September-October 1980

After reviewing the negotiating package with President Carter, Deputy Secretary of State Warren Christopher departed for Germany. He met secretly in Bonn with Iranian Minister of State Sadeq Tabatabai on September 16 and 18, 1980, in the presence of German Foreign Minister Hans-Dietrich Genscher. In these meetings, Christopher outlined a U.S. response to the Iranian requests. It was phrased in a positive manner but it also served to educate Tabatabai about some of the technical difficulties that might be expected in a negotiated settlement.

Christopher outlined for Tabatabai the various types and locations of Iranian assets, noting that upon release of the hostages some would be available immediately (for example, the gold and letters of credit on deposit with the Federal Reserve Bank) or after only a short delay (for example, deposits in foreign branches of U.S. banks). Together, these two categories comprised some $5.5 billion. It was proposed that these funds be placed in escrow with a third party (possibly the German Bundesbank) until certification was received that the hostages had been released.

A third category was the assets on deposit in banks in the United States. All of these deposits had been placed under court attachment by Americans who had claims against Iran. This amount, estimated at more than $2 billion, could not be freed immediately.

When Tabatabai alluded to the question of military spare parts, Christopher acknowledged that several million dollars worth of military spares that Iran had ordered and paid for were presently in storage in the United States. Christopher said that the inclusion of military equipment would complicate any agreement, but he did not exclude the possibility that this matériel might be made available to Iran if all other aspects of the dispute were resolved. Indeed, an "unfreezing" of Iranian assets would technically make such Iranian-owned equipment available. Nevertheless, normal munitions control and other restrictions governing the transfer of military equipment would continue to apply. A "sanitized" package of military equipment had been selected earlier by Christopher's team in Washington and approved by President Carter for use if essential. The list included only those items regarded as unclassified and nonsensitive spare parts.

On the issue of the shah's assets, Christopher outlined the steps that the United States government would be prepared to take to facilitate Iran's claims in U.S. courts. Christopher informed Tabatabai that it was the considered judgment of the U.S. Treasury that the value of any assets owned by the shah in the United States was much less than the Iranians apparently believed--indeed, probably less than the interest earned on the funds frozen by the United States. Consequently, he told Tabatabai, Iran should not anticipate locating and retrieving large quantities of money or property belonging to the shah. The magnitude of the shah's personal wealth was not known to the government, but almost certainly little of it was held in a form that could be identified or retrieved through the courts.

Other elements of the Iranian position were discussed at some length, with Christopher spelling out in each instance the degree to which the United States would be able--or unable--to respond. Valuable support was provided by German Foreign Minister Genscher, who, for example, assured the Iranian envoy that the U.S. position on the shah's wealth was reasonable and that it went further than would have been possible under German law.

Tabatabai listened carefully to the presentation without raising serious objections. After the second meeting, he informed Christopher that he intended to return to Iran on September 22 to meet with Khomeini and others. Following that meeting, a decision would be made about how to follow up on the initial discussions. A further meeting was anticipated near the end of the month. Both Genscher and Christopher indicated satisfaction with this schedule.

Ironically, on the very day Tabatabai was scheduled to return to Iran from Germany, the conflict that had been simmering along the border between Iran and Iraq broke out into full-scale hostilities. Iraqi aircraft bombed targets in Iran, and Iraqi military forces poured across the border into the oil-rich province of Khuzestan. With normal air traffic in and out of Iran suspended, Tabatabai remained in Germany, maintaining occasional telephone contact with Tehran.

Despite the war, the Majlis debated the hostage issue in late September and established a seven-man commission which was empowered to define the precise terms of Iran's demands on the United States. However, the committee was prohibited from having any direct contact with U.S. officials, and any agreement approved by the Majlis had to be consistent with Khomeini's original formulation. Despite this restrictive mandate, produced only after a raucous public session where members came close to blows, Tabatabai assured his German hosts that the scenario was proceeding on track. This message was reiterated on October 10 after Tabatabai had returned to Iran and met with all the top leadership.

At the same time, it became evident that the Iranian leaders were becoming increasingly concerned about the war with Iraq and the lack of military supplies and spare parts. Also on October 10, with Tabatabai in Tehran, the Iranians sent a message through the Germans requesting an inventory from the United States of all goods ordered from the United States under the shah but not yet delivered. Almost by definition, such a listing would include military equipment, since there was relatively little other matériel that had been held in storage in the United States, with the exception of a large quantity of oil and gas equipment that had been trapped when the embargo was imposed. An answer was prepared in Washington which held out the possibility of a sanitized but sizable package of spare parts (but not munitions) that Iran had previously ordered and paid for, to be made available if and when the hostages were released.

This issue of military supply and spare parts was never again mentioned by the Iranian side. The subject was never raised during the lengthy negotiations conducted through the Algerians.

Enter the Algerians

In mid-October Iranian Prime Minister Mohammed Ali Rajai paid a visit to the United Nations in New York to present Iran's case against Iraq as a result of the September invasion. His reception at the United Nations was exceptionally cool. Rajai, who had been a provincial school teacher and was generally regarded as a rather simple man with blind faith in Islam, Khomeini, and the revolution, was astonished to discover that his interlocutors at the United Nations were, almost without exception, much more interested in the hostage crisis than in Iran's plight in its war with Iraq. The tightly controlled press and radio in

Iran restricted its broadcasts and publications to
reports suggesting that most of the world understood
and sympathized with Iran's actions in the hostage
taking, and this visit (Rajai's first outside Iran) may
have been his first acquaintance with the considerable
hostility this act had aroused throughout the world.

On October 18 Rajai met in New York with several
Algerian officials who argued persuasively that termination of the hostage crisis would be in the best
interests of the revolution and Iran's national security. The Algerians had been contacted by the United
States in advance of this conversation, and it represented one of the earliest instances of direct Algerian
involvement in a quasi-intermediary role.   Rajai
stopped in Algiers on his return trip to Tehran, and
there were indications that the Algerians took advantage of this second opportunity to discuss the hostage
issue with the Iranian prime minister.

When Rajai returned to Tehran on October 22, he
took an uncharacteristically conciliatory line.   In
answer to questions, he said he was sure that the
United States was prepared to respond to the conditions
posed by Khomeini. He added that "the hostages are not
really a problem for us. We are in the process of
resolving [the crisis]. The nature of the hostage-
taking was important for us. We got the results long
ago." Significantly, he explicitly excluded military
equipment from any role in a settlement: "We do not
link the release of the hostages with spare parts," he
said.   It appeared that the Algerian discussions with
Rajai had made a considerable impression.

In the meantime, however, the Majlis delayed
taking up the report of the special commission on the
hostage issue. First, the Iranian legislature postponed the report, then began to debate it in open session, and finally moved into closed session to continue
the debate. On October 30 a key vote was prevented by
a number of die-hard members who disapproved the terms
offered by the commission. By their failure to appear
in the Majlis, they succeeded in preventing a quorum,
thus thwarting the majority in favor of a resolution.

The Iranian inability to come to terms with the
issue was given special poignancy by the fact that the
American election campaign was nearing its conclusion.
In the last week before the presidential election on
November 4, the media speculation about a last-minute
deal that could swing the election became almost hys-
terical. In fact, it was not until Sunday, November 2,
that the Majlis was finally able to take action. The
text of the commission report, which was approved on
that date, contained a number of elements that were
unacceptable or impossible for the U.S. side, including
a demand that all American court actions against
Iranian assets in the United States be voided by the

president. Although President Carter returned to the
White House from a campaign trip to review these
demands, it was quickly evident that the Iranian proposal had to be regarded as the basis for continued
negotiation, rather than as a final demand.

On November 3 the Algerian ambassador to
Washington delivered to Christopher the official
text of the Majlis decision. The Algerians, in their
transmittal note, observed that they were delivering
the message at the request of the Iranian Foreign
Ministry.   More significantly, Ambassador Malek
informed the United States that Algeria had been
charged by Iran with implementation of the Majlis
declaration. Although Washington would have preferred
dealing with Iran directly, the participation of
Algeria was regarded as an important breakthrough.

Ambassador Malek was immediately provided with a
paper detailing the formal U.S. position as it had been
developed over the previous eight months. From that
point on, all communications with Iran were conducted
through the good offices of the government of Algeria.

Act II: Mediation Begins

One week later Christopher and a small group of
officials from the State Department and the Treasury
Department arrived in Algiers for the first formal
discussion of the U.S. response to the action of the
Iranian Majlis. On that first night, more than three
hours were spent in discussions between Christopher and
Algerian Foreign Minister Mohammed Behyahia and the
other members of the Algerian team, which now consisted
of Ambassador Malek, Algerian Ambassador Gharaib who
had returned from Tehran, and Seghir Mostafai, governor
of the Algerian central bank. The Algerians made clear
from the outset that they reviewed their role strictly
as that of an intermediary. However, they left open
the possibility that they might assume a more direct
role if that seemed to be required at some point.

During that long first night, the Algerians
established a method of operation that was to become
routine over the months that followed. They took the
statement of the U.S. position--in the form of a
response to the Iranian Majlis decision--and subjected
it to careful scrutiny and a stream of questions.
Politely but firmly they raised specific issues that
they anticipated would be of concern to the Iranians
and then pressed the U.S. team to explain the reasons
for its position as clearly as possible. In some
cases, the Algerians explored possible changes in
wording, which the U.S. side then considered and on
occasion incorporated into the text of its response.

These exchanges accomplished two purposes. First, they provided an external check--by a group sensitive to the ideological requirements of the Iranian revolutionaries--on the drafting work that had been done in Washington. In some cases, a possible clash was averted by a simple change of words that had no legal effect; in others, substantive problems were brought to light and remedied.

Second, the American negotiators were given an opportunity to present in great detail the constitutional, legal, financial and other considerations that had gone into the preparation of the U.S. response and thereby to provide the ammunition the Algerian intermediaries would need in order to make a persuasive presentation in Tehran.

Although it was never acknowledged directly, the Algerians must have been aware that the underlying U.S. objective in these lengthy talks was to persuade them that the U.S. position was honorable, just, defensible, and at the outer limits of what the United States could deliver in practice. In this way it was hoped that the Algerians could be transformed into advocates for the U.S. position.

By the end of the first night of meetings, some minor problems were identified, but the main thrust of the U.S. position had held up well under Algerian probing. However, the Algerians made it clear that, in their judgment, the mere delivery of the U.S. position to the Iranians would be a disaster. They believed the U.S. position would be regarded as too general in nature and as failing to address positively certain key points in the Iranian resolution, for example, the cancelation of all claims against Iran. At the same time, the Algerians appreciated the constraints on U.S. action. Consequently, the U.S. team devised a procedure in which the Algerians would present the U.S. position paper in conjunction with copies of proposed presidential draft orders, thus lending the paper additional weight and legal substance.

This written presentation would be augmented by oral explanations from the three-man Algerian team, based on their detailed conversations with Christopher and his team. The Algerians believed--correctly as it turned out--that such a presentation would engage the Iranians in the substance of the U.S. position while avoiding the likelihood of an immediate rejection.

Christopher made it clear to the Algerian team that the United States, while prepared to demonstrate flexibility on form and wording, had almost no room for maneuver on substance. After lengthy and exhaustive probing, the Algerian team seemed to understand this very well by the time they left for Tehran. They arrived in Tehran on November 12 and delivered their initial presentation to the Iranian commission the same day. (The text of this and other documents later made public are available in the appendix.)

During this first round of indirect discussions, there was considerable concern on the part of both the Algerian and the U.S. teams about the problem of maintaining some degree of confidentiality. On the one hand, it was feared that the Iranian side would immediately publicize the details of the U.S. position, thereby forcing a public debate and complicating the negotiating process. That did not occur. The Iranian committee under Behzad Nabavi remained totally out of public view, and the substance of the Iranian-Algerian discussions during these initial exchanges remained entirely confidential.

There was also the endemic danger of press leaks on the American side. This also did not occur, for several related reasons. First, substantive knowledge about the U.S. position was limited to a tiny group of individuals in the departments of State, Treasury, and Justice and in the White House. Every member of this small group understood that a premature leak could directly affect the lives of the hostages in Tehran—many of whom were personal friends and former colleagues. That realization inhibited what is normally an irresistible urge for Washington officials to demonstrate access to inside information by whispering it to the press. The incentive to leak was also reduced by the fact that the lame-duck Carter administration was free during this period of many of the political pressures that encourage leaks. Finally, the choice of Warren Christopher as the chief U.S. negotiator was a major factor in maintaining an unusual degree of confidentiality. Christopher is a highly disciplined man who, by instinct and conviction, shuns personal publicity.

Finally, there was the danger of mixed signals emanating from Iran itself. The Nabavi commission established by the Iranian Majlis was composed exclusively of what might be considered the clerical faction in Iranian politics. Although that fact endowed the commission with great credibility, growing out of presumed access to Khomeini, it also excluded members of rival political factions, including those closest to President Abolhassan Bani-Sadr. The rivalry between these hard-line clerics and the more Westernized "liberals" was already quite visible in late 1980; within the following eighteen months it would explode into full-scale internecine warfare.

At the same time the Algerian team was making its first visit to Tehran, Washington was receiving a variety of messages and signals from the faction around Bani-Sadr, including the head of the Iranian Central Bank, Ali Nobari, who was determined not to be left out of a negotiation involving billions of dollars of Iran-

ian assets.   Nobari hired several Western lawyers,
established contact with the various American banks,
put out lines to Washington, and began his own set of
negotiations at the same time discussions were getting
under way with the Algerians in Tehran.
     Initially, it was not clear whether the signals
emanating from Nobari and the Iranian Foreign Ministry
were an integral thread of the negotiating process or
whether they were independent--or even competitive.
Through the Algerians, it was determined that these
alternative channels were not in fact authorized by the
Nabavi group.   Consequently, the various would-be
interlocutors on the Iranian side were informed that
the United States would conduct talks only through the
Algerians to the Nabavi group.
     There was some concern, however, that the
American lawyers retained by the Iranians would offer
advice conflicting with that coming to Iran through
official channels.   There was no way to control what
advice an American lawyer might offer to an Iranian
client under such circumstances, but the State Department, the Treasury Department, and others in Washington
made every effort to acquaint these lawyers with
Washington's views on various key legal issues, for
example, limitations on the president's ability to
annul court actions.   The objective was to ensure that
the Iranians did not receive from their private counsel
an unrealistic view of what they might expect to
achieve in the negotiations.
     During the course of these initial talks between
the Algerians and the Iranians in Tehran--as well as in
subsequent rounds--Washington received almost no substantive information about the course of the talks.   At
one point, the Algerian Foreign Ministry informed the
U.S. ambassador in Algiers that there were several
points of dispute.   It was no surprise to learn that
these points related, first, to Iran's insistence on
the need to release all Iranian assets (as opposed to
leaving some under attachment), and second, to Iranian
demands for access to what they believed to be the
shah's massive fortune in the United States.
     From the diplomatic circuit in Tehran, Washington
heard that Nabavi was dissatisfied with the American
response. He let it be known that he had anticipated a
yes-or-no answer; he regarded the response the
Algerians had relayed to Tehran as a new proposal.
That was, of course, an accurate representation of the
U.S. reply; but the report provided no grounds for
optimism.
     In view of the extremely tight control over
information in Tehran, it is very likely that this
report was part of the Iranian negotiating strategy and
was intended to reach American ears.   In any event, it
proved prophetic with regard to the Iranian formal

response, which was delivered to the Algerians on November 21 and relayed to the State Department on November 26.

The Second Exchange of Notes

The Iranian note characterized the U.S. response as being "not to the point" and as straying from the demands spelled out by the Majlis. It claimed that the Iranian government had no authority to deviate from the resolutions of the Majlis and therefore could not reply to "unrelated" proposals such as those included in the U.S. paper. It asked for a positive or negative response or for a request for clarification. It then reiterated what Iran regarded as the key points left unresolved by the American paper. As expected, these centered on annulment of claims, transfer of all assets without exception to Iran, and access to the assets belonging to the shah. One senior U.S. official dismissed the Iranian response as "insulting" and recommended rejecting it out of hand.

The Christopher group, however, chose to interpret the Iranian message as the opening gambit in a negotiating stategy, and President Carter authorized Christopher to proceed on that basis. The trick was to find a formula that appeared to respond to Iran's purported requirement for a simple yes-or-no answer while maintaining the substance of the U.S. position. In the course of two intense days of discussions and drafting, the U.S. prepared an answer that provided very brief and positive responses to each of the Iranian requests. In each case, however, the reader was referred to a separate set of "comments" or "procedural steps" that would be required to carry out the necessary measures. In this way the Iranians could have their brief, positive answer--if only for public consumption--while the U.S. conditions were preserved in the "small print" at the back.

Iran had also requested detailed information about the lawsuits pending in U.S. courts, a survey of all Iranian assets, and other data in areas where Iran's information was presumably scanty or nonexistent. In each case, the U.S. reply referred the Iranians to their own American lawyers, who could provide such information, or else informed them that the United States government had no precise information of the sort they were seeking. Orally, Christopher made it clear to the Algerians that Tehran could not expect to receive any cooperation from the United States regarding the location of assets so long as they were unwilling to provide a detailed accounting of the location and condition of each of the American hostages.

Although the U.S. written reply was stated in the neutral language of the legal profession, it was as much a rebuke of the Iranian request as their own response had been from the U.S. point of view.

Back to Algiers and Tehran

Christopher carried this paper to Algiers for a new set of discussions on December 1. One of the most significant points to emerge from this second round of discussions was a proposal that all claims against Iran be channeled into a mutually agreed claims-settlement procedure. Such a mechanism would permit Iran to claim technically that attachments and court proceedings had been annulled (on the grounds that settlement action had been transferred from the courts to the claims-settlement procedure) while at the same time protecting the U.S. claimants.

The Christopher group had not proposed such a solution, thinking that the Iranians would perceive it as contrary to their own interests. In fact, relying on traditional claims of sovereign immunity, Iran's position in the U.S. courts was very strong; but if all claims were transferred to a settlement procedure-- where Iran would necessarily have to agree to accept adjudication--Iran would likely be required to pay far more in compensation in the end. However, the Algerians believed that Iran would find such an arrangement attractive since it would permit them to contend (as the Majlis resolution required) that all claims against Iran had been terminated and all assets transferred out of direct U.S. control. Although no one on the Algerian side ever expressed it in such bald terms, what they were actually suggesting was that Iran was less interested in protecting its tangible interests than in finding an acceptable political formula to escape the intolerable corner into which they had painted themselves. That judgment again proved to be insightful.

On December 3 the Algerian team returned to Tehran with the clear intention of pressing hard for a resolution of the stalemate by the end of the year. (For the text of the U.S. position paper, see the appendix.) All participants were keenly aware that time was slipping away. If the issue was not resolved satisfactorily by the time a new president was inaugurated on January 20, 1981, no one could predict what would happen. Certainly, any new team of U.S. officials would have to spend a considerable period of time studying the negotiating history and preparing a new U.S. position under the intense light of international publicity. At a minimum, that process would delay a settlement; more important, it would risk

reigniting the crisis on a more dangerous level of
confrontation. The Algerians understood this very
well, and although they were careful not to discuss the
nature of their conversations with the Iranians, they
presumably made this point with some vigor when they
returned to Tehran for their second round of discussions.

Several days after the Algerian team arrived back
in Tehran, a Third World diplomat in Tehran provided
his own interpretation of the course of events.
According to this observer, the Algerians believed that
the United States had accepted 80 percent of what Iran
wanted, and they were cautiously optimistic that a
resolution of the problem could be achieved by
Christmas. However, given the difficult political
situation in Iran, where the least deviation from the
formal conditions of the Majlis could have drastic
political repercussions, the outcome was not entirely
predictable. This diplomat believed that the Algerians
would seriously consider withdrawing from the process
if the Iranians rejected the most recent U.S. proposals. The Algerians did not share their personal
assessments or intentions with the United States, but
this independent interpretation had the ring of
credibility.

The Third Exchange of Notes

On December 11 the Algerian team relayed a message from the Iranian commission to Washington. In
this message, the Iranians agreed not to press for the
information in the five lists attached to their previous note, which Christopher had flatly refused. They
did ask, however, for an accounting of the total value
of assets belonging to the shah and his relatives in
the United States. That information, they said, was
necessary for them to respond properly to the latest
U.S. position. Perhaps significantly, they asked for
the amount of the shah's assets in the United States on
November 4, 1979 (the date of the hostage-taking), and
the total remaining in the United States now that more
than a year had gone by. This suggested a recognition
on their part that the shah and his family might have
chosen to transfer assets out of the United States as a
consequence of the hostage crisis.

A second Iranian demand in the December 11 message related to their renunciation of all U.S. claims
arising out of the seizure of the U.S. embassy in
Tehran and the holding of American hostages. This
posed a particularly difficult question, for it would
prevent individual hostages and their families, for
example, from asserting claims against Iran for its
actions. In practical terms, such a renunciation would

mean very little, for the collection of private claims
against a foreign government has virtually no chance of
success.   The administration conferred on this point
with members of the hostage families, who had formed an
organization   known   as   FLAG--Family   Liaison   Action
Group.   The families agreed that it would be futile to
insist on the claims as a matter of abstract principle
while letting the crisis drag on even longer.   Consequently, draft presidential orders were drawn up agreeing to withdraw and to forgo prosecution of any claims
arising out of the seizure of the embassy in Tehran.

On the question of the shah's assets, however,
there was simply no information available. Christopher
informed the Algerian foreign minister that, even if
the United States were willing to launch an immediate
investigation into the suspected holdings of the shah
and his family in the United States, there was no
possibility that such a survey could be completed
before the change of administration.   Nevertheless,
Christopher accepted as deadly serious the evidence
that this point was of critical importance for the
Iranians.   Therefore, as an attempt to square the
circle, the U.S. reply to the Algerians included a
draft executive order blocking all assets of the shah
and his family once the hostages had been released.
The U.S. response also made reference to the sum of
$56.5 billion as being the amount that Iran's lawyers
had claimed as the shah's wealth in the United States.
The United States (and presumably the Iranians) recognized that that number was totally speculative--if not
entirely fictitious--and the U.S. note carefully
avoided suggesting that it had any validity.   However,
the American side recognized that, for political reasons, the Iranians could not officially accept the fact
that the shah's wealth, whatever its size, had almost
certainly fled from the United States and would no
doubt prove as elusive for the Iranians as claims for
personal damages would have been for the hostages and
their families.

The new American message, incorporating responses
to Iranian questions on the shah's assets and renunciation of claims, was reviewed and approved by President
Carter at his regular Friday morning foreign policy
breakfast with key advisors on December 12.   The message was transmitted to Algiers late the same night,
giving the Algerian foreign minister the choice of
transmitting it directly to Tehran or requesting clarification or changes. In the event, he chose to send the
message to Tehran without further contact with Washington, and the Algerian team presented it to the Iranians
on December 15.

Act III: The $24 Billion Misunderstanding

On December 17 Washington learned that the Algerian team had received an answer from the Iranians and had begun making preparations to return to Algiers. However, Washington did not receive the 3,000-word text of the Iranian note until December 19.   The note included some recommendations for minor wording changes in the text of the U.S. response, reflecting Iranian political sensitivities.   But the most startling feature of the reply was its proposal for the handling of financial assets.

First, the message demanded that $9.6 billion of Iranian assets, plus interest, together with the gold deposited in Iran's account with the Federal Reserve Bank of New York, be delivered to the central bank of Algeria prior to the release of the hostages.   Immediately upon release, these assets were to be placed at the disposal of the Iranian government.   In addition, the U.S. government was to deposit $4 billion with the Algerian central bank as security for eventual repayment to Iran of Iranian funds held under attachment in the United States.   The message repeated a request for the United States to accept liability for any claims against Iran for damages associated with the embassy takeover and incarceration of the hostages.   It further demanded a full accounting of Iranian assets and a and a written U.S. commitment to return any assets that might be identified in the future but were not included in the existing lists.

In turn, Iran agreed to bring current the outstanding payments on loans from U.S. banks and authorized the Algerian central bank to hold $1 billion as a guarantee against future payments of loan installments. Most significantly, the Iranian response formally accepted the concept of some form of claims-settlement procedure, and it offered to set aside another fund of $1 billion to cover payment of such claims against Iran.   The note agreed to replenish this account as necessary to ensure that it never dropped below a level of $500 million until the claims-settlement process was complete.

It was, however, the question of the shah's putative assets in the United States that caused the greatest difficulty.   The Iranian message asked that the United States establish a thirty-day deadline for collecting information about the size and location of the shah's assets in the United States.   Until that process was complete, a freeze was to be maintained on such assets, and the U.S. government was to deposit $10 billion with the central bank of Algeria as a guarantee of the proper "discharge of its obligations."

Taken as a whole, the Iranian message was so thoroughly outrageous in its demands that the instinc-

tive reaction of U.S. officials was to regard it as a
rejection. In the face of such a response, it was felt
that further negotiation could only be futile and
humiliating. The Iranian side had almost totally
disregarded the detailed breakdown of frozen assets
provided to them through the Algerians, and they had
replaced the actual figures with numbers seemingly of
their own invention. (For example, their request for
$9.6 billion in assets included $800 million in the
Defense Department trust fund--a figure ten times
higher than the actual amount in the fund at the time.)
Moreover, when one considered the $10 billion requested
to guarantee the shah's assets, together with the
demand that the United States accept financial liability for all of Iran's litigations and claims in the
U.S. courts, the Iranian message appeared so far
removed from the reality of what was possible--legally
or morally--for the United States as to constitute a
calculated insult.

That impression was given some credence when the
Algerians replied to a U.S. query about a possible
further meeting with the bland statement that they had
nothing further to add to the Iranian message. Clearly
the Algerians did not wish to associate themselves with
a set of demands that they knew were not only outside
the realm of the practical but that strained the limits
of credibility.

Within Christopher's small group, the Iranian
message was immediately dubbed the "$24 billion misun-
derstanding." To make matters worse, on December 21
the Iranians published a summary of their message to
the United States as part of a propaganda effort to
justify their position. This, in turn, led the United
States to publish the texts of its own communications
with Tehran to set the record straight (see appendix).
Given the immense gap between the Iranian and U.S.
positions, the apparent Algerian withdrawal, the breakdown of confidentiality, and the rapid passage of time
(less than one month remained before the inauguration),
it seemed that the mediation process had broken down
totally and irrevocably.

Second Thoughts

That was the initial response in Washington.
However, within the small group of individuals around
Christopher, two alternative views emerged which held
out the possibility of a different U.S. strategy. The
first of these maintained that the Iranians were merely
engaging in traditional bazaar haggling. The $24 bil-l
lion figure should, in this view, be regarded as nothing more than an opening gambit to which the United
States should respond with a counter offer. This

interpretation was offered, as might have been anticipated, by an individual who had served in Iran.

The second point of view, which ultimately pre-
vailed, held that the Iranians genuinely wanted to
terminate the crisis but found themselves boxed in by
political circumstances that prevented them from dealing with the problem directly. A careful reading of
the December 19 message revealed a number of positive
elements. The Iranian note accepted the basic concept
of a claims-settlement procedure and an escrow agreement with the Bank of Algeria. Iran also agreed to pay
U.S. banks all overdue installments of loans made under
the shah. The Iranian negotiators had shrugged off the
U.S. refusal to provide additional detailed information
without making it an issue. They had also accepted--in
a left-handed sort of way--the principle that the
shah's assets would be attainable only through the
courts and that attachments on assets frozen in the
United States could be undone only through court action
over time. However, to cover themselves politically,
and to avoid the appearance that they were simply being
taken in by the Americans, they had proposed financial
guarantees. In that way, they would not be seen as
relying solely on the word of the Great Satan. The
size of the guarantees was essentially arbitrary
(although Iran would have a natural incentive to make
them as high as possible), and some of the ambiguity
could be attributed to the U.S. refusal to provide the
detailed accounting that the Iranians had obviously
sought for that purpose.

In other words, putting aside the instinctive
U.S. emotional response to what seemed to be an insult,
it was possible to see the Iranian response as a rather
far-reaching effort to accommodate the U.S. position,
but with some protective factors built in to ensure
that they would not be cheated by an enemy they hated
and distrusted. After the initial shock, it was this
interpretation that came to be accepted within Christopher's "core group," and President Carter authorized
the group to proceed on that basis. Nevertheless, the
gap between the Iranian position--now public--and what
the United States could offer was immense. Was it
possible to close this gap in less than one month?

On December 21, after conferring with President
Carter, Christopher sent a message to the Algerians,
relaying the American reaction to the "deeply dis-
appointing" message from the Iranians. The U.S. note
provided some new draft material and requested Algerian
comments. Christopher also asked the Algerians whether
or not it would be worth sending still another message
to Iran or whether the talks should simply be permitted
to remain dormant until the Reagan administration took
office. He left open the possibility of another meeting with the Algerian team if the latter felt such a

meeting would be worthwhile. Christopher noted that, to judge from the lack of understanding reflected in the Iranian message, Washington had only a "slight expectation" that the original timetable could be preserved, but remained willing to explore whatever possibility might remain.

The principal new element in the U.S. position presented to the Algerians in late December was a draft memorandum of understanding that Iran and the United States would each sign with the Algerians. The memorandum did not substantially change the basic U.S. position, but attempted to reformulate it more in accordance with what Washington understood to be the essential political requirements of the Nabavi commission in Tehran. Thus, the memorandum called for the transfer of as many of the Iranian assets as possible to escrow outside the United States in advance of the hostage release, with arrangements for their further transfer to Iran as soon as the release had been accomplished. This new approach expressly rejected Iran's request for $24 billion as being inconsistent with the principle of reestablishing the status quo prior to the hostage-taking and as legally infeasible, but it maximized the amount of Iranian assets that could realistically be collected short of court action. The Iranians, it was felt, might prefer to take what they could reasonably expect to get in the short run, rather than prolong the negotiations in the dubious hope of squeezing more out of the next administration.

The new U.S. proposal established a deadline of January 16, 1981, as the final date by which a settlement might be reached. If this deadline was exceeded, the United States reserved the right to withdraw from whatever arrangements had been concluded up to that time.

The Algerians welcomed the new U.S. proposal. They had originally been led to believe that the Iranians regarded the United States' December 15 position as positive and requiring only a few minor changes, so the Iranian reply had taken them by surprise. Nevertheless, on reflection, the Algerians had come to the same conclusion as the members of the American team, that is, that the "$24 billion misunderstanding" was in fact an ill-fated attempt by the Iranians to solve the political problem of how to implement the agreement.

On December 23 Ambassador Haynes was called to the Algerian Foreign Ministry and informed that Algeria was prepared to proceed with its mediation efforts on the basis of the latest U.S. position. However, before deciding whether or not to transmit the U.S. paper to Tehran, the Algerian team felt that further in-depth discussions with Christopher and his associates were needed. Consequently, the Algerians said they were

prepared to leave immediately for Washington if this
were acceptable to the U.S. side.

On the following day, December 24, there was a
significant change in the situation in Tehran. Through
the Swiss embassy, the United States was notified that
the three U.S. diplomats who had until then been held
at the Iranian Foreign Ministry (Chargé d'Affaires
Bruce Laingen, Political Counselor Victor Tomseth, and
Security Officer Michael Howland) had been removed from
the Foreign Ministry to join the other hostages.
According to this report, all fifty-two hostages were
now in "the safekeeping of the government."

Also on Christmas Eve, the Algerian ambassador in
Tehran and his deputy visited the hostages. Two days
later Washington was informed that all fifty-two hostages had been positively sighted. This was the first
visit by outside officials to the hostages since before
the failed rescue mission exactly eight months earlier
and the only positive confirmation in nearly fourteen
months that all of the hostages were physically safe.
Paradoxically, however, the Algerians in Tehran
reported that Bruce Laingen and his two colleagues were
visited in a different site from the others, thus
leaving open the question of whether a transfer of all
the hostages to government control had actually
occurred.

It was difficult to know how to interpret the
meaning of these events. It had been a basic objective
of the United States from the earliest days of the
crisis to get the hostages out of the hands of the
student radicals and into the official custody of the
government. On the basis of the contradictory evidence
available, it was not clear that this had finally been
accomplished. On balance, it seemed that Iran was at
least moving toward asserting government control over
the hostages, paving the way for their eventual
release. That view was strongly reinforced by the
Algerian team when they arrived in Washington on the
night of December 29.

Talks began the following morning and continued
through a luncheon hosted by Secretary of State Muskie.
By the end of the afternoon of December 30, after more
than eight hours of intensive consultations, a
thoroughly revised package had been put together.

Act IV: Endgame

This new package, which the Algerians carried
back to their own country on New Year's Eve, was in the
form of a "declaration" by the government of Algeria,
incorporating the points of agreement between the two
parties. By this device, Iran and the United States
would each be making promises to Algeria, not to each

other--a point of great psychological importance for the Iranians.

The new package addressed each of the four points in the original Majlis resolution and described how the agreement would be implemented.

-- It provided for an escrow account, with funds in the value of approximately $9.5 billion to be turned over to Iran when Algeria certified the safe release of all the hostages.

-- It established a claims-settlement procedure with binding arbitration, and incorporated the Iranian idea of a $1 billion Iranian account designated for payment of claims, to be replenished so as never to fall below a level of $500 million.

-- With respect to the shah's assets, the United States reiterated its willingness to freeze existing assets, to direct the collection of information about the size and location of assets, and to facilitate Iran's access to U.S. courts.

On January 3 the Algerians met with Nabavi in Tehran to explain the latest American proposal. They emphasized that time was running out if an agreement was to be reached before the change of administrations in Washington. (The new package identified January 16 as the date when the United States was authorized to withdraw unilaterally from any obligations.) Nabavi acknowledged the point and indicated than an Iranian response would be forthcoming within two or three days.

In Washington there was still great uncertainty about the location of the three diplomats in the Foreign Ministry. There was also grave concern that, if agreement were not reached, the Iranians would put all of the hostages on trial. Plans were prepared to deal with that eventuality. Late on January 5 Washington was notified that the three diplomats had been transferred to an unknown location with the other forty-nine hostages as of January 4. In relaying this information, the Algerians counseled the Americans to remain cool and provided personal assurances from the Iranians that all fifty-two hostages were now in the hands of the government. (Subsequent personal accounts by the hostages suggested that Iranian government control over the student militants remained problematic to the very end of the ordeal.)

On January 6 Ambassador Haynes was informed that the Algerian team felt it was not far from a solution and was much more optimistic than before. It was suggested that the United States avoid mention of the January 16 deadline, apparently to avoid the impression that Iran was working under a U.S. ultimatum.

Return to Algiers

At this juncture, Washington began to receive requests for clarifications or changes on many different points. These requests would be presented to the Algerian team in Tehran, relayed to Algiers, and passed to the U.S. ambassador, who sent them to Washington. The entire process was then repeated in reverse with Washington's reply. A question and answer required eight exchanges and four translations (Farsi-French, French-English, and vice versa). In order to streamline this cumbersome procedure, on January 7 Christopher flew to Algiers with a small group of aides in order to have direct contact with the Algerian side and to deal directly with questions as they were relayed from Tehran. Although the participants originally expected this process to continue only for a brief period of time (one member of the team packed only enough clothes for an overnight visit), the team in fact was required to remain in Algiers until after the hostages had been released on January 20.

As Christopher began his consultation in Algiers on January 8, it was becoming evident that the Iranians were prepared to accept most of the Algerian declaration in principle. However, the details of handling the vast quantities of money and goods involved in this immense transaction were emerging as very serious issues as each side got down to the fine print. The most troublesome of these issues was the prospective transfer of Iranian assets frozen in accounts of American banks overseas. Some of these assets had been offset against outstanding Iranian loans, and it would be necessary for Iran to settle the loan accounts before the remaining balance could be determined. Negotiations between the Iranian Bank Markazi and the American banks had been under way for almost a year, and a variety of plans had been developed to deal with the problem. However, final agreement remained elusive.

Also, the Iranians had to be persuaded that the United States was unable to terminate attachments on the $2.2 billion of Iranian deposits in U.S. banks prior to the actual release of the hostages. These funds could not be placed in escrow—and hence would not be available in cash form—at the time of the exchange. For the Iranians, this was extremely serious. They had publicly identified some $9.5 billion in frozen assets for immediate return, and to this sum they had added $14 billion more in "guarantees." They were now being asked to accept a grand total of $7.3 billion, with an additional $2.2 billion to follow upon completion of U.S. court action. The fact that they had chosen to publicize their demands in December must have been a matter of great embarrassment as they struggled with the realities of a settlement in January.

The Algerians also found it exceedingly difficult to believe that the Iranians would ever agree to reduce their demands below the level of $9.5 billion. Christopher's return to Algiers and his analysis for Foreign Minister Benyahia of what the United States would and could not do was critical in persuading the Algerians to raise the question of the $7.3 billion with the Iranians. The argument Christopher finally used with telling effect was that the Iranians had the choice of taking the $7.3 billion now, with the remainder to come later, or else wait for the entire $9.5 billion until spring, after the administration had changed.

During this period, there was a flood of cabled messages between Algiers and Tehran. Every word of the declaration and the supporting documentation was the subject of scrutiny, queries, and suggested changes. Copies of this message traffic were dutifully relayed to Washington, where they piled up in mounds. Those of us in Washington, who were involved only indirectly in most of this trilingual swirl, could only watch with respect bordering on awe as the small American team in Algiers managed to deal with each new issue calmly and precisely, never losing sight of the larger picture. Just keeping the telegrams in order was virtually a full-time occupation.

By January 10 the $7.3 billion escrow proposal had been presented to the Iranians, who promised to study it. The Algerians felt. at this stage that, despite the flurry of minor changes and alterations, the momentum of negotiation was well established and that almost nothing stood in the way of an agreement except the amount of money to be placed in escrow. The American side, almost submerged under the blizzard of details, was less sanguine. Among other things, time was rapidly running out. Reports from Tehran indicated that Iran planned to respond to the latest U.S. posi-tion on about January 15. That was only one day from the orignal deadline--selected on the basis of practi-cal considerations, not as a negotiating strategy--and there was growing awareness that every hour that passed represented one more hour of the previous time needed to complete the complex and unprecedented arrangements necessary for a succesful transfer.

Benyahia indicated he would be willing to travel personally to Tehran if absolutely necessary, and he formally requested that Deputy Secretary Christopher remain in Algiers for the time being. Christopher agreed to remain at least one more day. Then on January 12 he again acceded to Benyahia's request. In this fashion, the length of his visit was gradually extended, one day at a time. However, by early on the

13th, as rumors began to circulate about a formal
meeting of the Majlis on the hostage issue, Christopher
had personally concluded that the chances of completing
a settlement by January 20 were remote.

Not the least of Christopher's concerns during
this tense period of waiting for an Iranian reply was
the status of negotiations between the Bank Markazi and
the American banks being conducted in New York under
the supervision of Deputy Secretary of the Treasury
Robert Carswell and presidential counsel Lloyd Cutler.
The Iranians balked at the demand of the American banks
that they should be required to maintain a guarantee
fund greater than the total value of the loans themselves.   They were also quite unhappy about the interest rates being offered by the American banks.

Iran Blinks

This deadlock continued until January 15 when, to
the astonishment and relief of the American side, the
Iranians unilaterally introduced a new memorandum
offering not only to bring their loans current but to
pay them off entirely, thus eliminating the issue.
This option had been considered from the very beginning
of the bank negotiations, but it had been dropped along
the way since it had appeared to be too costly to the
Iranians.   Now the Iranians chose to reintroduce it in
order to break what was rapidly developing into a
deadlock.   Although this decision was a major breakthrough, it also meant that virtually every paper that
had been prepared during the long bank negotiations had
to be completely redrafted under the most stringent
time limits.

Also on January 15, U.S. Treasury General Counsel
Robert Munheim and State Department Legal Advisor
William Lake were dispatched to London to assist in the
financial arrangements.   Iran had by this time agreed
that the Bank of England would be acceptable as the
escrow ban, and the financial activities associated
with the transfer and certification of billions of
dollars of assets from a wide variety of sources were
increasingly focused in "the City."

The Majlis met as scheduled and voted approval on
January 14.   The questions presented to the Majlis were
intentionally restricted to approval of the claims-
settlement procedure and the nationalization of the
shah's assets, apparently in an attempt to avoid a
prolonged political wrangle about the actual text of
what was now being referred to as the Algiers
declaration.

However, it was not until January 17 that the
Nabavi commission formally notified the Algerians that
it was prepared to reduce its demands below the $9.5

billion level. To this concession, the Iranians added two caveats: first, they insisted that the actual level of assets, including interest, should be no less than $8.1 billion; second, they insisted on a U.S. guarantee that the remaining $2.2 billion under attachment in the United States would be freed no later than May 31, 1981.

Although the United States recognized the major concession that Iran had made in lowering its publicly stated goal, there was still considerable doubt that $8.1 billion could in fact be produced. Part of the problem was the fluctuation in the price of gold on the world market. Iranian bullion in the Federal Reserve had lost some $150 million in value since the talks had begun some three months earlier. Moreover, the Iranian securities on deposit with the Federal Reserve also fluctuated in value.

After some extended computation and soul-searching, the United States agreed to accept an aggregate figure of $7.955 billion as the required "trigger" to free the hostages. The Algerians were able within a matter of hours to persuade the Iranians to accept this figure, which was then written into a series of formal documents prepared and signed in Washington on January 18 (for texts, see appendix).

The Final Rollercoaster

The Iranians formally acceded to the agreement early on the morning of January 19, and Deputy Secretary Christopher initialed the documents in Algiers as the authorized representative of the president of the United States. At that point, the crisis appeared to be over. The transfer of funds began from various accounts into the Federal Reserve preparatory to transfer to the escrow account in the Bank of England. Although the transfer mechanism was complex and cumbersome, it appeared for a time on January 19 that only matters of technical compliance remained. Two Algerian aircraft had already been dispatched to Tehran for the hostages. The stage seemed to be set.

But in the Iranian crisis nothing ever went according to schedule. Within hours, the exhilarated and exhausted team in Algiers learned that the Iranians had rejected a technical supplement to the basic escrow agreements, thus halting the banking transfer process that had just begun. The clause that Iran found offensive (denouncing it repeatedly as an "underhanded" maneuver) was a conventional statement that transfer of specified deposit amounts to the Federal Reserve would release deposit banks from further liability. The Bank Markazi, whose records were incomplete and in some

cases at variance with the American banks, saw this as
a trick to avoid resolving such inconsistencies later.
Their point was valid, if overstated.

After nearly a full day of wrangling and Iranian
accusations of bad faith, the offending supplement was
removed from the basic document. It was then redrafted
by Bank Markazi's lawyers, agreed to by all parties,
and sent out by telex as an order to begin the financial transfer.

This telex also turned into a nightmare. The
text was full of typographical errors which, in a normal banking transaction, would have had to be resolved
by laborious retransmission until the text was perfect.
However, by this time (early on the morning of January
20, Inauguration Day) there was no time left. All of
the banking officials conferred by telephone to no
avail, until Secretary of the Treasury William Miller
finally gave oral instructions to the U.S. banks to
proceed on the basis of the order as received.

At 4:17 A.M., January 20, the Federal Reserve
transferred a total of $7.955 billion to the Bank of
England. Another technical problem at that point
delayed for two more hours the transfer of this
amount--within the Bank of England itself--from the
account of the Federal Reserve to the escrow account of
the Algerian central bank. The holdings of that
account were then verified painstakingly, line by line,
by telephone between London and Algiers, where the
formal certificate was finally presented at 8:04 A.M.,
Washington time. Two minutes later the certification
was passed from Algiers to Tehran, successfully completing what was probably the largest private transfer
of funds in a single transaction in history.

Again, the crisis appeared to be over. In
Washington, President Carter was in the Oval Office
with his key aides awaiting word from Tehran that the
hostages had been released. The president had spent
the night in the Oval Office, following the intricacies
of the bank negotiations on a minute-by-minute basis
and intervening at critical moments with support or
essential authorization for a process that had no
precedent and no existing set of rules. He had, in
fact, scarcely slept for forty-eight hours as the final
stage of the negotiations was completed.

But the ordeal was not yet over. There was no
word from Tehran. Although Iran was notified that the
"trigger" amount was in the escrow account at 8:06
A.M., Washington time, they did not acknowledge it
until 12:05 P.M.--five minutes after President Carter's
term ended. The hostages themselves did not depart
until shortly after 12:30, while the former president
was en route home from the inaugural ceremony. The
Algerians, who were on the scene in Tehran, later
insisted that this delay was merely typical ineffi-

ciency on the part of the Iranians; but to those in the
Oval Office it appeared to be one final gouge at the
Great Satan.

In the weeks that followed, however, it was the
Iranians who found themselves embarrassed. The figures
in the final agreement that Iran had accepted were
startling, even to those who had followed the negotiations closely. At the beginning of the hostage crisis,
some $11 to $12 billion of Iranian assets were frozen
by the United States; but because of attachments and
other limitations, only about $8 billion could in fact
be transferred to the escrow account before the
hostagerelease. Once the release took place, these
funds were distributed as follows: $3.67 billion to
pay off U.S. bank loans contracted by the shah's
regime; $1.42 billion to remain in escrow as security
against payment on disputed claims between U.S. banks
and Iran; and $2.88 billion to Iran.

In addition, approximately $2.2 billion was to be
freed of attachment and the claims referred to an
international tribunal. Of those funds, Iran agreed to
place $1 billion in an escrow account to secure pay-
ments of claims by U.S. citizens and companies against
Iran as decided by the arbitral tribunal.

In short, Iran received only slightly more than
$4 billion in cash, or approximately one-fourth of the
total it had originally lost as a result of the hostage-taking. The political opposition in Tehran was
not shy about drawing attention to the very considerable financial concessions the Iranian team had
accepted in the course of these negotiations. Certainly, if anyone had proposed such an outcome when the
talks began in September or October 1980, it would have
been rejected as unthinkable.

Some General Observations

The negotiating process that led to this outcome
was tortuous and unpredictable, but it seems in retrospect to have been composed of the following elements:

--   Once the Iranians had decided (in early
September 1980 that the hostages had ceased to be a
political asset, they were prepared to go quite far in
finding a way out of the political predicament they had
created for themselves.

--   To a considerable degree, the Iranians relied
on the United States, and the small team of experts
around Christopher, to conduct the staff work, drafting,
and legal craftsmanship required to find a mutually
acceptable position. The Iranians posed objectives in

terms of their own political requirements, leaving the
Christopher team to find formulas that would square
Iran's political needs with the moral, legal, financial,
and constitutional realities affecting the president of
the United States.   When the United States found it
could not square the circle, it was Iran that repeatedly
shifted ground to permit the process to go forward.   In
some respects, the longer Iran negotiated, the less it
got.

        --   The Iran-Iraq war was probably an obstacle to
a settlement in the first two months, since it distracted Iranian attention from the hostage crisis and
delayed development of a formal position until the final
days   before   the   U.S.   election   (when   agreement   was
impossible).   Later, however, as the costs of the war
began to mount, the war probably increased pressure on
the Iranian clerics to find a settlement.

        --   The menacing posture adopted by President-
elect Reagan during the transition period unquestionably
increased the pressure on Tehran to reach agreement
before January 20.   Both Carter administration officials
and the Algerians made full use of Iran's uncertainties
about the incoming U.S. leadership to press hard for
Iranian acceptance of what had to be considered, from
the Iranian perspective, a thoroughly distasteful final
package.

        Finally, and most important, the settlement could
never   had   been   completed   without   the   assistance   of
Foreign   Minister   Benyahia,   ambassadors   Malek   and
Gharaib and Governor Mostafai of the central bank,
together with their very able staffs.   The Algerian team
was   everything   one   could   hope   mediators   to   be: dis-
creet,   intelligent,   perceptive,   persistent,   skeptical,
and inexhaustible.   Their careful questioning of the
successive U.S. position papers consistently improved
and sharpened them.   The team was skillful at presenting
unpalatable messages to either side when necessary, and
with very few exceptions their judgments proved accurate.   When it was necessary to push, they pushed; when
discretion called for them to hold back, they showed
restraint.   In the end, they succeeded in improving
their stature with both parties.
        What did Algeria hope to achieve for itself by
accepting this onerous and potentially thankless task?
On   the   American   side,   there   was   little   doubt   that
Algeria hoped to establish a position of greater respect
and trust with the United States which might lay the
foundations for a more friendly relationship.   Ironically, the Algerians were in some measure cheated out of
their triumph by the arrival of the administration of
Ronald Reagan.

President Reagan and his aides had not worked
closely with the Algerians, as had President Carter,
Deputy Secretary Christopher, and others in the Carter
administration. Moreover, Reagan and his advisors were
uncomfortable with the hostage-release agreement and
wished to preserve a certain distance from a process
that they regarded as perilously close to ransom. The
new administration also arrived with well-established
notions about terrorism, which included deep suspicions
of Algerian attitudes and political associations. As a
result, official U.S. relations with Algeria did not
bloom in the same manner as might have been expected had
the Carter administration remained in office.

That is not to suggest that the Algerians would or
should regard the hostage-release episode as a failure.
Quite the contrary. In the first place, the Algerians
were the recipients of a remarkable popular outpouring
of emotion. The Algerian embassy in Washington was
deluged with letters, telegrams, flowers, gifts, and
every conceivable token of appreciation from individual
Americans. Despite the relative coolness of the Reagan
administration, the Algerians had accumulated a reser-
voir of goodwill and affection with the American people
that might serve them well in the future.

They had also achieved two additional objectives
that may have been of equal or greater importance than
the immediate status of their relations with the United
States. By successfully negotiating the release of the
hostages, the Algerian leaders significantly burnished
their international reputation as skilled mediators--a
recognition they seemed to seek. More significantly,
they had the considerable satisfaction of having
resolved a crisis that had bedeviled the international
community for more than a year, that undermined principles of international law important to Third World
nations, that divided members of the Third World against
one another, and that risked a wider conflict between a
Third World nation and the United States. On each of
these accounts, the Algerians had an enlightened self-
interest in bringing the crisis to a peaceful resolution
and ample grounds to be gratified with the success of
their efforts.

Unlike some other cases, the mediator in this
instance was not required to cajole the two parties into
negotiations or to persuade them of the value of a
settlement. The United States had sought such an outcome from the very start; and by September 1980 the
peculiar rhythms of revolutionary politics had finally
led the Iranians to the same point. For similar reasons, neither party was eager to drop out of the process. Although the mediator presumably felt it necessary on occasion to exert pressure on one or both parties to make concessions, it was sufficient to draw the
parties' attention to the dangers of failure. There is

no evidence that the Algerians ever found it necessary to resort to side payments or to suggest that they might join the adversary.

The degree to which the Algerians were prepared to evoke the risks of failure may never be known in any detail.   Most of the pressure was directed at the Iranians, and neither they nor the Algerians are likely soon to provide a public account of how politically unpopular concessions were wrung from a reluctant regime in Tehran.   However, it seems certain that the most important pressure factor was the existence of an irrevocable deadline--the inauguration of a new president in Washington.

The menacing posture of the incoming president effectively removed any illusions Tehran may have harbored that delay would work in their favor.   In reality, the Reagan administration had no plan for dealing with the crisis beyond an understandable anxiety at the prospect of being tarred with the same brush as its predecessor.   However, the Iranians had no reason to believe that Reagan would be more forthcoming than Carter, and the Algerians presumably played on Iranian doubts and uncertainties to set in motion the remarkable flurry of last-minute changes and concessions on the Iranian side that made the agreement possible.

Equally important, however, was the great skill with which the Algerians performed the classic role of the mediator, that is, understanding the position of each party and conveying that position accurately and with sensitivity to the other.   In the hostage negotiation, the Algerian mediators never proposed solutions of their own.   However, on the U.S. side at least, they reviewed each proposal in great detail and, through their questions and comments, greatly influenced the form, if not the substance, of each successive communication.

It is supposed to be the role of the mediator to urge the parties back to the table when the going gets rough, but the roles were reversed on at least one occasion during the hostage negotiations.   In late December 1980, after Iran insisted on transmitting its "$24 billion misunderstanding" despite the mediators' objections, the Algerians virtually withdrew. They were induced to return only when the U.S. side decided to persevere by building on the positive elements of the Iranian message (while ignoring the provocative misperceptions of the rest).

Ultimately, the role of the Algerians was to stand as a cool screen between two angry adversaries.   Iran was burning with revolutionary and religious passion in the wake of the seemingly miraculous overthrow of the monarchy, while the United States seethed with righteous wrath at Iran's flouting of international law and elementary human rights.   Direct conversation was impossible under these circumstances, and a translator or interpreter was required to permit each party to listen to what the other had to say.

In retrospect, it is much too easy to assume that a successful mediator would have inevitably appeared once both parties had concluded that their respective national interests would best be served by a settlement. There was nothing inevitable about the outcome. It was produced by an improbable blend of circumstances, personalities, skills, perseverance, and more than a bit of luck. The mere fact that more than fifty Americans survived for fourteen months of haphazard imprisonment with no severe physical injuries or deaths was itself something of a miracle. If a hostage had died, for whatever reasons, at certain emotional junctures, the outcome could have been quite different. If the Algerians had refused to undertake a most uncertain task--perhaps on the entirely realistic grounds that any benefits to their own national interests were potentially outweighed by the risks--the results would have been very different. If the Algerians had fielded a less skillful team, if the American team had spent its time watching the headlines instead of the auguries out of Tehran, if the president had been less willing to master the complexities of the issues and to participate personally in an improvised last act, if the Iranians had let their revolutionary rhetoric overwhelm their better judgment as it had so often in the past, if the new administration in Washington had been faced with a complex and emotional international crisis on its first day in office. . . . The ifs could be extended almost indefinitely.

It is enough to note that, without mediation, the crisis between Iran and the United States over the hostages could well have had a much different and possibly tragic outcome. For that reason above all, the Algerians who accepted this task and carried it through with such skill deserve the gratitude and respect of the United States, Iran, and the international community.

Appendix

A.   The U.S. message of November 11, 1980

The Government of the United States has received and has carefully reviewed the resolution adopted on November 2, 1980, by the Islamic Consultative Assembly of Iran.

The United States accepts in principle the resolution as the basis for ending the crisis and hereby proposes the following series of Presidential orders and declarations in response to the resolution. Each of the Presidential orders and declarations is to be made public and become effective upon safe departure from Iran of the 52 hostages.

I

The United States is prepared to deliver to the Government of Algeria a copy of a formal declaration signed by the President of the United States in which the United States states its policy, which is to refrain from interfering either directly or indirectly, politically or militarily, in the internal affairs of Iran.

II

A.   The United States is prepared to deliver to the Government of Algeria a copy of a signed Presidential order unblocking all of the capital and assets of Iran within the jurisdiction of the United States, whether located in the U.S. or other countries, in order to allow the parties to move expeditiously toward a resumption of normal financial relations as they existed before Nov. 14, 1979.

B.   An accompanying Presidential order will direct the Federal Reserve Bank of New York to make available to the Government of Iran all Iranian capital, assets and properties held by the bank, amounting to approximately $2.5 billion.

C.   An additional accompanying Presidential order will also remove all U.S. legal restrictions from an additional sum of approximately $3 billion on deposit with the U.S. banks abroad.

D.   In order to bring about the cancellation of all judicial orders and attachments relating to the capital and assets of Iran within U.S. jurisdiction, the United States is prepared to deliver to the Government of Algeria a copy of a signed Presidential declaration committing the United States to join with the Government of Iran in a claims settlement procedure which will lead to the cancellation of such orders and attachments as rapidly as possible.

III

A.   The United States is prepared to deliver to the Government of Algeria a copy of a signed Presidential order revoking all economic and financial sanctions and all legal prohibitions imposed since the seizure of the hostages against exports to, imports from and transactions with Iran in order to allow trade between the two countries to be resumed on the basis of conditions prior to Nov. 14, 1979.

B.   The United States is prepared to deliver to the Government of Algeria a copy of a signed Presidential declaration committing the United States to withdraw all claims pending against Iran in the International Court of Justice and to refrain from pursuing any other claims for financial damages on account of injuries or harm emanating from the seizure and detention of the U.S. Embassy and the hostages in Teheran.

C.   In addition, as indicated in paragraph 2(D) above, the United States is prepared to commit itself to join with the Government of Iran in a claims settlement procedure which will lead to the cancellation and annulment of all claims asserted by U.S. nationals, including U.S. companies, and by agencies, instrumentalities and controlled entities of the U.S. Government against Iran.

IV

A.   The United States is prepared to deliver to the Government of Algeria a copy of a signed Presidential order prohibiting the transfer out of the United States of any properties owned by or derived from the estate of the former Shah.

B.   The same order will require the compilation, for delivery to the Government of Iran, of all information which is in the possession of U.S. nationals or in the financial records of the U.S. Government and which may serve to identify any properties of the former Shah in the United States.

C.   The order will also direct the Attorney General of the United States to give notice to all appropriate U.S. courts that it is the position of the United States Government that (1) no claim of the Government of Iran to the property of the former Shah should be considered legally barred either by principles of sovereign immunity or the act of state doctrine and (2) that all decrees and judgments of the Government of Iran relating to such property may be enforced in the courts of the United States in accordance with U.S. law.

V

A.   The United States believes that this response to the decision of the Iranian Majlis represents the completion of the penultimate stage in resolving the hostage issue. The final step, which the United States believes should be taken in the next several days, would be to arrange, through the good offices of the Government of Algeria, release of all hostages concurrent with the United States taking all the specific steps noted above.

B.   To implement this final step, the United States will deposit with the Government of Algeria copies of the Presidential declarations and orders noted above, to be effective upon the safe departure of all the hostages from Iran. When their safe departure is confirmed by the Government of Algeria, the Government of the United States will publicly release the Presidential orders and declarations.

B.   The U.S. message of December 3, 1980

The response of the Government of the United States to the resolution of the Islamic Consultative Assembly of Iran, as delivered in Teheran by the Algerian delegation on Nov. 12, was a positive answer. In accepting the resolution as the basis for ending the crisis, the United States described the steps that it is prepared to take within its constitutional system to carry out each of the points in the Assembly's resolution upon the safe return of the 52 hostages.

On Nov. 26–27, 1980, the Algerian delegation delivered to the United States a message from Iran requesting answers to each of nine points relating to the response of the United States. The answers of the United States, which are premised upon the safe return of the 52 hostages from Iran, are set forth below, together with certain additional comments which are intended to clarify the answers.

I

Resolution No. II

A guiding principle of the answers under this heading is that the United States shall restore the financial position of Iran insofar as possible to that which existed prior to November 1979.

A.   The United States will order that Iran's deposits in United States bank offices outside the United States be transferred to Iran. The necessary procedural steps are set forth in comment No. 1.

B.   The United States Government will order that the setoffs previously taken by the United States' bank in Europe be canceled. The procedural steps are also explained in comment No. 1.

C.   The United States specifically commits itself to insure the mobility and free transfer of the Iranian assets. The necessary procedural steps are set forth in comment No. 2.

II

Resolution No. III

A.   All claims by American institutions and companies against Iran in United States courts will be canceled and nullified. The procedural steps necessary to the achievement of such cancellation and nullification are set forth in comment No. 2.

B.   The U.S. is willing to cancel and nullify all claims previously or hereafter made by any U.S. individual or institution against Iran concerning the occupation of the embassy or the taking of the hostages. The commitment is explained in comment No. 3.

C.   The undertaking set forth in paragraph (B) above will result in relieving Iran from the risk of any charges or losses resulting from such claims.

III

Resolution No. IV

A. The United States will put into force a freeze order requiring any person having custody or possession of any property or assets of the former Shah to retain such property and assets.

B. All undertakings by the United States with respect to the property and assets of the former Shah include the properties and assets of the close relatives of the former Shah.

C. Transfer of the properties and assets of the former Shah and his close relatives can occur pursuant to the procedures described in comment No. 4.

U.S. Comments on Its Answers

1

With respect to the U.S. answers to Paragraphs (A) and (B), it is understood that Iran is willing to honor and bring current all loans made to Iran or its instrumentalities by U.S. banks (and by syndicates including U.S. banks) which hold Iranian deposits outside the United States and which have taken setoffs against such deposits. As each such loan is brought current and affirmed by the Government of Iran and the parties consult concerning the normalization of their banking relationships, the United States will require such U.S. bank to cancel the underlying setoff and transfer all Iranian deposits in its possession to Iran or to any other recipient designated by Iran.

2

With respect to the U.S. answer to Paragraph I(C), it is understood that Iran is willing to pay all of its legitimate debts to U.S. persons and institutions and that it wishes to terminate all related litigation. Accordingly, the United States agrees, in the context of the safe return of the hostages, to terminate all legal proceedings in U.S. courts involving claims of U.S. persons and institutions against Iran and its state enterprises, to nullify all attachments and judgments obtained therein and to prohibit all future litigation by U.S. persons and institutions based on existing claims against Iran, when Iran agrees to submit all existing claims of U.S. persons and institutions (except those to be canceled and nullified pursuant to section II(B) of the answers of the United States) to an international claims settlement process for the determination and payment of such claims. This process would include binding third party arbitration of any claim not settled by mutual agreement. The United States agrees that such arbitration may be conducted, at Iran's election, by and under rules of the International Chamber of Commerce or the World Bank's International Center for the Settlement of Investment Disputes or such other tribunal as may be agreed upon by Iran and the United States. The judgments and awards of the arbitral tribunal shall be enforceable in the courts of any nation in accordance with its laws. The United States is willing to consider applying the above international claims settlement process to specific claims of Iran against the United States.

3

With respect to the U.S. answer to Paragraph II(B), the United States has previously confirmed that it is prepared to withdraw all claims pending against Iran in the International Court of Justice and to refrain from pursuing any other claims for financial damages on account of injuries emanating from the seizure of the United States Embassy and the detention of the hostages in Teheran. The United States undertaking will include the cancellation or nullification of claims previously or hereafter made by United States individuals or institutions concerning the occupation of the embassy and the taking of the hostages.

4

With respect to the U.S. answer to Paragraph III(C), under the laws of the United States, the only entity within the United States Government which could lawfully transfer the property or assets of the former Shah or his relatives to the Government of Iran would be a U.S. court acting pursuant to a legal proceeding brought by the Government of Iran. In fact, Iran has brought such a proceeding, which is now pending in an American court (Islamic Republic of Iran v. Mohammed Riza Pahlevi and Farah Diba Pahlevi, pending in the Supreme Court of the State of New York, Index No. 22013/79), and that pending case affords Iran an opportunity to prove its right to have the properties and assets in question transferred to Iran. The United States Government will facilitate efforts of the Government of Iran to obtain and enforce a judgment in the manner described in the United States position delivered by the Algerian delegation on Nov. 12, 1980.

C.   The Algiers Declaration

Declaration of the Government of the Democratic and
Popular Republic of Algeria

The Government of the Democratic and Popular Republic of Algeria, having been requested by the Governments of the Islamic Republic of Iran and the United States of America to serve as an intermediary in seeking a mutually acceptable resolution of the crisis in their relations arising out of the detention of the 52 United States nationals in Iran, has consulted extensively with the two governments as to the commitments which each is willing to make in order to resolve the crisis within the framework of the four points stated in the resolution of November 2, 1980, of the Islamic Consultative Assembly of Iran. On the basis of formal adherences received from Iran and the United States, the Government of Algeria now declares that the following interdependent commitments have been made by the two governments:

General Principles

The undertakings reflected in this Declaration are based on the following general principles:

A. Within the framework of and pursuant to the provisions of the two Declarations of the Government of the Democratic and Popular Republic of Algeria, the United States will restore the financial position of Iran, in so far as possible, to that which existed prior to November 14, 1979. In this context, the United States commits itself to ensure the mobility and free transfer of all Iranian assets within its jurisdiction, as set forth in Paragraphs 4-9.

B. It is the purpose of both parties, within the framework of and pursuant to the provisions of the two Declarations of the Government of the Democratic and Popular Republic of Algeria, to terminate all litigation as between the Government of each party and the nationals of the other, and to bring about the settlement and termination of all such claims through binding arbitration. Through the procedures provided in the Declaration relating to the Claims Settlement Agreement, the United States agrees to terminate all legal proceedings in United States courts involving claims of United States persons and institutions against Iran and its state enterprises, to nullify all attachments and judgments obtained therein, to prohibit all further litigation based on such claims, and to bring about the termination of such claims through binding arbitration.

Point I: Non-Intervention in Iranian Affairs

1. The United States pledges that it is and from now on will be the policy of the United States not to intervene, directly or indirectly, politically or militarily, in Iran's internal affairs.

Points II and II: Return of Iranian Assets and Settlement of U.S. Claims

2. Iran and the United States (hereinafter "the parties") will immediately select a mutually agreeable central bank (hereinafter "the Central Bank") to act, under the instructions of the Government of Algeria and the Central Bank of Algeria (hereinafter "The Algerian Central Bank") as depositary of the escrow and security funds hereinafter prescribed and will promptly enter into depositary arrangements with the Central Bank in accordance with the terms of this declaration. All funds placed in escrow with the Central Bank pursuant to this declaration shall be held in an account in the name of the Algerian Central Bank.

3. The depositary arrangements shall provide that, in the event that the Government of Algeria certifies to the Algerian

Central Bank that the 52 U.S. nationals have safely departed from Iran, the Algerian Central Bank will thereupon instruct the Central Bank to transfer as provided in Annex A attached hereto all monies or other assets in escrow with the Central Bank pursuant to this declaration, provided that at any time prior to the making of such certification by the Government of Algeria, each of the two parties, Iran and the United States, shall have the right on seventy-two hours' notice to terminate its commitments under this declaration.

If such notice is given by the United States and the foregoing certification is made by the Government of Algeria within the seventy-two hour period of notice, the Algerian Central Bank will thereupon instruct the Central Bank to transfer such monies and assets as provided in Annex A. If the seventy-two hour period of notice by the United States expires without such a certification having been made, or if the notice of termination is delivered by Iran, the Algerian Central Bank will thereupon instruct the Central Bank to return all such monies and assets to the United States, and thereafter the commitments reflected in this declaration shall be of no further force and effect.

Assets in the Federal Reserve Bank

4.   Commencing upon completion of the requisite escrow arrangements with the Central Bank, the United States will bring about the transfer to the Central Bank of all gold bullion which is owned by Iran and which is in the custody of the Federal Reserve Bank of New York, together with all other Iranian assets (or the cash equivalent thereof) in the custody of the Federal Reserve Bank of New York, to be held by the Central Bank in escrow until such time as their transfer or return is required by Paragraph 3 above.

Assets in Foreign Branches of U.S. Banks

5(A). Commencing upon the completion of the requisite escrow arrangements with the Central Bank, the United States will bring about the transfer to the Central Bank of all Iranian deposits and securities which on or after November 14, 1979, stood upon the books of overseas banking offices of U.S. banks, together with interest thereon through December 31, 1980, to be held by the Central Bank in escrow until such time as their transfer or return is required in accordance with Paragraph 3 of this agreement.

B. At such time as the Central Bank notifies the Government of Algeria, Iran and the United States that the Central Bank has received pursuant to Paragraphs 4 and 5(A) above 1,632,917.779 ounces of gold, world bank securities in the face amount of $35 million, and not less than $6.895 billion, Iran shall immediately bring about the safe departure of the 52 U.S. nationals detained in Iran. Upon the making by the Government of Algeria of the certification described in Paragraph 3 above, the Algerian Central Bank shall instruct the Central Bank to make such transfers, and to retain in escrow such funds, as are specified in Annex A to this declaration.

Assets in U.S. Branches of U.S. Banks

6.   Commencing with the adherence by Iran and the United States to this declaration and the claims settlement agreement attached hereto, and following the conclusion of arrangements with the Central Bank for the establishment of the interest-bearing security account specified in that agreement and Paragraph 7 below (which arrangements will be concluded within 30 days from the date of this Declaration), the United States will act to bring about the transfer to the Central Bank (within six months from such date) of all Iranian deposits and securities in U.S. banking institutions in the United States, together with interest thereon, to be held by the Central Bank in escrow until such time as their transfer or return is required by Paragraph 3.

7.   As funds are received by the Central Bank pursuant to Paragraph 6 above, the Algerian Central Bank shall direct the Central Bank to (1) transfer one-half of each such receipt to Iran and (2) place the other half in a special interest-bearing security account in the Central Bank, until the balance in the security account has reached the level of $1 billion. After the $1 billion balance has been achieved, the Algerian Central Bank shall direct all funds received pursuant to Paragraph 6 to be transferred to Iran.   All funds in the security account are to be used for the sole purpose of securing the payment, and paying, claims against Iran in accordance with the claims settlement agreement. Whenever the Central Bank shall thereafter notify Iran that the balance in the security account has fallen below $500 million, Iran shall promptly make new deposits sufficient to maintain a minimum balance of $500 million in the account. The account shall be so maintained until the President of the Arbitral Tribunal established pursuant to the claims settlement agreement has certified to the Central Bank of Algeria that all arbitral awards against Iran have been satisfied in accordance with the claims settlement agreement, at which point any amount remaining in the security account shall be transferred to Iran.

Other Assets in the U.S. and Abroad

8.   Commencing with the adherence of Iran and the United States to this declaration and the attached claims settlement agreement and the conclusion of arrangements for the establishment of the security account, the United States will act to bring about the transfer to the Central Bank of all Iranian financial assets (meaning funds or securities) which are located in the United States and abroad, apart from those assets referred to in Paragraph 5 and 6 above, to be held by the Central Bank in escrow until their transfer or return is required by Paragraph 3 above.

9.   Commencing with the adherence of Iran and the United States to this declaration and the attached claims settlement

agreement and the making by the Government of Algeria of the certification described in Paragraph 3 above, the United States will arrange, subject to the provisions of U.S. law applicable prior to November 14, 1979, for the transfer to Iran of all Iranian properties which are located in the United States and abroad and which are not within the scope of the preceding paragraphs.

Nullification of Sanctions and Claims

10.   Upon the making by the Government of Algeria of the certification described in Paragraph 3 above, the United States will revoke all trade sanctions which were directed against Iran in the period November 4, 1979, to date.

11.   Upon the making by the Government of Algeria of the certification described in Paragraph 3 above, the United States will promptly withdraw all claims now pending against Iran before the International Court of Justice and will thereafter bar and preclude prosecution against Iran of any pending or future claim of the United States or a United States national arising out of events occurring before the date of this declaration related to (A) the seizure of the 52 United States nationals on November 4, 1979, (B) their subsequent detention, (C) injury to United States property or property of the United States nationals within the United States Embassy compound in Tehran after November 3, 1979, and (D) injury to the United States nationals or their property as a result of popular movements in the course of the Islamic Revolution in Iran which were not an act of the Government of Iran.   The United States will also bar and preclude the prosecution against Iran in the courts of the United States of any pending or future claim asserted by persons other than the United States nationals arising out of the events specified in the preceding sentence.

Point IV: Return of the Assets of the Family of the Former Shah

12.   Upon the making by the Government of Algeria of the certification described in Paragraph 3 above, the United States will freeze, and prohibit any transfer of, property and assets in the United States within the control of the estate of the former Shah or of any close relative of the former Shah served as a defendant in U.S. litigation brought by Iran to recover such property and assets as belonging to Iran.   As to any such defendant, including the estate of the former Shah, the freeze order will remain in effect until such litigation is finally terminated. Violation of the freeze order shall be subject to the civil and criminal penalties prescribed by U.S. law.

13.   Upon the making by the Government of Algeria of the certification described in Paragraph 3 above, the United States will order all persons within U.S. juris diction to report to the U.S. Treasury within 30 days, for transmission to Iran, all information known to them, as of November 3, 1979, and as of the date of the order, with respect to the property and assets referred

to in Paragraph 12. Violation of the requirement will be subject to the civil and criminal penalties prescribed by U.S. law.

14. Upon the making by the Government of Algeria of the certification described in Paragraph 3 above, the United States will make known, to all appropriate U.S. courts, that in any litigation of the kind described in Paragraph 12 above the claims of Iran should not be considered legally barred either by sovereign immunity principles or by the act of state doctrine and that Iranian decrees and judgments relating to such assets should be enforced by such courts in accordance with United States law.

15. As to any judgment of a U.S. court which calls for the transfer of any property or assets to Iran, the United States hereby guarantees the enforcement of the final judgment to the extent that the property or assets exist within the United States.

16. If any dispute arises between the parties as to whether the United States has fulfilled any obligation imposed upon it by Paragraphs 12–15, inclusive, Iran may submit the dispute to binding arbitration by the tribunal established by, and in accordance with the provisions of, the claims settlement agreement. If the tribunal determines that Iran has suffered a loss as a result of a failure by the United States to fulfill such obligation, it shall make an appropriate award in favor of Iran which may be enforced by Iran in the courts of any nation in accordance with its laws.

Settlement of Disputes

17. If any other dispute arises between the parties as to the interpretation or performance of any provision of this declaration, either party may submit the dispute to binding arbitration by the tribunal established by, and in accordance with the provisions of, the claims settlement agreement. Any decision of the tribunal with respect to such dispute, including any award of damages to compensate for a loss resulting from a breach of this declaration or the claims settlement agreement, may be enforced by the prevailing party in the courts of any nation in accordance with its laws.

Annex A

Undertakings of the Government of the United States of America and the Government of the Islamic Republic of Iran with Respect to the Declaration of the Government of the Democratic and Popular Republic of Algeria

Iran, having affirmed its intention to pay all its debts, and those of its controlled institutions, and having agreed to the dismissal of all litigation relating to the blocking or withholding of overseas deposits in U.S. banks, the Algerian Central Bank acting pursuant to Paragraph 5(A) of the accompanying declaration will issue the following instructions to the Central Bank:

(A)   To transfer $3.667 billion to the Federal Reserve Bank of New York to pay the unpaid principal of and interest through December 31, 1980, owing on (1) all loans and credits made by a syndicate of banking institutions, of which a U.S. banking institution is a member, to the Government of Iran, its agencies, instrumentalities or controlled entities, and (2) all loans and credits made by such a syndicate which are guaranteed by the Government of Iran or any of its agencies, instrumentalities or controlled entities, or in such other manner as the United States and the banks holding such overseas deposits shall mutually agree.

(B)   To retain $1.333 billion in the escrow account for the purpose of paying the unpaid principal of and interest owing, if any, on the loans and credits referred to in paragraph (A) after application of the $3.667 billion and on all other indebtedness held by United States banking institutions of, or guaranteed by, the Government of Iran, its agencies, instrumentalities or controlled entities not previously paid, and for the purpose of paying disputed amounts of interest, if any, not exceeding $130 million on Iranian deposits in U.S. banking institutions.   Bank Markazi and the appropriate United States banking institutions shall promptly meet in an effort to agree upon the amounts due under these loans, or the amount of such disputed interest.   In the event of such agreement, the Bank Markazi and the approprivate banking institution shall certify the amount owing to the Central Bank of Algeria which shall instruct the Bank of England to credit, as appropriate, to the account of the Bank Markazi or of the Federal Reserve Bank of New York in order to permit payment to the creditor banking institution.   In the event that within 30 days any U.S. banking institution and the Bank Markazi are unable to agree upon the amounts owed, either party may refer such dispute to binding arbitration by such international arbitration panel as the parties may agree, or failing such agreement within 30 additional days after such reference, by the Iran-United States claims tribunal.   The presiding officer of such panel or tribunal shall certify to the Central Bank of Algeria the amount, if any, determined by it to be owed, whereupon the Central Bank of Algeria shall instruct the Bank of England to credit such amount to the account of the Bank Markazi or of the Federal Reserve Bank of New York in order to permit payment to the appropriate banking institution.   After all disputes are resolved either by agreement or by arbitration award and appropriate payment has been made, the balance of the funds referred to in this Paragraph (B) shall be paid to Bank Markazi.

(C)   To transfer immediately to, or upon the order of, the Bank Markazi all assets in the escrow account in excess of the amounts referred to in Paragraphs (A) and (B).

Chapter 1: Note

1.   For a full account of the hostage crisis and negotiations, see Harold H. Saunders et al., The Iranian Hostage Crisis (New Haven: Yale University Press, 1984), and Gary Sick, 444 Days (New York: Morrow, 1985).

2.
IRAN AND IRAQ AT ALGIERS, 1975

Diane Lieb

At the closing session of the first thirteen-nation summit conference of the Organization of Petroleum Exporting Countries (OPEC), Algeria's president, Houari Boumedienne, declared: "I am happy to announce that last night an agreement was signed that completely eliminated the conflict between the two brotherly countries, Iran and Iraq."[1] The surprise was total, and only after a moment of stupor did the audience rise to give the mediator a standing ovation. This coup de theatre resulted from two private, intensive discussions in which the Algerian leader brought Muhammed Reza Pahlavi, shah of Iran, and Saddam Hussein, deputy chairman of Iraq's leftist junta, together for the first time. The text of the communique, issued later that day of March 6, 1975, consisted of four points by which the two high-level contracting parties decided:

1. To proceed with a permanent demarcation of their land frontiers on the basis of the 1913 Constantinople Protocol and the reports of the 1914 Commission for Delimitation of the Frontier.

2. To delimit their river frontier according to the Thalweg Line (the median line of the Shatt al-Arab navigation channel leading into the Persian Gulf).

3. To reestablish security and confidence along their common frontiers and to undertake to exercise strong and effective control over these frontiers with the aim of putting an end to all infiltrations of a subversive character from either side.

Diane Lieb received her Ph.D. in political science from New York University in 1983 and is currently engaged in postdoctoral research.

4.   To consider the above provisions as insep-
arable elements of a comprehensive settlement, any
breach of which would be incompatible with the spirit of
the accord as a whole. [2]

Moreover, the agreement--which came to be known as
the Algiers Accord--specified that the two contracting
parties would meet with Algeria's foreign minister in
Tehran "to determine the working conditions of the mixed
Iranian-Iraqi commission, created with the aim of putting into practice the decisions fixed above by common
accord." Finally, the communique stated that Iran and
Iraq would invite Algeria to all the joint commission's
future meetings to help prepare the details necessary
for implementing the agreement. As anticipated, Iranian
representative Abbas Ali Khalatbari met with Saadoun
Hammadi of Iraq on March 15 in Tehran. After two days
and one night of difficult negotiations in the presence
of Algerian Foreign Minister Abdul-Aziz Bouteflika, the
two countries agreed to set up three working commissions: one to delimit their common land frontier, one
to delimit their common river frontier, and one to work
out a system of common surveillance along both
frontiers. [3]
The second foreign ministers' meeting took place
in Baghdad on April 19. For two days the Iranian and
Iraqi representatives, again with Bouteflika's help,
deliberated over the findings of the three committees.
Out of these sessions came four documents, the most
important of which defined the border line of the Shatt
al-Arab. The median line of the main channel was demarcated and recognized as the river frontier between the
two countries. [4]
The third and last meeting took place on May 18 in
Algiers.   There the three foreign ministers heard
reports from the three tripartite committees concerning
the delimitation of land and river frontiers and security matters along both borders. [5] During a closed
session on May 20 the parties ratified the essential
elements for a demarcation of their common land frontier. In a communique issued at the end of this session, Iran and Iraq announced that a committee had been
formed to prepare the final documents for an accord
based on the principles of the March 6 formula and its
implementing details, as agreed upon in the Tehran,
Baghdad, and Algiers protocols. After three successive
meetings in Algiers, Tehran, and Baghdad, a Treaty on
International Borders and Good-Neighborly Relations was
signed at Baghdad on June 13, 1975. [6] In addition to the
three protocols and appendices establishing land and
river frontiers and those on border security, the two
governments exchanged a letter and memorandum binding
them to settle the still-unresolved issues of navigation

in the Shatt al-Arab, grazing rights in the border pas-
tures, and border guards on both sides of the frontier.
     The Algiers Accord represents a curious diplomatic
breakthrough in the long and violent history of Irano-
Iraqi history.   It is also a good example of step-by-
step mediation.   During the first cycle of third-party
intervention, the United Nations played a key role in
reinforcing a highly unstable ceasefire along a poorly
demarcated central border.   This effort was followed by
Egyptian offers of Arab support for the shah's Persian
Gulf policies in return for Tehran's agreeing to a peace
with Baghdad. 7   This interlude of "quiet contacts"
between Muslim actors culminated in a third and final
mediating cycle in which Algeria's leader provided the
setting that allowed both sides to acknowledge in public
what they had already conceded in private.
     At Algiers the two main military protagonists in
the Persian Gulf area put an end (at least temporarily)
to long-standing disputes that had sapped their energies
in periodic flare-ups of violence since 1969.   In a
skillfully drafted communique, Iraq agreed to considerable territorial concessions: First, by agreeing to the
principle of the Thalweg Line as the new boundary, it
abandoned an ancient claim to sovereignty in the Shatt
al-Arab; second, Baghdad agreed to delimit its land
frontier with Iran on the basis of agreements that
predated the British presence in Iraq.   In return for
these concessions, the shah promised to halt his substantial assistance to Kurdish rebels fighting for
autonomy in northeastern Iraq. Thanks to Boumedienne's
careful attention to the wording of the document, Iraq's
territorial concessions were not spelled out in detail;
nor was any reference made to the Kurds by name, an
allusion that might have caused considerable embarrassment to the shah.
     While each of these disputes generated more than
enough tension and bitterness to spill over into all-out
war, these and many other grievances reflected deeper
animosities rooted in the historical, ideological, and
political makeup of the Gulf.   The historical threads of
Irano-Iraqi border disputes can be traced back to
Persian-Ottoman rivalries for cultural and political
supremacy in the region.   Since 1520 these imperial
states had concluded and terminated eighteen treaties
dealing with their fluvial and terrestrial frontiers. 8
In the modern period, the ideological chasm separating
the Iranian monarchy from the revolutionary, socialist-
oriented regimes in Baghdad led the shah to resent the
expanding Soviet presence in the Gulf.   In turn, Iraq
disdained Iran's excessive reliance on the United
States.   These ideological differences also heightened
the shah's fears that Iraq might successfully export
instability and political radicalism to other Gulf
states, and that its socialist system might serve as a

model for Iranian opposition to his rule. Indeed, another source of conflict between the two governments had been Iraq's support for antigovernment Iranians, who had traditionally sought refuge in the Iraqi cites of Karbala and An-Najaf, holy cities of Shi'a worship.[9] The search for military supremacy in the Persian Gulf following Britain's announcement to withdraw its forces in 1968 constituted a third source of conflict.[10]

Thus, the dispute between Iran and Iraq went far beyond an immediate conflict over real estate; indeed, the number of issues dividing them encompassed the entire range of their relations. The contrasting nature of their political systems, the active support lent to indigenous minorities and political exiles seeking to weaken and overthrow the existing regimes, the opposing pulls of the superpowers, and the legacy of 460 years of competition in the Persian Gulf--all these sources of conflict convinced many observers of Gulf affairs of the impossibility of reconciling Iran and Iraq. Indeed, the increasing number of frontier incidents along the central border, the growing hostility generated by Iraq's expulsion of Iranian residents, and Hussein's decision to crush the Kurdish separatist movement all pointed to full-scale war once the warmth of spring had melted the snow in the Kurdish highlands. This is why the news of the Algiers Accord was received with such surprise. How can we explain this unexpected shift in the way Iran and Iraq managed their conflict?

History proceeds more in paradox than in logic, and it is this paradox that explains why Iran and Iraq chose a diplomatic solution over a violent one at this time in their history. Iran and Iraq had to go to the brink of total war before they could restructure the values they had previously attached to the underlying issues of their conflict. In the new construction, the cost of winning or losing in Iraqi Kurdestan became, for both countries, greater than the cost of an agreement. Meanwhile, changes in the regional and international environments in the 1970s had created some confluence of foreign policy interests, adding value to a negotiated solution. Houari Boumedienne's specific contribution to the agreement lay in providing the setting for the initial agreement and in implementing the March formula.

The Disputed Issues: The Kurds and the Shatt al-Arab

Like so many others in the Mideast, the Kurdish movement for greater autonomy from Iraq's central government became enmeshed in the balance of the external forces on which it depended for its survival and success.[11] In the early years of the rebellion, no neighboring country except Iran gave consistent support to the separatist movement.[12] Until 1974 even Iran's sup-

port had been limited and inconsistent, coming mainly in
the form of light arms, money, food, medicine, and
refuge for Kurdish women and children, whose menfolk
carried on their guerrilla-style war across the border.[13]
Why did Iran, with its own history of Kurdish troubles,
support (however sparingly) these mountain tribesmen
during their earlier cycles of revolt? The answer, in
short, is that the shah's pattern of controlled,
camouflaged aid reflected a deliberate strategy designed
to keep the despised Iraqi leadership sufficiently weak
to deter it from flexing its muscles in the Persian Gulf
and thwarting the shah's ambitions there.[14] With the
prospect of Britain evacuating its forces from the area
by 1971, the shah had begun to formulate and implement
grandiose strategies that were to bring Iran dominance
of the treasured waterway. Thus it was to his advantage
to keep the Kurdish issue open, obliging successive
Iraqi governments to attend to it from time to time.
Meanwhile, the shah, having seized the initiative,
played out his imperial ambitions in the region.[15]

        The second issue in dispute between Iran and Iraq
was the Shatt al-Arab boundary. One element of the
dispute was the unresolved status of the waterway since
the signing of the July 1937 Frontier Treaty between the
Kingdom of Iraq and the Empire of Iran.[16] In articles 3
and 5 of that treaty, Iran and Iraq agreed to set up a
mixed commission to define their common frontier and
administer the waterway. However, the two sides could
not agree on the nature and degree of the commission's
authority. After conclusion of the Baghdad Pact twenty
years later, Iraq agreed to an Iranian proposal for a
Swedish arbitrator to faciliate the resolution of differences, but the bloody overthrow of the Iraqi monarchy
in 1958 cut short this earlier effort at a diplomatic
solution.[17]

        In December 1959 a crisis erupted in the Persian
Gulf when Iraq's new leader claimed a three-mile stretch
of water opposite the Abadan port that had been ceded to
Iran in the 1937 treaty.[18] The Iranian response was to
reiterate its traditional position; namely, that the
boundary between the two countries along the entire
length of the Shatt al-Arab (and not just opposite
Abadan port) should run through the middle of the
deepwater channel. These verbal exchanges touched off a
series of hostile actions, foreshadowing a pattern in
which one aspect of the conflict was to spill over into
other disputed areas. Thus, while both sides alerted
their armed forces and fortified their frontier, the
Iraqi government vented its frustration by harassing
Iranian residents and Shi'a pilgrims in the holy cities.

        This early crisis along the river frontier fizzled
out by mid-January 1960. The shah did not cede the
three-mile strip of water, nor did Qasim retract his
claim to the entire waterway and exclusive Iraqi admin-

istration of it.   The border remained relatively calm
until the British announced their intention to withdraw
forces from the Persian Gulf in 1968.   A brief hope for
negotiations appeared in 1967, when Iraq's new leader,
Abd al-Rahman Arif, came to Tehran to discuss a wide
range of issues.   Yet, as Ramazani notes with regard to
the waterway, it never became clear what was agreed
upon. [19] Moreover, even if the leaders had made some
headway on substance, a diplomatic solution could not
have survived the turbulence of Iraqi domestic politics.
Hardly a year was to pass before the next storm broke
the short lull in relations between the two countries.
That tempest came in April 1969.

To the Brink--1969-74

The momentous British decision to remove its
forces from the Gulf area after 150 years of Pax
Britannica created new opportunities and new dangers for
Iran and Iraq.   As both countries spun out complex
strategies in the Gulf, their major and minor controversies became entangled in the webs, pulling both sides to
the brink of war in the spring of 1975.   The period from
1969 to 1975 is marked by a serious deterioration in
Irano-Iraqi relations, by the shah's expanding power in
the Gulf (paralleled by Iraq's growing frustration at
its inability to thwart Iran's objectives there), and by
the increased value that each side attached to all of
the major issues in dispute.
In April 1969 the Shatt al-Arab controversy again
reached a crisis point. [20]   The need to counter Iranian
support for the opposition to the new Ba'thist regime
may well have led al-Bakr, Iraq's new strong man, to
renew Iraq's claim in the waterway.   The region had also
taken on new importance with the growth of industry in
southern Iraq.   Since Iraq considered the Shatt as an
integral part of its sovereign domain, al-Bakr demanded
that all Iranian ships lower their flags in the river.
Iran, now more confident of its ability to deal
with Iraq, abrogated the 1937 treaty, placed its forces
on full alert, and sent two large freighters with raised
flags into the river with an impressive military escort.
The shah's swift response brought results: the
Iraqi government quickly backed down behind a face-
saving device that linked the conflict to the Arab-
Israeli one.   Arguing that since Iran's actions were
designed to weaken Iraq's contribution to the more vital
"Israeli front," Iraq would not be drawn into war with
Iran at this time. [21] Iran's fait accompli established a
precedent, however, allowing it to use the river as if
the border had passed to the Thalweg Line.   The shah had
clearly won this second round.

The 1969 crisis at the Shatt al-Arab differed from the 1959 incident in three important ways. First, Iran had become a military power; its monarch had effectively concentrated control over foreign policy, successfully courted "moderate" Arab friends in the Gulf, and was on good terms with both superpowers. In contrast, Iraq's chronically unstable political factions had few regional friends. This shift in political fortunes heightened Iraq's ancient fear of Persian dominance in the Gulf. Later, the country's dependence on the Soviet Union was to become a double-edged sword. The more military aid Baghdad received from the Kremlin in support of its effort against the Kurds, the more it paid in conces- sions in the Gulf (for example, the Soviets were given docking privileges at Umm Qasr).

The second difference was the increased value both sides now attached to the Shatt al-Arab, both in eco- nomic and strategic terms. [22] Given the ever-increasing economic importance of the Gulf to both oil-producers, the opposing ideological orientations and foreign-policy objectives of both countries, and the looming prospect of Gulf insecurity left by the British vacuum, forced the Shatt al-Arab dispute into the larger regional struggle for power and prestige at the head of the Gulf. Iran and Iraq were playing for high stakes: Who would be the power in the Gulf? Although the Shatt al-Arab itself was not the scene of further violence between 1969 and 1975, the dispute had become caught in the web of Gulf power politics. The level of military force that each side had committed to it was high enough to keep the stalemate dangerously unstable.

The third element distinguishing the 1969 escala- tion from the earlier period was the effect of one area of dispute spilling over into another. As a result, the level of hostilities (except for brief lulls) remained high, and as each dispute escalated and spilled back into another area, the values attached to it took on increasing symbolic and substantive importance. Let us briefly trace this process in three areas.

First, we recall that in 1959 the Iraqi response to what was regarded as Iranian provocation in the Shatt was to single out Iranian residents and Shi'a pilgrims as targets of harassment. But now, Iraq's frustration with the shah's growing military superiority in the Gulf resulted in an intensified campaign of violence against the Iranian community. [23]

A second spillover took the form of attempts by each side to discredit and subvert the government of the other. While the shah continued to assist the Kurds, Iraq used anti-shah dissidents as a political instrument against Iran. [24] The third area in which the spillover continued to escalate the violence involved a strip of land extending approximately 200 miles into central Iraq. The ancient dispute over this land, like that

concerning the river, was to have been resolved under
the terms of the 1937 treaty. Article 1 of this treaty
stipulated that the border line between the two countries was to be the line fixed and plotted by the 1914
Turco-Persian Border Commission. Moreover, Article 3 of
the treaty called for the formation of a committee to
erect border pillars, whose sites were fixed by the 1914
commission. [25] The commission began its work but never
completed demarcating the central boundary.

Beginning in 1972, this border became the site of
numerous shooting incidents that resulted in both sides
placing complaints before the U.N. Security Council.
These grievances were usually followed by more complaints of Iraqi expulsion of Iranian residents and
Iranian attempts to undermine the Iraqi regime by
supporting the rebellious Kurds. When the 1973 war
between Israel and the Arabs broke out, some believed
that relations between the two sides might improve, but
in the very month that Iran and Iraq resumed diplomatic
relations after a three-year hiatus, a new round of
fighting broke out in the central border district and
reached serious proportions.

Iraq appeared to have changed its perceptions of
the boundary dispute by the spring of 1974, ceasing to
see the problem as one of isolated border incidents, but
rather as one of territorial encroachment by Iran; boundary change was allegedly Iran's goal in abrogating the
1937 treaty on the Shatt al-Arab River. [26] In this way,
the central border dispute became caught in the web of
the river controversy for the first time and, as a
result, took on greater symbolic value.

U.N. Mediation: Heightening Awareness of Stalemate

We have seen in the last section how the 1969
crisis in the Shatt al-Arab triggered a cycle of
conflict between Iran and Iraq that went from bad to
worse. This state of affairs resulted from three
related elements: (1) the reality of Iranian power
throughout the Gulf; (2) the growing importance of the
Shatt al-Arab within the context of power politics in
the Gulf; and (3) the spillover effects of Irano-Iraqi
controversies. By the spring of 1974, these spillovers
heightened the tensions along the entire length of the
borders. Each side feared that the next round of
aggression would be more costly than the last.

Accompanying this escalation was a marked increase
in the number of complaints to the U.N. Security Council
in the early months of 1974. On February 12 of that
year, the Iraqi government asked for an urgent meeting
of the council, following a serious frontier incident
two days before. [27] When the council met on February 15,
Iran's representative, Fereydoun Hoveyda, stated his

government's readiness to settle the border dispute through direct talks. Iraq's representative, Talib el-Shibib, agreed, provided that Iran first accept its obligations under the 1937 boundary treaty. This demand was countered by a long, familiar argument explaining why Iran no longer considered the treaty valid. Then, on February 28, the council adopted a consensus statement asking U.N. Secretary-General Kurt Waldheim to appoint a special representative to investigate the events leading to the latest clash. [28]   Both sides accepted Waldheim's invitation and gave assurances that they would cooperate fully with his representative, Luis Weckmann, Mexico's ambassador in Bonn. Waldheim's goal was clearly to "freeze a situation which was developing into an all-out war." [29]   The Security Council mandate instructed Weckmann to prepare a detailed report of his investigation upon his return from the Mideast.

This fact-finding mission was limited to the 200-mile stretch of land along the central border, from Qasr as-Shirin to Mehran in Iran, and from Khanaqin to Badra in Iraq. However, what began as an investigative task with the special purpose of determining a way to defuse and contain this dimension of the conflict turned out to encompass a far more comprehensive third-party role. The unexpected turn of events arose, in part, from the enormous difficulties the ambassador experienced in telephoning Waldheim for further instructions. [30]   When Weckmann saw a moment ripe for more active mediation, he seized it.

Ambassador Weckmann made two important discoveries in his role as fact-finder. First, he found that the frontier in the area of the recent incidents had never been formally demarcated. There was a de facto boundary that varied from the one shown on maps drawn up by former boundary commissions. The ambassador conveyed his observation that each side was using different sets of maps with different border tracings. After correcting this discrepancy, Iran and Iraq agreed on the need to establish a new, mixed commission to set the boundary line once and for all. [31]

The second discovery had to do with the nature of the military buildup along the border. Evidently, neither side was fully aware of the instability inherent in the concentration of forces and heavy weaponry. Ambassador Weckmann attempted to instill in both parties a heightened sense of the situation on the ground. As proof of success, he reported that both sides expressed a desire not only to observe the March 7 ceasefire, but also to "begin a prompt and simultaneous withdrawal of concentrations of armed forces along the entire border in accordance with an arrangement to be agreed upon between the appropriate authorities of the two countries." [32]

After an hour-long conversation with the shah, Weckmann saw a chance to negotiate a full agreement. Following the interview with the Iranian monarch, Foreign Minister Khalatbari gave out signals that Iran was, indeed, ready to settle the entire range of its problems with Iraq, although the Kurdish problem was not mentioned explicitly. Weckmann carried the idea to Baghdad, where it was received favorably by Saddam Hussein. [33] The Iraqis gave the mediator an extensive river tour from Basra to Abadan in the course of which they clarified the Iraqi position on a variety of issues in the waterway including hazards in the Shatt due to navigation problems, the extent of territorial waters, fishing zones, and exploitation of the continental shelf.

Thus, what began as a U.N. fact-finding mission with the very limited goal of reinforcing an unstable ceasefire evolved into a mediating cycle, setting diplomatic processes in motion. These processes culminated in Boumedienne's successful mediation twelve months later when Iranian and Iraqi leaders met for the first time in Algiers. Thanks to Weckmann's careful preparation, and his meticulous efforts to inspect all of the areas in dispute, he was able not only to reinforce the March 7 ceasefire; he also altered Iranian and Iraqi perceptions of their opponent's motivations, at least in the central district, and made more salient the danger inherent in the situation on the ground. Having uncoupled the problem of the border frontier from the larger, emotion-laden issue of "territorial encroachment," the mediator helped the parties discover the formula that ultimately settled the dispute. The fact that both sides willingly agreed to abide by the findings of the new, mixed commission to delimit the frontier attests to the mediator's success in accurately portraying both a reality (hidden by centuries of deep animosity) and a range of negotiated solutions based on redrawing the boundary line somewhere down the middle of the disputed territory.

Upon Weckmann's return from his four-week mission to the Mideast, he filed a detailed report to the Security Council. [34] Although this first mediating attempt went far beyond the fact-finding role mandated by the council, and although it appeared that there was a real opportunity to manage at least one aspect of the conflict, the Security Council evidently did not see the need to follow up on the ambassador's findings and conclusions—conclusions that pointed to a continued U.N. role in the diplomatic cycle the mediator had begun. In Weckmann's view, both sides could have made considerable progress in settling the border problem in the central district at this time. However, some role for the United Nations was clearly indicated. This is particularly true in the area of disengagement. Both

sides had agreed to pull back their forces along the
entire border as a part of future bilateral negotiations. Yet, as Tomasek points out, "the Security Council made no provisions for following up in the future
negotiations what progress had been made, or even check-
ing to determine if a military withdrawal had taken
place and would continue." [35]

   This lost opportunity was most unfortunate. Seen
in the light of history, a major stumbling block in the
conflict has been the strain put on both sides to agree
bilaterally on the nature and powers of a mixed commission to demarcate borders. [36] Indeed, as we shall see, a
major ingredient in Boumedienne's success lay in his
provision for a continued Algerian presence to ease this
strain. That is why his foreign minister took part in
all three of the meetings in which the joint commissions
implemented the details of the Algiers formula. No such
function was envisioned for the United Nations in 1974.
The United Nations could have contributed to the resolution process by providing observers to check on the
actual process of disengagement. [37] Yet the entire load
of this first negotiating step seems to have been put on
the parties themselves, not only to maintain a highly
vulnerable ceasefire, but also to negotiate both the
procedure and substance of their deep-seated
differences. Clearly, any jolt in the tenuous
stalemates along the Kurdish border, the central border,
or the river border, would deal a serious blow to the
mediator's achievements; and that is exactly what
happened in the late spring of 1974, when Saddam
Hussein, now Iraq's leader, began his all-out war
against the Kurdish community.

The Hurting Escalation

   The events and developments leading up to the
collapse of the four-year old stalemate in the Kurdish
revolt need not concern us here. [38] What is important to
note is that, by the fall of 1974, it was clear that the
next round of fighting would be different from all previous ones. Hussein, well aware that past stalemates
with the Kurds had doomed former regimes, was committing
his political career to total victory. He took this
enormous gamble because Iraq was stronger than ever
before, thanks to Soviet supplies of arms and training
for Iraqi soldiers. By September Hussein's "go for
broke" strategy appeared to be working: Only one supply
route to the Iranian border remained open, and Iraqi
troops had captured almost every Kurdish city and town.
As a result, some 130,000 Kurds had fled en masse to
Iran.
   As the level of fighting increased, Iran found
itself involved in more military operations than had

been the case in the past. With each Kurdish setback,
Iranian border forces became further involved, so that
by late summer Iraq protested to the Security Council
that Iran was putting troops in the central border
frontier in violation of the March ceasefire. Tomasek
documents that it was then that the Kurdish conflict
spilled over into the central border conflict for the
first time. [39] This made the entire nature of the
fighting riskier for everyone. By September the Kurds
seemed to be hanging on by a thread. The shah then
brought in more artillery, including some very sophisticated weapons that had never been used before (radar-
guided antiaircraft, Hawk missile batteries, and anti-
tank weapons). With this substantial escalation in
assistance, the Kurds managed to blunt the Iraqi drive
as the winter snows set in.
     The situation on the ground had now reached a
turning point. In the past, the pattern of the Kurdish
flare-ups had been an Iraqi offensive in spring and
summer, followed by limited Iranian assistance to the
Kurds, winter stalemate, and an Iraqi decision to negotiate before spring. But this winter, Hussein was not
going to negotiate. Instead, he kept up Iraqi pressure
on the Kurds all through the winter months, preparing to
deal the rebels a death blow in the spring. Clearly the
ball was now in the Iranian court. The shah had to make
the momentous decision whether or not to save the Kurds
from total defeat when the spring season arrived for
renewed military operations. His decision not to make a
major military commitment to the Kurds resulted from a
complex set of factors that together made the benefits
of an agreement appear to outweigh those of more
conflict.

Secret Diplomacy: The Egyptian, Jordanian and Turkish Mediating Roles

     Playing the Kurdish Card. We recall that the
shah's policy of support for the Kurds had always been a
means, not an end. Now the time was ripe to use this
bargaining card. Three reasons explain why the moment
was ripe. First, the policy had become an expensive and
risky one. Until the summer of 1974 the shah had been
able to keep the Kurdish sore raw using only limited
means; but now, continued assistance would mean more
sophisticated weapons, more advisors and personnel, more
refugees, and the increased possibility of bombed oil
fields and refineries. On the other hand, if the shah
did nothing for the insurgents (and at the same time
chose not to negotiate with Hussein), he would lose his
leverage with Baghdad in the continuing border wars.
     The second reason that caused the scales of choice
to tip in favor of diplomacy had to do with changes in

regional goals and the global balance of power in the 1970s. Iraq had begun to signal an interest in loosening its ties with the Soviet Union, with which it signed a treaty of friendship in 1972. If the shah were to raise the ante in the spring, Hussein might be forced to maintain or increase his dependence on the Soviets. The shah, ever insecure about Russian influence in the Persian Gulf, must have weighed this into the scales as he evaluated the cost of conflict.

Finally, the shah's decision to seek a diplomatic way out of his dispute with Iraq was tied to his regional goal of cultivating friends and allies with Arab states, not only in the Gulf, but in the rest of the Mideast as well. Before and after the British withdrawal from the region, the shah curried favor with all of the oil-producing states in the Gulf (except Iraq) by economic, military, and diplomatic means. Beyond the immediate Gulf area, the Iranian monarch resumed diplomatic ties with Lebanon and ended his ten-year feud with Egypt. These hard-won political realignments might have been endangered by an Iranian war in Iraq. If the shah chose war, the oil-producing Arab states, fearing the unstable effects of war on OPEC cooperation, might close ranks and isolate Iran. There was more to be gained by agreement among all OPEC members to keep oil prices high and avoid conflict. Choosing more conflict would also seriously strain relations with other Arab states, which sought not to divert Iraq from assisting them in any future confrontation with Israel.

This concern for Arab friendship was strong enough to cause the shah to have second thoughts about his Iraqi policy as early as 1974. Weckmann's reflections on his meeting with the Iranian leader point out the degree to which the shah had thought through the advantages of settlement for his Arab policy. [40] But it was hurting escalation that heightened the shah's need to resolve this dilemma before the approaching deadline. The major new factor introduced during the winter stage of the Kurdish war was the increase of outside aid to both sides. In response to Iran's stepped-up assistance to the Kurds, the Soviet Union supplied its ally with tactical ground-to-ground missiles; moreover, it was reported that Soviet pilots, flying MIG-23 jets, were engaged in combat missions. Although these reports were unconfirmed and even may be untrue, they must have aggravated the shah's obsession with Soviet involvement in Gulf affairs. [41]

As the military stalemate continued to take its toll on both parties in spite of the biting winter weather, Egypt, Turkey, and Jordan offered mediation. What lay behind the decision to facilitate a rapprochement, and what kinds of leverage could be brought to bear on the shah of Iran?

Enhancing Interests and Exercising Leverage. When
Nasser died in September 1970, bequeathing the leadership to Sadat, the new Egyptian president began to mas-
termind complex global, regional, and domestic strategies to attain his goals for Egypt. As Iran and Iraq
moved closer to the brink of war, Sadat found a role to
play in settling this dispute--a role that harmonized
well with two of his objectives for his country. First,
we recall that in 1974 Sadat was determined to recover
yet another slice of the Egyptian territory in the Sinai
that had been lost to Israel in the 1967 War. Because
the United States alone could persuade Israel to return
territory, Sadat sought to influence Washington to be
more "evenhanded" in the Arab-Israeli conflict. One
path led through Tehran, which had close relations with
both the United States and Israel. Sadat believed that
the shah might use his connections to improve Cairo's
bargaining position over Sinai land; in return, Sadat
could bring Arab support for the shah's Persian Gulf
policies. 42
     Sadat's second objective for Egypt was to regain
his country's traditional leadership within the Arab
world. Following the first Sinai disengagement agreement with Israel in 1974 and Egypt's subsequent drift
toward the West, Sadat found himself more and more
isolated from regional affairs as the so-called rejec-
tionist group of Arab states (Libya, Iraq, and Algeria)
condemned Sadat's cooperation with Henry Kissinger's
"step-by-step" diplomacy. The Irano-Iraqi conflict
provided a rare opportunity to put cracks in the wall of
anti-Sadat hostility. Thus, when Baghdad indicated that
it was prepared to cooperate with Iran, Sadat used his
leverage in Tehran and extracted a promise from the shah
to cease all subversive activity against Hussein's
government, including aid to the Kurds. Sadat needed
better relations with Iraq to balance his relations with
Syria. Although Iraqi-Egyptian relations remained
strained, the effect of Sadat's quiet diplomacy was
appreciated by Iraq's leader, who continued to feel the
debilitating effects of the Kurdish revolt.
     Third, Egypt needed good relations with Iraq as
well for his own sake. Iraq could furnish Egypt with
financial aid, and in fact gave it as much as $1 billion
over the years. In addition, Iraq could and did absorb
a large number of Egyptian workers at all levels in
order to help ease Egypt's growing population pressure.
Egypt had interests on both sides of the conflict.
     Now that the game of secret diplomacy had elicited
the necessary concessions from both sides (Iraq would
concede the sovereignty issue in the Shatt al-Arab in
return for an end to Iranian aid to the Kurds), all that
remained was to find the appropriate public forum in
which to ratify the substance of an agreement that had
already been worked out privately. Here Sadat found a

second opportunity to mend his fences with another Arab
member of the anti-Sadat coalition. In choosing Algeria
to act as go-between for Iraq and Iran, Sadat offered
Boumedienne a chance to enhance his own prestige in the
region--an objective long pursued by the Algerian head
of state. In return for this "subcontracted" mediating
role, Boumedienne was to adopt a more conciliatory
attitude toward Cairo.

Another element in setting the stage for Egyptian
and Algerian mediation was the failure of other Mideast
attempts at mediation.[43] During the last two weeks of
August 1974, direct negotiations between Iran and Iraq
took place in Istanbul, punctuated by incidents on the
battlefield. Some progress was made and at least a
better atmosphere was begun; under Turkish mediation,
the two countries' ministers agreed to meet again to
continue negotiations. At the same time, King Hussein
of Jordan offered his good offices to the shah while he
was on a visit to Amman, and the shah accepted, adding
to the atmosphere of conciliation. Yet neither mediatory attempt produced enough movement to bring about
agreement, even though both contributed to the momentum
that Egypt then accelerated and Algeria utilized to the
fullest extent.

The Algerian Contribution

By the time the two sides arrived in Algeria for
the first OPEC summit, Iran and Iraq had reassessed the
values previously attached to the issues in dispute.
The shah, aware of the importance of the Kurdish revolt
for Hussein's future, knew that the moment had come to
trade his "Kurdish card" for complete sovereignty in the
Shatt al-Arab waterway.[44] Hussein, having faced up to the
reality of Persian power, conceded that it was less
risky to live on a Gulf dominated by Iran than to oppose
it. Given the new perceptions, the formula for agreement was in place well before the meeting in Algiers.
All that was now required was a forum in which both
sides could communicate these concessions to each other
without losing face and then proceed to implement the
details of their agreement. In these two areas Boumedienne's contribution was essential.

Providing the Proper Setting. Boumedienne's
intervention allowed Iran and Iraq publicly to set out
the substance of an accord that had been previously
worked out through secret contacts. That the Algerian
leader was able to do this reflects first the nation's
place in the international relations of the Persian
Gulf. Algeria is a peripheral actor in Gulf affairs;
hence, this oil-producing state was not caught in the
web of Irano-Iraqi politics--a web that spun through and
politicized the area of oil cooperation. All three

states, and ten other major oil-exporting nations, had
gathered together for the first OPEC summit to prepare a
united stand on oil prices for the preliminary meeting
in Paris with the representatives of the oil-consuming
nations. Through the fact of the OPEC meeting, Boumedienne was in the position to communicate to both sides
the virtue of transcending their differences and closing
ranks in the common OPEC cause.

The second reason why Boumedienne was so well
positioned to mediate this part of the Irano-Iraqi conflict reflects the important place of Islam in Mideast
conflicts. Although Boumedienne was far removed from
the core of Persian Gulf politics, he was, nevertheless,
a Muslim leader; and in Mideast political culture, this
affiliation is often a prerequisite for mediating disputes between Muslim sister-nations. Further, a major
theme running through the violent history of Irano-Iraqi
border disputes has been the Persian-Arab rivalry for
cultural and political hegemony in the region. Now, by
stressing the Muslim component of their relationship,
Boumedienne helped the parties transcend their ethnic
differences; and as a member of the larger "community of
believers," he possessed an impeccable credential needed
to perform the traditional role of a fellow Muslim--
reconciling differences between "members of the same
family."

Implementing the Formula. Boumedienne recognized
the necessity for a continued Algerian intervention
throughout the bargaining process. As noted, in the
first mediating cycle the Security Council made no provisions for a sustained third-party role in the deliberations that followed Ambassador Weckmann's mission.
Thus, when the foreign ministers of Iran and Iraq held
their Istanbul negotiating sessions in the fall of 1974
and in January 1975 for the purpose of implementing
their earlier understandings, the diplomatic process
immediately bogged down in legal arguments and mutual
recriminations. Clearly a different structure was
needed to sustain the atmosphere of pragmatic decision-
making that the ambassador had so artfully created. Now
at Algiers, Boumedienne seemed determined to make his
presence felt and help the parties write a peace treaty
based on the Algiers formula. Thus, the accord specified that the Iranian and Iraqi foreign ministers should
meet in Tehran, in the presence of the Algerian foreign
minister, to determine the modalities by which the mixed
commissions would come into existence. The Tehran Protocol of March 15 was the result of extremely difficult
negotiations over details. Foreign Minister Bouteflika's efforts in keeping the bargaining on a pragmatic
track appear to have been critical during those demanding encounters.

Not only did Boumedienne ensure that Algeria's
representative would participate in the procedural phase

of the bargaining; he also provided for Algerian participation in the deliberations of all three working commissions. The Baghdad and Algiers protocols, of April
20 and May 20 respectively, were the products of these
intense tripartite meetings. Again, Bouteflika demonstrated his mediating skills by encouraging the parties
to make concessions of a highly practical nature, while
discussions of sovereignty and security principles were
avoided. During this phase of the diplomatic process,
one might argue that mediation was necessary to sustain,
not so much the atmosphere of trust as that of pragmatic
problem-solving. The Algerian president carefully cul-
tivated this approach during his intensive talks with
the shah of Iran and Saddam Hussein. Out of these discussions came a tactfully worded formula for an agreement on March 6, 1975. Boumedienne's foreign minister
successfully nurtured this pragmatic approach throughout
the following three months of tedious bargaining over
detail. The working commissions met continuously, and
by mid-June both governments accepted an eighty-page
treaty, based on the principles of the March 6 formula
and its implementing details, as agreed upon in the
Tehran, Baghdad, and Algiers protocols.

Extending and Protecting the Mediator's Interests

Boumedienne's motives in accepting the role of
peacemaker were based primarily on self-interest.
During his tenure as Algeria's head of state,
Boumedienne tried to enhance his international status
and secure a leadership role in the Third World.
Throughout 1975 Algeria continued to be the spokesman
for the developing nations in promoting the "New
International Economic Order." [45] In February representatives of 104 developing nations held a conference
in Algiers to seek a joint stand before a U.N. conference on industrial development scheduled to take place
in Peru. Then, on March 6, Boumedienne assembled
leaders from the major oil-producing countries to the
Algerian capital for the first official OPEC summit
meeting. Here were the chiefs of Saudi Arabia, Kuwait,
Libya, Qatar, and the United Arab Emirates, as well as
Iran and Iraq--all wealthy Mideast nations whose leaders
accorded Boumedienne the honor of speaking in their
name. If Algeria's leader now accepted Sadat's offer to
act as go-between for Iran and Iraq during this two-day
conference, bringing the protagonists together for the
first time in face-to-face talks, he had reason to
believe he might further advance his reputation. In
Mideastern political culture, the mediation of disputes
between Muslim sister-states brings honor and prestige
to the mediating regime and strengthens its legitimacy.
To engage in mediation is to obtain credit for Algeria;

indeed, following the dazzling peace announcement at a reception marking the end of the OPEC summit, Boumedienne continued to express his willingness to undertake mediation. In a flurry of diplomatic activity, he tried to patch up relations between Iraq and Syria in their conflict over the Euphrates, and between Iraq and Kuwait over the islands situated at the approaches to Iraq's Gulf ports. Later that year, he also tried to eradicate the tensions between Egypt and Syria that arose during Kissinger's diplomacy in the Arab-Israeli conflict. [46]

Boumedienne had another motive in accepting mediation beyond that of extending his influence and enhancing his prestige. That motive, defensive in nature, is related to the politics of oil. The Algiers agreement reflects, to a certain degree, the shared concerns about OPEC's future and, as such, reflects the concerns of Algeria, a leading actor in the oil cartel. In 1974 scarcity was the rule in the oil world. By 1975 this had changed to glut, and some oil-rich countries were feeling the effects on their national economies. Algeria saw its crude-oil production fall from 48.7 million metric tons in 1974 to 42.6 million in 1975, and began to experience difficulties in finding markets despite prices. [47] These reverses were danger signals for Boumedienne's ambitious industrialization programs designed to promote Algeria's financial independence. With its relatively large population, this oil-rich nation could not afford to cut back production to maintain the 1975 oil price. So it was not only Iran and Iraq who had a vested interest in preserving OPEC unity; Algeria, too, needed that consensus. A rapprochement between the two countries in the Gulf would limit the damage to OPEC's fortunes. Under the circumstances, the mediator's goal was to obtain an agreement that would bring stability to the Gulf and depoliticize the oil issue within the cartel. If that meant transferring half of the Shatt al-Arab waterway to the shah of Iran and dooming the Kurdish struggle, that was an acceptable solution.

Discovering and Selling the Negotiating Formula

We have seen how the painful escalation in late 1974 contributed to an Irano-Iraqi reassessment of the major issues in dispute and of the ways to resolve them. Neither side wanted an all-out conflagration because the costs of more conflict outweighed the possible benefits. Once this perception was in place, a quid pro quo formula on the two most salient issues became a distinct possibility. In these circumstances, the shah's decision to accept Sadat's (and later Boumedienne's) mediation and agree to a comprehensive peace with Iraq had logical antecedents. The Iranian monarch had already thought out the benefits of a trade-off settlement. First, in return for the shah's sacrifice of the Kurds, Baghdad might agree to end its support of Iranians opposing the shah's regime from Iraq; second, the shah might achieve his grandiose objective of dominating the entire Persian Gulf from the Shatt al-Arab to the Strait of Hormuz, and a concession by Baghdad on the Thalweg Line was the concrete expression of this hegemony; third, an accord with Iraq would be the final chapter in the shah's policy of earning Arab friendship. Thus, when Sadat signaled his willingness to embellish the shah in Arab eyes in return for Tehran's support in Washington, the Egyptian president merely heightened the shah's awareness of the benefits of a diplomatic solution.

Likewise, Hussein's decision to accept mediation was taken in light of the reality of Persian Gulf power. As the spring approached, the threat of all-out Iranian assistance to the Kurds was made painfully credible by the fact of Iranian military superiority. By conceding the Thalweg Line in the Shatt al-Arab, Hussein guaranteed himself a military victory over the Kurds--a victory that also guaranteed his political future as the Iraqi strongman.

These new perceptions may very well have been heightened by third-party actors with a stake in a peaceful settlement. But a more satisfactory explanation seems to lie in the harmony of Iranian and Iraqi foreign-policy objectives--objectives that tempered basic differences. The global expression of Irano-Iraqi rivalry in the Gulf had become a double-edged sword for both Gulf powers; by the mid-1970s, Hussein seemed as interested as the shah in taking the East-West conflict out of Gulf politics. The price the Soviets demanded for helping to solve Iraq's domestic troubles had become too high. So when Hussein began to signal a willingness to reduce his dependence on the Soviet Union, a shared perception of what constituted Persian Gulf security began to develop. Both Iran and Iraq were now inclined to keep the two superpowers far from the waterway.

This switch in Iraqi perceptions of Persian Gulf security made it easier to concede the Shatt al-Arab sovereignty issue. Hussein no longer needed to maintain the pretense that he controlled the Shatt. His regime at home had been stabilized and he could make concessions. The shah, however, regarded the issue as most salient, as it concretely expressed Iraq's recognition of Iranian power in the Gulf's destiny. Since Hussein's future depended on a military victory over the Kurds, conceding the Shatt al-Arab was worth the Kurdish prize.

Thus we have seen that a complex set of factors ranging from domestic concerns for elite legitimacy to a degree of harmony in foreign-policy interests helped bring about the ripe moment for mediation and settle-

ment. Once the perception took hold that it was possible equitably to exchange values with regard to the
disputed issues, other Arab actors stepped into the
conflict to help translate these new attitudes into a
bargaining process. Almost everyone benefited from the
Algiers accord: The shah took another giant step in his
Persian Gulf policies; Hussein consolidated his power at
home; Sadat strengthened his friendship with the shah;
and Boumedienne enhanced his influence in the developing
world. The only losers in this surprising reconciliation were the Iraqi Kurds.[48] Within hours of the March
settlement, the shah closed his border to further military supplies and withdrew his forces operating inside
Iraqi territory. The Iraqi army then opened its offensive along the Kurdish front and, after two weeks of
fighting, the Kurdish resistance collapsed.

Chapter 2: Notes

1.   New York Times, March 7, 1975.

2.   For the full text of the communique, see the New York
Times, March 8, 1975.

3.   Arab Report & Record, no. 6 (March 1975): 192.

4.   Arab Report & Record, no. 8 (April 1975): 248.

5.   Arab Report & Record, no. 10 (May 1975): 307-08.

6.   The full text of the treaty can be found in
"Selections from the Iraqi-Iranian Dispute" (mimeographed)
(Baghdad: Ministry of Foreign Affairs, January 1981), 183-97.

7.   A high-ranking Egyptian official provided the author
with evidence of Sadat's third-party role and of his motives for
mediation. (Interview held in Washington, June 1982.)   Edmund
Ghareeb cites corrborating evidence of an earlier Egyptian
mediation. (Interview with a high-ranking U.S. State Department
official, March 15, 1977.)   See Edmund Ghareeb, The Kurdish
Question in Iraq (New York: Syracuse University Press, 1981), 171.
Dr. Ghareeb has made useful comments on this chapter.

8.   For a history of these treaties, see Vahe J. Sevian,
"The Evolution of the Boundary Between Iraq and Iran," in Charles
A. Fisher, ed., Essays in Political Geography (London: Methuen &
Co., 1968), 211-23.

9.   The Ayatollah Khomeini had been granted asylum in Iraq
after being exiled by the shah in 1964.   For twelve years, Baghdad
allowed him to wage a war of rhetoric against the shah.   But after
the March settlement (which put an end to meddling in each other's
affairs), Khomeini's activities became troublesome to Hussein.   In
the fall of 1978 the Iraqi leader acceded to the shah's request and
removed Khomeini from Iraq.   The Ayatollah went to Paris and
remained there until his triumphal return to Tehran in February
1979.   Relations between the two countries immediately deteriorated
and slipped back into war in September 1980, following Iraq's
abrogation of the Algiers agreement.

10.   A detailed history of Persian Gulf politics after the
British departure appears in Rouhallah K. Ramazani, Iran's Foreign
Policy, 1941-1973 (Charlottesville: University Press of Virginia,
1975), 427-38.

11.   From 1961 to 1970 the Iraqi government undertook four
unsuccessful military campaigns to crush the Kurdish rebellion.   In
1970 the Baghdad regime reluctantly signed a comprehensive
agreement conceding substantial autonomy to the Kurdish community.
Four years later, this fragile peace unraveled.   The most detailed

coverage of these events can be found in Edgar O'Ballance, The Kurdish Revolt: 1961-1970 (Westport, Conn.: Archon Books, 1973).

12.   Turkey's correct relations with all the Baghdad regimes and its concern for the loyalty of its own four million Kurds precluded any help to the Kurdish revolt. In spite of their deteriorating relations with the Iraqi leadership, neither the Syrian elite nor Egypt's President Nasser paid more the lip-service to the Kurdish cause. As for the Soviet Union, at no time did its commitment to the doctrine of "national liberation" lead to a consistent policy of Kurdish support.

13.   Robert A. Tomasek, "The Resolution of Major Controversies Between Iran and Iraq," World Affairs 139 (Winter 1976-77): 220-21.

14.   A comprehensive treatment of the shah's Persian Gulf policies before the British withdrawal is given in Ramazani, Iran's Foreign Policy, 395-427.

15.   The shah's aggressive policies in the Gulf are marked by his unilateral abrogation of the 1937 Boundary Treaty in 1969 (which placed the Shatt al-Arab frontier on Iran's eastern bank); his seizure of the strategic islands of the Greater and Lesser Tunbs and Abu Musa in 1971; and his appropriation of the Strait of Hormuz in 1973.

16.   For the complete text of this treaty, see "Selections from the Iraqi-Iranian Dispute," 149-51.

17.   The Iraqi Revolution of 1958 is probably the single most important event that turned the shah's attention to the Persian Gulf. Eight months after Qasim's coup, he terminated Iraq's association with the Baghdad Pact. This rupture in the region's western security system aggravated the shah's fear that postrevolutionary Iraq would export political radicalism and instability to the rest of the Gulf.

18.   The 1959 crisis at the Shatt al-Arab is carefully documented in Shahram Chubin and Sepehr Zabih, The Foreign Relations of Iran (Berkeley: University of California Press, 1974), 172-74; Ramazani, Iran's Foreign Policy, 400-02.

19.   Ibid., 403-04.

20.   The best accounts of the 1969 crisis at the Shatt al-Arab can be found in Chubin and Zabih, The Foreign Relations of Iran, 185-87; Ramazani, Iran's Foreign Policy, 417-18.

21.   This linkage of the Irano-Iraqi dispute with the Arab-Israeli conflict was also invoked by the Iraqi government as the primary reason for Baghdad's acceptance of Boumedienne's mediating offer at Algiers. See "The Iraqi-Iranian Conflict, Documentary Dossier," mimeographed (Baghdad: Ministry of Foreign

Affairs, January 1981), 24.   The mirror image of this linkage appears in Iran's efforts to discredit the Baghdad regime: the Iraqi government was depicted by the shah as anti-Arab because it conspicuously failed to aid the Arab cause of Palestine.   Chubin & Zabih, The Foreign Relations of Iran, 190.

22.   Tomasek, "The Resolution of Major Controversies Between Iran and Iraq," 209-11.

23.   In 1970, a policy of Iranian expulsions reached serious proportions.   According to one report, 8,317 Iranians were evicted from Iraq in October 1971.   This number reached 30,000 by December of the same year, and at the beginning of 1973 passed the 60,000 mark.   These figures are taken from Mohammed Reza Djalili, "Le Rapprochement Irano-Irakien et ses consequences," Politique Etrangere 40 (Fall 1975): 281.

24.   For example, Teymour Bakhtiar (Iran's former security chief) was encouraged by Baghdad to organize subversive activities against Iran.   Ibid., 280.

25.   "Selections from the Irano-Iraqi Dispute," 149-50.

26.   Tomasek, "The Resolution of Major Controversies Between Iran and Iraq," 216.

27.   According to the Iraqi version of the February incident, Iran suffered more than 70 casualties, including the dead and wounded.   See U.N. Document S/11216, February 12, 1974.   See also documents S/11230, March 6, 1974; S/11231, March 6, 1974; S/11233, March 12, 1974; S/11241, March 27, 1974.

28.   U.N. Document S/11229, February 28, 1974.

29.   Correspondence between author and Ambassador Luis Weckmann, June 1982.

30.   Ibid.

31.   U.N. Document S/11291, May 20, 1974.

32.   Ibid.

33.   Correspondence between author and Ambassador Luis Weckmann, June 1982.

34.   U.N. Document S/11291, May 20, 1974.

35.   Tomasek, "The Resolution of Major Controversies Between Iran and Iraq," 218.

36.   For a penetrating analysis of the element of trust in conflict resolution, see I. William Zartman, "Explaining Disengagement," in Jeffrey Z. Rubin, ed., Dynamics of Third Party

Intervention: Kissinger in the Middle East (New York: Praeger,
1981).

        37.   This lost opportunity is noted in Tomasek, "The
Resolution of Major Controversies Between Iran and Iraq," 218.

        38.   For a detailed analysis of these events, see Honore M.
Catudel, Jr., "The War in Kurdistan: End of a Nationalist
Struggle?"   International Relations 5 (May 1976): 1033–38, and
Ghareeb, The Kurdish Question.

        39.   Tomasek, "The Resolution of Major Controversies
Between Iran and Iraq," 222.

        40.   Correspondence between author and ambassador Luis
Weckmann, June 1982.

        41.   Keesing's Contemporary Archives, April 7–13, 1975,
27053.

        42.   Interview with a high-ranking Egyptian official, June
1982.

        43.   Majid Khadduri, Socialist Iraq (Washington: Middle
East Institute, 1978), 151.

        44.   On the importance of the trade-off in reaching a
settlement, see Tomasek, "The Resolution of Major Controversies
Between Iran and Iraq," 207.

        45.   Arab Report & Record: 1975 in Retrospect (1975), 4.

        46.   Ibid.

        47.   Ibid.

        48.   For a detailed account of the collapse of the Kurdish
struggle, see Catudel, "The War in Kurdistan," 1040–44.

3.
THE ZIMBABWE SETTLEMENT, 1976-1979

Stephen Low

British efforts to resolve the conflict between the minority white government and black majority population of Rhodesia stretch back to the period before the colony's Unilateral Declaration of Independence in November 1965. Negotiations between British and Rhodesian governments from 1963 through 1965, and settlement proposals made in 1966, in 1968, and in 1979 (the Home-Smith Agreement) were all ultimately unsuccessful.

The effort that finally resulted in a settlement agreement in December 1979 began in March 1976 with a statement in the British Parliament by Prime Minister James Callaghan, followed by a speech in Lusaka the following month by U.S. Secretary of State Henry Kissinger. Thus begun, the movement toward settlement continued through various stages or rounds to its ultimately successful conclusion. Callaghan's proposal contained the formula that, with some modifications, served as the basis for subsequent efforts in each of the succeeding rounds. The prime minister had proposed a settlement based on white acceptance of majority rule, with elections to be followed by independence and, later, negotiation of a constitution. He offered British economic assistance for the independent country's development and volunteered to participate in the negotiations toward a settlement on this basis. The following month in Lusaka, Kissinger added the commitment of U.S. support. This, too, remained a constant feature of further efforts. Unspoken but implied in Callaghan's response to a question posed following his remarks was the final major element in the settlement--resumption of British authority following the agreement and administration of a transitional period that was to include the elections.

Stephen Low is director of the Foreign Service Institute, the U.S. Department of State. Dr. Low was U.S. ambassador to Zambia from 1976 to 1979, and ambassador to Nigeria from 1979 to 1981. He also served on the U.S.-U.K. mission to southern African, which assisted in negotiating the resolution of the Rhodesia-Zimbabwe problem.

There were some differences in the conduct and context of the successive rounds. In the first round, Kissinger and then Ivor Richards, the British permanent representative to the U.N. Security Council, carried on the negotiations alone while keeping the Rhodesian government fully informed. The second round was conducted almost entirely by means of negotiations between the British and the Americans. The third was conducted solely by the British, working with strong behind-the-scenes support from the United States.

Modifications were made to the plan as it developed. For example, Callaghan's proposed two-year transition to independence was reduced to two months by Margaret Thatcher, his successor as prime minister, and her foreign minister, Lord Carrington. There were also minor differences in the proposed independence constitution between the second and third rounds. The Anglo-American proposal of the second round called for a U.N. peacekeeping force, which was changed to a Commonwealth force in the third round. Finally, the second round bogged down in negotiations over power-sharing formulas for the transition period. Basically, however, Callaghan's March 1976 proposal was the one agreed to in December 1979, and the continuity of the negotiation effort was never significantly interrupted from its inception.

Kissinger's April 1976 trip to Africa was followed by intensive discussions between the Americans and the British on a proposal for governing the country during the transition period that was to be negotiated with the parties. In September Kissinger put the plan before President Julius Nyerere of Tanzania, President Kenneth Kaunda of Zambia, Joshua Nkomo of the Zimbabwe African Peoples Union (ZAPU), Prime Minister John Vorster of South Africa, and finally the Rhodesian leader, Ian Smith. Smith's dramatic acceptance of the proposals (as he understood them) the next month marked a major step forward in the negotiations. The reservations expressed soon after by the chiefs of state of Tanzania, Zambia, Mozambique, Angola, and Botswana (the Front-line states) was a bargaining gambit that left plenty of room for continuing the negotiations.

All parties agreed to meet in Geneva in October to discuss implementation of the new understanding. Many reasons have been given for the breakdown of that conference two months later. Certainly a major factor was Gerald Ford's electoral defeat shortly after the opening of the meeting. There were other reasons, as well, including misunderstanding of what had been agreed to, inflexibility on both sides, and--perhaps basic to both--the absence of a "hurting stalemate." Put another way, each side still believed it had more to gain by continuing the warfare than making the compromises asked of it.

Ivor Richards's attempts to narrow the differences in the course of travels through southern Africa in January and February 1977 were ultimately rejected by Smith in Salisbury where, to the annoyance of the Patriotic Front (PF, the recently formed alliance of Nkomo's ZAPU and Robert Mugabe's Zimbabwe African National Union--ZANU), Richards abandoned his effort, signaling an end to the first round of negotiations.

The second round began with the appointment of David Owen as British foreign secretary following the sudden death of Anthony Crosland. Owen shared the optimistic findings of a get-acqainted trip through Africa with the new U.S. secretary of state, Cyrus Vance. Together they decided to embark upon a joint mediating effort based essentially on the Callaghan proposals with one refinement. This time it was to be made clear that majority rule meant one-person-one-vote. An Anglo-American Consultative Group was appointed (Graham from the United Kingdom and Low from the United States) to consult with all parties and draw up a proposal for an independence constitution, on which it might be easier to achieve agreement than on the transitional arrangements that had already proved so difficult. The group traveled through southern Africa in May 1977 and again in July. A plan that came to be known as the Anglo-American proposal was prepared and presented to the Front-line in late August. It was presented to Ian Smith in Salisbury on September 1. Neither side accepted the proposals but neither broke off negotiations. President Kaunda of Zambia and Joshua Nkomo demanded that the PF be installed as the governing authority during the transition period, while Smith objected to the proposal that the independent army should be "based on the liberation forces" as proposed by the U.S.-U.K. mediators. In November Smith surprised the mediators and many Africans by announcing his intention to form a government with several internal parties--Bishop Abel Muzorewa of the United African National Congress and Ndabaningi Sithole of Mugabe's ZANU.

The mediators countered by sending a new mission to Africa. Led by retired British field marshal Lord Carver and including an American representative, the mission was intended to reassure the Rhodesians on the issue of the army in the new state. Meeting first in Dar es Salaam with PF leaders Nkomo and Mugabe, a new conference of all parties was proposed. Smith, at work on his internal settlement, refused to attend this conference, and the mediators, led by David Owen and U.S. ambassador to the U.N., Andrew Young, met with the PF and Front-line representatives in Malta in February 1978. There, proposals were made to introduce a formula for power sharing (originally suggested by Mozambique) during the transition period.

Though some progress was made at Malta, Smith proceeded with his internal settlement plans. On March 3 he signed an agreement on a constitution with the three internal African leaders. Shortly thereafter, a government was set up in which the chairmanship of the Council of Ministers was to rotate monthly among Smith, Muzorewa, Sithole, and Chief Jeremiah Chirau until elections could be held. Another meeting between the mediators, this time including David Owen, Cyrus Vance, Andrew Young, and the PF, with Front-line representatives, took place in Dar es Salaam in April. Again some progress was made, but it was clear that the African side was willing to make no further substantial concessions until the mediators could bring Smith to commit himself to the negotiations.

Graham and Low returned in June to Salisbury, where they remained until the fall. Their stay was broken by periodic trips to Front-line capitals. However, none of the three tracks then being followed was prospering: Inside Rhodesia no significant progress had been made in ending violence and achieving acceptance of the internal settlement; the negotiations toward acceptance of the Anglo-American proposal had not advanced; and the PF's campaign against the internal settlement had not abated. Smith's exploration of the possibility of reversing alliances by meeting with Nkomo and Kaunda in Lusaka, and Nkomo's destruction of a civilian airliner with a ground-to-air missile worsened matters and rendered further negotiations even more difficult.

Smith sought support in the United States by accepting the invitation of a number of senators to visit the country together with his African colleagues, but he was unable to gain a lifting of the sanctions then in force against Rhodesia. Returning to Salisbury, Smith was forced to postpone elections because of the worsening security situation. In December Prime Minister Callaghan sent out a new British mission, this time headed by parliamentary leader Cledwyn Hughes, again with U.S. participation, to see whether the conditions existed for an "all-parties" meeting and to keep up some momentum in the negotiations. Again the results were negative.

The stalemate was not broken by the Rhodesian elections that took place in April 1979. Although Muzorewa won the leadership with significant popular participation (more than 60 percent), no progress was being made to end the war. The area of the country under martial law had expanded until by the end of 1978 virtually the entire countryside was covered. The numbers of PF fighters grew in proportion to the martial law, and the violence and bloodshed steadily increased. After the elections, the Muzorewa government failed to win international recognition. This was not enough to assure the success of the PF, however, which had been unable to prevent the April elections and was now being seriously punished by the integrated Zimbabwe-Rhodesian forces. South African military support was growing.

It was at this point that the Thatcher government came to power in Britain. Thatcher's public statements prior to assuming office on May 4 had indicated that if Lord Boyd's commission of inquiry were to conclude that the elections in Rhodesia had been "free and fair," her government would not try to reimpose sanctions but instead would move toward recognition of the Muzorewa government. However, at a Commonwealth conference convened on August 1 in Lusaka, Mrs. Thatcher faced united opposition from other Commonwealth nations, including Australia and Nigeria, as well as the Front-line. As a result, the prime minister backed away from her position and agreed to renew the search for an internationally acceptable settlement. Britain was specifically charged by the conference with responsibility to carry out free and fair elections under its authority and to grant legal independence to Zimbabwe.

The Lancaster House talks that convened soon after returned to the Anglo-American Consultative Group's concept of negotiating an independence constitution and of supplying a Commonwealth military force instead of one from the United Nations. The main difference this time was that the British government was willing to commit forces to the effort. Although the talks were on the verge of breakdown several times, agreement was achieved. The British governor, Lord Soames, hoisted the Union Jack over Salisbury on December 14, nearly fourteen years after Rhodesia's unilateral declaration of independence.

Initiation of the Mediation Effort

Why. By the spring of 1976 violence in Rhodesia had reached a level of almost daily incidents and significant casualties. Efforts by the British, South Africans, and the Front-line states to encourage a settlement had all failed, and there was little prospect of a successful new effort. Nevertheless, no British prime minister or foreign minister wished to be seen as avoiding a problem that increasingly strained Britain's relations with the Commonwealth, embarrassed it in Africa and the United Nations, and created growing unhappiness among its citizens who had close ties to the Rhodesian whites. Prime Minister Callaghan's offer in March 1976 was the latest effort to move things toward a settlement. Although it seemed at first to have little chance of success, it was reinforced in April by U.S. Secretary of State Henry Kissinger, speaking in Lusaka.

In the spring of 1976 the United States found itself in a position similar to that of Britain. The

Portuguese coup in April 1974 and the subsequent installation of radical regimes in Mozambique and Angola
reduced the likelihood that white-minority regimes could
survive in Rhodesia and Namibia. With the end of the
Vietnam War, the United States was able to turn its
attention to other areas. Kissinger's decision to
travel to Africa led to a reexamination of southern
African policy. The secretary's speech, which listed
ten points on Rhodesia, supported the Callaghan proposals, declaring for the first time U.S. support for
majority rule and independence. Kissinger warned
Rhodesia that it could not depend upon U.S. assistance.
At the same time, he offered assistance to the Front-
line nations and to an independent Zimbabwe, and, most
important, committed the United States to participate
actively in an effort to find a "rapid, just, and
African solution to the issue of Rhodesia." [2]

It is often said that the United States in general
and Henry Kissinger in particular were single-mindedly
bent on opposing Soviet expansion in southern Africa;
that Kissinger realized that white rule was doomed in
Rhodesia and that the longer the conflict continued the
more radical and Soviet-oriented would be the government
that resulted. Having failed at direct, covert intervention in Angola, he now recognized that the United
States would have to depend on overt diplomacy. Was the
U.S. mediation primarily motivated by concern over growing Soviet influence? It can be argued that there was
much more to it than that. For instance, even if the PF
had been obliged to rely on arms captured from Rhodesian
forces rather than imported from Communist sources, the
conflict still would have presented the same great problems for the United States in the United Nations and the
Third World. Even without Soviet involvement, circumstances would probably have led to direct United States
participation in the mediation effort, although it might
have received a lower priority and less attention. In
any event, in the spring of 1976 both the United States
and the United Kingdom were impelled by reasons of
self-interest to commit themselves to an active
mediation effort.

Ian Smith and the African nationalist leaders (who
at this point had not yet split into external/violent
and internal/cooperative wings) accepted the mediation
offer for different reasons. Because the nationalist
leaders had met with Smith the previous August (with
Vorster and Kaunda in attendance), and because Smith had
met with Nkomo in January, no party could claim indif-
ference to good-faith settlement efforts.

It is unlikely that either side was particularly
impressed with the "impartiality" of the volunteer
mediators. On the contrary, during the negotiations
each side constantly claimed, and largely believed, that
the United States and United Kingdom were strongly par-

tial to the other side.   What chiefly motivated each
side to accept the mediation was the belief that the
United States and United Kingdom could induce the other
side to make concessions through sanctions or through
financial and political incentives.   The so-called
linear attributes of trustworthiness, credibility,
empathy, impartiality, and rapport of the mediators
probably played a relatively minor role in the decision
by the parties to accept mediation. [3] Each saw mediation
principally as a means of exerting more pressure on the
other.   To put it another way, each saw mediation as a
possible, though unlikely, means of achieving its aims
by negotiation rather than by warfare.

   <u>When</u>.   The actual timing of the mediation was much
more a function of the mediators' interests than of the
conflict itself.   Coming so soon after the failure of
the last effort, the March-April intervention did not
involve a difficult decision on the part of the parties
to the conflict.   Though each would have welcomed a settlement, both were confident of ultimate victory and
neither felt an immediate need for relief from the warfare.   Both recognized that the mediators wanted a settlement as much, if not more, than they did.   Throughout
the negotiation this recognition seriously reduced the
leverage available to the mediators.   The participants
often appeared to believe they were doing the mediators
a favor by permitting them to try to solve the conflict,
and sometimes threatened to deny them the opportunity to
continue.   In part, this was a technique adopted by the
parties to exert counterpressure against the mediators.

   In spite of this, however, pressures from supporters left the parties little choice but to continue negotiating.   Equally important, each of the parties realized that if it adopted too intransigent a position,
refusing to negotiate, it risked alienating the United
Kingdom and the United States, and perhaps causing them
to ally themselves with the other side.   This fear provided the mediators with the leverage to keep the negotiations going.

   Beyond these reasons, the fact of negotiations gave
leaders of the participant forces a degree of international recognition and a political forum that they might
not otherwise have had.   While this was important to Ian
Smith, it was perhaps even more so to the African
nationalist leaders, who needed to assert their authority over their military commanders.   Another advantage
to the continuation of negotiations may have been the
trauma to participants in military action (particularly
on the African nationalist side) of crossing the threshold into negotiations.   Once the step was taken, it may
have seemed better to the African leaders to maintain
it.   In the event, both sides sought to keep the two
tracks going simultaneously--the war effort and negotiations.   They viewed them as means to the same end.

It is evident that in every successful mediation, there comes a crucial point in the conflict at which settlement becomes possible. The experience of the Zimbabwean negotiations indicates that the mediating process should be in train when the crucial moment arrives. Because it is so difficult to judge when this moment will occur--or to identify it once it has occurred--there is real advantage to starting mediation early and keeping it going until it is successful. Throughout the negotiation process it was often stated that each effort was the "last chance in Rhodesia." While there may be circumstances in which unsuccessful mediation can prejudice the chances of ultimate resolution of a conflict, this does not appear to have happened in Zimbabwe. There is no evidence that the repeated near-misses ever damaged the chances of succeeding efforts.

Basis. Each of the three rounds of the mediation effort began with a declaration of the basis of the mediators' participation in the negotiation. The public statements of Callaghan and Kissinger constituted a sort of charter for further discussion. While not initially public, the Anglo-American effort in the second round was based on a set of principles and a working procedure made known to both sides by the mediators from the beginning. In substance, the mediators established that a settlement had to be based on restoration of British authority, a one-person-one-vote election, and independence within two years for the government so elected. The third-round negotiations were based on the public agreement reached at the Lusaka Commonwealth Conference in August 1979.

These declared bases for negotiation, while not always accepted by both parties from the beginning, provided a basis for discussion and negotiation. They were the platform upon which the structure of a wider settlement was to be built--a minimum basis of agreement the mediators believed would be acceptable to the parties and to their own domestic constituencies. They were an integral part of the initiation of negotiations.

The Goals of the Mediators. The motivations of the United States and the United Kingdom determined their goals. The two countries intervened in the Rhodesian conflict because continuation of the conflict threatened their relations with Africa and the Third World and presented an opportunity for the Soviet Union to increase its influence. It was already clear that white rule could not last. Although the mediators had certain preferences among the black nationalist leaders (and were constantly being accused of manipulation in favor of one or the other), they were prepared to deal with any victor. Halfhearted efforts (primarily by the British) to favor one or the other of the African leaders had little effect.

If the two governments remained relatively impartial, popular opinion in the two countries was much more partisan. It favored Nkomo at one point and the "moderate," internal leaders at another. This weakened the mediators' ability to bring pressure on the parties since one of their major strengths lay in the position that it was up to the people of the country to decide its leadership.

Inevitably, the principle of popular self-determination led to problems. While some contended that international support would have enabled the internal group to pacify the countryside, most on-the-spot observers did not believe so. Thus, to the British and the Americans, the objective of ending the conflict required that Smith's attempted internal settlement not be accepted unless and until it resulted in a government able to control the country and end the violence. It became clear to the mediators as early as May 1978 that the internal settlement was not going to resolve the conflict. In their view, to throw their support behind it would have contributed to the prolongation of conflict and a perhaps irredeemable loss of credibility. There was furthermore the unacceptable risk of being drawn into military action in order to sustain the internal settlement.

There is evidence to indicate that the United States and the United Kingdom would have supported an internal settlement had it shown signs of succeeding. The statements of both governments upon learning in November 1977 of Smith's intention to form an internal settlement were relatively cautious and guarded, as were their reactions to the agreement on a constitution by the internal-settlement groups in March 1978 and the elections the next month. Moreover, public support for the internal settlement in both the United States and United Kingdom was so broad that neither government could probably have done otherwise. Had Muzorewa been able to consolidate his leadership and had the fighting significantly decreased, the United States and United Kingdom would have had little choice but to lift sanctions and recognize the new government.

Evidence that resolving the conflict was more important to the mediators than the precise terms of the settlement also exists in the actions of the British (and secondarily the United States) during the two-month restoration of British authority in Zimbabwe. No one could avoid the impression that Robert Mugabe, the leader of ZANU, was the favored candidate in either country. Yet no serious effort was made to thwart him. Though accusations of favoritism were made against the British, the elections were fairly administered and the results quickly accepted by both countries.

Means of Operation

The Zimbabwe mediation, like that in Namibia, was somewhat unusual in that one of the parties accepted formal "defeat" and replacement, if not diminished influence, early in the negotiations. When Ian Smith agreed to Kissinger's proposals in his speech of October 24, 1976, he acknowledged the end of the white population's formal control of government. On the other side, the African nationalist leaders were deeply divided, not only between the internal leaders Muzorewa and Sithole and the external liberation forces of the Patriotic Front but also, within the PF, between ZANU and ZAPU. Each had very much in mind that it faced a winner-take-all situation. The lack of national consensus and internal communication was such that each leader could believe genuinely that he commanded majority popular support. As a result, while one set of negotiations proceeded between the primary parties--white Rhodesians and black nationalists--another went on among factions of each party. The success or failure of the overall effort depended as much on this level as on the primary struggle.

The Mediators' Roles. During all three rounds of the effort, the mediators made declarations concerning the nature of the ultimate settlement. Therefore, it was always clear that they recognized a need to play a larger role than that of providing good offices, that they should urge a solution on the parties through persuasion and the application of leverage, and that they should make substantive contributions to the matters under negotiation.

Although procedurally important, communication between the parties could not provide a settlement. The United States and the United Kingdom were aware of, and sometimes surprised by, the degree of communication that passed between the parties. Such contact was carried on through well-established, covert relationships, through a number of private mediators, and through frequent social and commercial intercourse. The parties often knew better what the other was thinking and doing than did the United States and the United Kingdom. That did not mean that they understood each other. Unfortunately, the mediators were unable to contribute significantly on this point.

The primary role of the mediators was to find a formula for settlement and have it accepted. The substance of the formula was not their most important concern, although they made clear from the beginning of the second round that a condition of their participation was an election based on one-person-one-vote. This condition was imposed for three reasons. The mediators had to protect their intervention from political opponents at home; they believed that a broad, rural elec-

torate prejudiced the position of the whites no more
than a narrow, urban one; and they did not believe that
any lesser formula had a chance of being accepted by the
PF or by the international community.

Throughout the negotiations the mediators were
aware that a deal might be struck behind their backs to
impose a government not having popular approval. Gradually, popular approval became synonymous with ending
the violence in the meditators' minds. Thus, it is
quite possible that if a formula for power-sharing could
have been found to end the conflict, the United States
and the United Kingdom would have accepted it even in
the absence of a test of popular approval. They
undoubtedly would have made very clear, however, that
it was not a product of their efforts, and that they
were not responsible for it.

Almost four years were spent hammering out a
formula acceptable to both sides. The first round
concentrated exclusively on the most difficult part of
the agreement: organization of the transition period.
The parties recognized all too well that this formula
would determine which of them would achieve power. It
was not until the beginning of the second round that the
second element of the formula--the independence consti-
tution--entered the picture. During the entire period,
hardly a week went by without a meeting between a mediator and one or another of the parties on one of these
two subjects.

Mediation Techniques

Process. During the first and second rounds the
mediation process was carried on by means of consultations led by the mediators. It was hoped that by con-
sulting closely with the parties on each subject, a
proposal could be built up which, taken as a package,
would be acceptable to all. No attempt was made to
obtain a commitment from any of the parties on the
individual provisions as they were discussed. It was
recognized that in the course of the bargaining process
the parties would only accept particular provisions in
the context of the whole agreement. When substantial
agreement had been achieved on the major points, a
meeting of all parties would be convened--chaired by the
mediators--to resolve lesser points and give final
approval to the document.

Though the first two rounds achieved substantial
progress, it proved impossible to adhere to this format,
and in the third round it was discarded. Kissinger's
proposals were formally accepted by Smith (as he
understood them), though not by the PF. As the going
got tougher in both rounds all parties began to meet

together in the hope that outstanding matters could be cleared up in this way.

Priorities. The Kissinger-Richards proposals left the structure of the eventual independent government to be worked out during the transition period. Reportedly at the suggestion of Joshua Nkomo, the next set of proposals began with a call to concentrate on a constitution for the independent country that would emerge after the transition period. It was thought that agreement on such a constitution would not be difficult to achieve and that the progress made would provide an incentive for agreement on the organization of the transition period. The consultative group spent many days debating with the Smith government over the provisions of the constitution, and some progress was made. However, the group was unable to engage the Africans in similar discussions, in spite of Nkomo's earlier position. The Africans appeared to be preoccupied with the struggle for the power inherent in the structure of the government during the transition period. Gradually the focus of negotiation shifted to the transition until this entirely dominated the discussions at Malta and Dar es Salaam. The structure of the independent government was of great importance to the white population of Rhodesia, but it was less so to the Africans and was therefore unsuitable as a natural basis for discussion. Occasionally, Africans would admit that power came first--rules and organic structures could always be changed afterwards. Nevertheless, developing adequate assurances for whites (and minorities) in the constitutional structure of the independent country continued to be seen as a way out of the impasse. In organizing the Lancaster House talks, Lord Carrington therefore reverted to the formula of seeking agreement on a constitution before considering the transition.

The Interlocutors. Through all three rounds the mediators adopted the principle that they must be free to meet with and talk to all parties on both sides. They traveled freely and met at various locations inside and out of Rhodesia. On occasion they even met with African parties in jail and once with the entire interned leadership of ZANU, who were brought out for a meeting at Britain's abandoned official residence in Salisbury. The principle of free access was not unfailingly respected, and each side tried to inhibit mediator contact with elements of the other. On at least one occasion on each side, the mediators passed up meetings with one of the parties. [4] The rule was so well and generally understood, however, that free movement and contact with all parties never became an issue during the negotiations. This was important in avoiding what would otherwise have been a major obstacle to the mediation process.

A Ceasefire. Each side tried to use the mediators to limit the military activities of the other. Smith repeatedly urged the mediators to call for a ceasefire while negotiations were being carried on. The Africans considered this simply an effort by Smith to relieve the pressure that they were bringing on him. They did not believe he would negotiate seriously once a ceasefire was in place. The mediators always made it clear to both parties that they understood that the war would continue until an agreement had been reached. Thus they resisted the efforts of both sides to use them to military advantage. They insisted, however, that a cease-fire must be part of a final agreement and that it had to be in place before the transition period began and elections were held. The mediators also did what they could to contain the level of hostilities by discouraging escalation. They publicly condemned Rhodesian military excursions into neighboring countries. They also anticipated ZAPU's use of SAM-7s against Rhodesian civilian airliners, and condemned atrocities against noncombatants from whatever source.

Factors in the Ultimate Success

Settlement was ultimately achieved by a combination of mediation and the "hurting stalemate" at which the parties arrived. The contribution of the mediation effort can be divided into three factors: finding an acceptable basis for settlement worked out by the mediators, application of significant outside influence or leverage, and, to a much less important extent, the application of mediation techniques.

The Formula. As long as both sides were directly disputing power, the zero-sum game did not allow adequate room for compromise. Even after Smith accepted the Kissinger proposals and took himself out of the game, he continued to dispute power with the Patriotic Front. An internal settlement based on an alliance between the Rhodesian Front (Smith's white political party) and African leaders who had no military forces, a constitution with an amendment procedure that the whites could block, and domination by whites of the armed forces, civil service, and judiciary did not constitute a surrender of power in the eyes of the PF or its Front-line supporters. Smith held on to this form of thinly disguised power as long as he could.

Once he abandoned any insistence on maintaining the trappings of power by accepting the Kissinger proposals, however, the white community began to separate its conditions of life from that power. As long as a constitution was respected, its assurances to the white community of a political voice and economic security could compensate for the loss of more active forms of power. The catch was, how long would a constitution be

respected without such power? The whites' confidence
could be strengthened by the acceptance of a constitution by all the African leaders, and by international
support for the agreement. As time went on, however,
whites simply became more willing to take a chance
rather than continue a war which, as described earlier,
was becoming increasingly hopeless. Once the separation
of security and power was accepted, the differences
between the white community and the African leadership
broke out of the zero-sum trap. The whites' demands
could be satisfied by an adequate constitution and those
of the African leaders by a transition period in which
each was confident he could win a free and fair
election.
        It took some time for the mediators to come to this
understanding. For a while they pressed the whites for
constitutional concessions that the Africans did not
value as highly as had been expected. This was particularly the case with the proposal that the army of the
independent country be "based on the liberation forces."
This idea frightened the whites and internal Africans
more than it appealed to the PF. But it was clear that
control of the well-trained and effective Rhodesian
armed forces was a real prize. It was Nyerere who
talked the United States into accepting the idea in
return for Front-line cooperation. The British had no
choice but go along. On another matter, the mediators
did not always understand the importance of the transition arrangements to the African leaders.
        It was Lord Carrington who saw clearly the possi-
bility of a settlement that would give each side what it
needed. Timing became his biggest problem. Agreement
on either one of the issues reduced the pressure for
concession on the other. There had to be a quid pro
quo. Thus, the PF strongly resisted final acceptance of
the constitution that had been negotiated until it could
see whether the election procedure of the transition
period would permit it a chance to win. It feared that
if negotiating on transition arrangements broke down,
the British would impose the constitution on them and
obtain international support for this move. Carrington
chose to interpret the PF's qualified acceptance as full
agreement and moved ahead with the transition arrangements. His understanding and management of the two
issues seems to have been a crucial element in the success of the conference.
        Outside Leverage. Kissinger's ability to bring
Smith to agree to seek a settlement on the basis of
majority rule in 1976 was based on several types of
leverage. The secretary of state's personal prestige
was very high. One did not lightly reject his offer of
mediation. Kissinger had already met twice with the
South Africans who, for their own reasons, saw advantages to moving toward a Rhodesian settlement. It was

widely believed that they had taken a step to encourage
Smith to cooperate with Kissinger's effort.   Finally,
Smith may have considered that he could use U.S. influence with the Front-line and other Africans to obtain
the kind of settlement he could live with.   That meant
giving up the trappings of power but preserving for the
white population ironclad constitutional guarantees of
position and rights and a certain amount of political
strength to protect the constitution.   He apparently
thought that the organization of the transition period,
which he understood Kissinger to imply would offer substantial white authority, would assure this.

Later Smith tried to work out unilateral settlements with the "moderates," or weaker, unarmed nationalists (Muzorewa, Sithole, and Chief Chirau), and with the
armed Patriotic Front (at the secret meeting arranged by
Zambia's president in Lusaka in August of 1978).   The
first would have given him the power he wanted but not
an end to the war; the second would have ended the war
but left him with insufficient authority. Thus, as the
situation became more desperate in late 1978, he had no
choice but, once again, to turn to outside help to get
his way with one or the other of the nationalist groups.

Smith's first gambit was to appeal directly to the
American people over the heads of the mediators.   His
trip to the United States along with Muzorewa and the
other black African members of the executive council in
the fall of 1978 was the culmination of this effort.   It
was an effort that very nearly succeeded.   The U.S.
Senate voted in June 1979 to lift sanctions, but the
House refused to go along and in July insisted on leaving the decision to President Carter.   It seems very
likely that if the House had supported the Senate and
required the president to lift sanctions, the Conservative party in Britain might have forced Prime Minister
Thatcher to do likewise.   She would then have been
deprived of the flexibility to make a new attempt at an
agreed settlement when she went to the Commonwealth
Conference in Lusaka later that month.

When the Lusaka Commonwealth Conference agreed on a
formula for a further attempt at an agreed settlement
along the lines of the second-round Anglo-American proposal (but with Commonwealth supervision of the transition period), Smith realized that his attempt to seek
outside support for the internal settlement had failed
in both the United States and the United Kingdom.   At
this point he realized that he had no choice but to turn
to an internationally acceptable settlement.   He agreed
to go to the Lancaster House talks on the assumption
that a conservative government in the United Kingdom
would give him as favorable a settlement with the
Patriotic Front as he could ever get and, if that did
not succeed, would help him achieve international support for an internal solution.

The Patriotic Front still had not abandoned its
maximum position of taking over power without negotiations or previous elections. It was perfectly willing
to discuss a constitution and schedule elections after
it had taken power. It recognized, however, that it was
still a long way from achieving this goal through military action and that too inflexible a position at the
Lancaster House talks could shift opinion in the United
Kingdom and the United States back to support for the
internal settlement, which would be a major setback.
Since the PF (including both of its component parts,
ZANU and ZAPU) was confident that it could win the
genuinely free and fair election promised by the mediators, it had both an interest in exploring such a solution and an incentive for compromise.

Thus the mediators' leverage was not inconsider-
able. Smith had tried unilateral settlements with each
of the nationalist groups and failed. He had tried to
appeal over the heads of the mediators and failed. He
now had no choice but to deal with both. For its part,
the PF believed it could achieve some of its objectives
through the mediators and feared failure of the talks.
Nevertheless, the mediators still had to use every bit
of their leverage to bring off a settlement.

The leverage the mediators enjoyed over Smith
derived from the ability of the mediators to bring an
end to the war through an internationally agreed settlement committing the United Kingdom (and the United
States), the PF, the Front-line, and the world community
to its support. The mediators could offer financial
support for the settlement. This enhanced leverage with
the PF as well as with Smith. On the PF side the mediators drew leverage from the fact that they could help
bring the PF what it wanted while reducing Western and
African support for the internal settlement in the event
of failure. The mediators offered financial support.
They maintained significant influence with the PF's most
important allies and supporters in the Front-line. By
this time both Zambia and Mozambique were anxious for a
settlement. They felt close enough to ultimate success
not to settle for anything less than a genuinely free
and fair election, and they probably would have accepted
a settlement that recognized any victor of such an election. The British government, as the principal mediator, was assisted by others besides the Front-line.
Through its secretary-general, Shridath Ramphal, the
Commonwealth secretariat also played an important role,
as did the United States.

Mediation Techniques. How much did the personality
of the mediators count? How important was good communication? There can be no doubt that personalities played
a role at moments during the various efforts. Kissinger's personal role in obtaining Smith's first acknowledgment of majority rule and independence was extremely

important.   His influence probably led South Africa to
press Smith to take the step.   Andrew Young's personal
credibility with the PF and the Front-line states probably kept negotiations going on a number of occasions.
And no one can fail to note the skill and profound
understanding with which Lord Carrington conducted the
Lancaster House talks.   In these cases, personality
probably played an important part.
    The level at which the mediation was undertaken
probably was significant.   There was considerable criticism of British Foreign Minister Anthony Crosland for
not chairing the Geneva Conference in late 1976.   Ivor
Richards did not have the cabinet status necessary to
commit his government.   Whether this conference would
have had a chance even with Crosland is a good question,
and he may have realized this.   Had it not been for the
personal involvement of British Foreign Minister David
Owen, U.S. Secretary of State Cyrus Vance, U.N. Ambassador Andrew Young, and parliamentary leader Cledwyn
Hughes during the second round, the negotiations probably could not have been sustained.   As it was, the
stature of the mediators was such that the parties could
not refuse to receive them and to take their efforts
seriously.   It is possible to argue that any lengthy
break in the mediation effort would have concentrated so
much attention on military activity that the negotiation
threshold would have been raised significantly and the
chances of achieving a settlement in 1979 seriously
damaged.

    The Zimbabwe settlement constitutes one of the few
recent examples of successful settlement in which mediation played a major role.   Its lessons, therefore, are
of particular importance.   These lessons are many, and
they are perceived very differently by different observers.   Perhaps the most important and least disputed lesson would be that no outside mediator in this conflict
was in a position to impose a settlement.   The British,
the Americans, the South Africans, the Front-line, even
the Soviets and Chinese, all would have liked to be able
to do so.   Each had a favorite solution.   Not only was
none able to impose a settlement, but each had significantly less leverage than appeared from the outside.
The Front-line might encourage or cajole the PF, but it
could not deliver it for a settlement in spite of the
fact that ZANU and ZAPU operated from Mozambican and
Zambian territory.   South Africa could threaten to
reduce or eliminate assistance to Rhodesia, but there
were limits on how far it could push Smith, who had
considerable influence inside South Africa (as did Nkomo
in Zambia and Mugabe in Mozambique).   More distant out-
siders had comparatively less leverage.   The final settlement could not come until the people of Rhodesia,

black and white, decided that they had more to lose than to gain from continuing the war.

Nevertheless, the mediation effort played an important role in the achievement of a settlement. It promoted acceptance of an agreement based on majority rule and independence following a brief restoration of British authority, and influenced many within the country, in the Front-line states, and in the West. Thus, the continuity of effort was important. The influence exerted by the mediators was limited but significant in the final analysis. It was aimed at keeping the negotiations alive over almost four years, and at achieving an acceptable settlement. The techniques that evolved were communicating with all parties, separating the constitution and transition agreements, accepting the existence of the war as the talks progressed, and keeping the talks going.

One final comment might be worth registering. The key concern of the mediators was to limit and, if possible, end a conflict that was gradually eroding their positions of influence in the area and in the global balance of power. As long as the United States continues to maintain its position of global power, it will be called upon to use its power on behalf of nations in conflict. It will be frequently condemned to act as a mediator. No major dispute is likely to arise without early appeals to the United States to exert its influence to prevent or resolve it. Over the last ten years a great deal of U.S. diplomatic energy has gone into mediation efforts, and progress through such efforts has strengthened U.S. influence in southern Africa and the Middle East, even though the successes have been few, and the credit small and fleeting. On the other hand, the failures have done little damage. The Soviets and the Communist world have stood on the sidelines and complained. By its good-faith efforts the United States has captured the high ground--as a Front-line African chief-of-state told one of the mediators near the end of the second round: "Well, you haven't succeeded, but I have to give you credit for trying."

Chapter 3: Notes

1.   The state with which we are concerned went through a progression of names from Southern Rhodesia to Rhodesia-Zimbabwe. It will be referred to by the name given it by the governing authority during the period under discussion.

2.   State Department Press Release 205, April 27, 1976.

3.   These "linear attributes" are discussed by Jeffrey Z. Rubin, ed., in Dynamics of Third Party Intervention (New York: Praeger, 1981), 40.

4.   Kissinger never met with Mugabe or a ZANU representative, though at that stage Mugabe was still in the bush somewhere in Mozambique and had not really established his leadership of ZANU over Sithole. The consultative group passed up seeing one of the internal leaders, Chief Chirau.

4.
THE NAMIBIA NEGOTIATIONS AND THE PROBLEM OF NEUTRALITY

Marianne A. Spiegel

The Namibia negotiations provide a useful case study regarding mediating efforts in which the United States has found it difficult to maintain sufficient neutrality. American policymakers cannot easily remain detached because the conflict involves many controversial issues that evoke emotional responses: a Soviet-backed insurgency, Cuban troops, an anticommunist government defending the status quo, apartheid, a struggle for national independence, and the denial of individual rights and freedoms. Whether an American mediator views policy primarily in terms of East-West competition or North-South dialogue, globalism or regionalism, power politics or humanitarian principles, he will more than likely address the Namibia question with some strong predispositions in favor of one side or the other.

At this writing, the Namibia negotiations have spanned two U.S. administrations (those of presidents Carter and Reagan), which have widely disparate views of fundamental American interests and have tended to side with different parties to the dispute. Skilled negotiators from both administrations have both succeeded and failed: They have employed creative techniques to overcome American handicaps as a partial mediator, they have

Marianne A. Spiegel is legislative assistant for Rep. Howard L. Berman (D.-Calif.) and was on the political planning staff, Africa Division, at the U.S. Department of State during the Carter administration. Ms. Spiegel is a candidate for the Ph.D. in the African Studies Program at SAIS.

made slow but real progress, but ultimately they have
complicated the peace process with their particular
biases. The purpose of this chapter is to examine these
successes and failures in the Namibia negotiations. It
is hoped that such an examination will demonstrate how
negotiators can learn either to overcome their biases or
to use them in attempting to reach settlements.

In 1920 the League of Nations gave the former
German colony of Namibia to South Africa as a "class-C"
mandate. Since that time, South Africa has ruled the
mineral-rich, sparsely populated desert and steppe-land
that stretches from South Africa's western border to the
Atlantic. South Africa's ruling National party, elected
in 1948, moved quickly to extend its white supremacist
policies of apartheid to the territory and to incorporate it as a fifth province. Representation in the South
African parliament was extended to Namibia's white
inhabitants in 1951, and Pretoria's Bantu Administration
Department extended its rule over the territories' black
majority in 1955.

A new wrinkle in South Africa's strategy for Namibia sparked the mediation effort now under discussion.
While South Africa was granting its peculiar brand of
independence to the fragmented black "homelands" that
comprise 13 percent of its own territory, it was also
preparing Namibia for an independence based on the
apartheid model, thus attempting to assure continued
South African dominance there. Neither the independence
to be granted the homelands nor that for Namibia would
be recognized by the international community. Pretoria
arranged a constitutional conference for Namibia called
the Turnhalle Conference. By early 1977 representatives
of eleven Namibian ethnic groups had agreed to a constitution on the apartheid model, providing for a confed-
eral system of autonomous ethnic homelands. The Turnhalle Conference set June 1977 as the date for the
installation of the new constitution.

South Africa's continuing control over Namibia, and
its extension of apartheid policies to the territory
faced two challenges: from Namibian nationalists,
represented by the South West African People's Organization (SWAPO), and from the United Nations. SWAPO had
been involved in political organization with Namibia,
but had turned to guerrilla warfare in 1966. With
Angola's independence in 1975, SWAPO gained bases from
which to operate and, so, intensified its attacks. By
the mid-1970s, clashes between South African and SWAPO
forces took place every month or so.

While SWAPO applied what military pressure it could
for Namibian independence, the United Nations applied
diplomatic pressure. The General Assembly withdrew the
League mandate from South Africa in 1966, established a
council and a commissioner to administer Namibia in
1967, recognized SWAPO as the sole and authentic repre-

sentative of the Namibian people in 1973, and in 1976 granted SWAPO permanent-observer status. In 1971 the International Court of Justice (ICJ) declared illegal the continued presence and actions of South Africa in Namibian territory. In 1976 the U.N. Security Council passed Resolution 385, calling for one-person-one-vote elections under U.N. supervision and control for the whole of Namibia as one political entity, withdrawal of the South African administration and its military forces, release of political prisoners, return of exiles, and an end to racial discrimination.[1]

For the United Nations and the independent nations of Africa, Namibia represents a remnant of colonial rule and part of the last bastion of official racial domination. For South Africa, Namibia represents a buffer against the spread of independence and black rule. On one side is the weight of world opinion, international law, and legitimacy, and on the other is the overwhelming military superiority of South Africa over SWAPO and the neighboring countries.

The Mediation Effort

The mediation effort discussed in this chapter began in April 1977, when after a period of joint planning the five Western members of the Security Council made a joint demarche to the South African government. Representatives of these nations traveled to South Africa and urged the South African government not to proceed with the Turnhalle proposals, but instead to participate in negotiations toward U.N.-supervised elections based on S.C. Resolution 385. The Western members of the Security Council asserted that if South Africa did not cooperate, they could not protect it from the inevitable sanctions-resolutions in the United Nations. Perhaps for a variety of reasons, South Africa agreed both to postpone implementation of the Turnhalle arrangements and to participate in negotiations. The five Western nations (the United States, the United Kingdom, France, West Germany, and Canada) formed a negotiating team, called the "Contact Group," which at this writing is still trying to mediate a resolution of the Namibia problem.

The parties almost came to formal agreement in 1978, when the Contact Group presented a "final package" to South Africa and SWAPO: one-person-one-vote elections for a constituent assembly under joint administration by the United Nations and South Africa; phased withdrawal of all but 1,500 South African troops over three months, with the remaining troops to be confined to two northern camps; return of exiles (including disarmed SWAPO troops) to participate in elections; dissolution of the paramilitary forces established by South

Africa; release of political prisoners; repeal of discriminatory legislation; and a sizable United Nations
Transition Assistance Group (UNTAG)--larger than the
South African force--with a civilian component to administer the transition. South Africa and SWAPO accepted
the package. The U.N. secretary-general submitted an
implementation plan, and the Security Council endorsed
it in Resolution 435.[2]   But within weeks, SWAPO
expressed some misgivings about the original package,
and South Africa balked at the implementation proposals.
The story of the Namibia mediation effort from this
point on is one of agreements reached, only to fall
apart because of details regarding implementation or
because the parties had second thoughts; of issues
resolved, only to be reopened months or years later; of
deadlines and target-dates set, only to pass unevent-
fully.

The conflict between South Africa and SWAPO has
intensified, although it has not reached the level
attained in preindependence Zimbabwe. Since 1978 South
Africa has launched major annual raids on southern
Angola, and from 1981 to 1984 South Africa maintained a
constant military presence inside Angola. By mid-1984
SWAPO was launching small sabotage expeditions, encoun-
tering South African forces in Namibia on an average of
once a day, although in 1982 and 1983 it had sent troops
into Namibia on larger raids. By 1982 the war was cost-
ing South Africa half a billion dollars and approximately eighty lives per year. Angolan losses were
twenty times greater, and the war's financial costs were
significantly greater for the impoverished new nation
than for South Africa.[3]

In addition to continuing their military efforts,
both sides have sought to keep their political options
open outside the negotiations. The South African government has moved forward with its plan to grant Namibia
a limited form of independence. In 1979 South Africa
held elections in Namibia for a constituent assembly and
turned the assembly into a legislature. In 1980 South
Africa transferred its authority over most governmental
matters (except foreign and financial affairs) to a new
Southwest Africa/Namibia executive council, made up of
Dirk Mudge and other members of the Democratic Turnhalle
Alliance (DTA). DTA is a multiracial coalition of the
parties that participated in the Turnhalle constitutional conference; DTA leader Dirk Mudge is white. The
South African government had hopes that the DTA would be
strengthened politically in Namibia by its authority to
repeal some discriminatory laws and regulations, and by
its allocation of greater resources to the black majority. In fact, the white backlash to the most minimal
reforms was so strong that Mudge and the DTA were able
to deliver few real benefits to the black majority. In

The Namibia Negotiations   115

November 1980 the DTA was defeated in an all-white election by Namibia's hard-line National party.

While South Africa retains its option to devise an internal settlement in Namibia, those pressing for an internationally acceptable agreement also retain an option: economic sanctions against South Africa. In 1978 the Contact Group met to consider possible sanctions should South Africa prove intransigent. It decided that sanctions would have to meet certain criteria. First, they would have to have a specific application to Namibia. For example, the United Nations could not very easily lift sanctions once South Africa agreed to a Namibia settlement if they related directly to South African enforcement of apartheid. Second, any trade cutoff would need to have maximum, immediate impact. Third, the sanctions would have to be enforceable. It was argued by some Contact Group experts, for example, that an oil embargo would be meaningless because of the abundance of oil on the world market and the ease with which renegade companies could circumvent it. Finally, sanctions would have to be sustainable. If the measures caused great economic hardship to any exporting country, for example, public opposition could force a premature suspension. Experts from the Contact Group countries reviewed a range of possible sanctions and agreed upon a short list that came closest to meeting all the criteria, although final approval by the governments would not be sought until the time came to impose sanctions. There were skeptics in both Washington and London about the list drawn up by the experts.

For a variety of reasons, the Contact Group has not sought Security Council approval of sanctions in order to secure final South African agreement. Although South Africa raises one obstacle after another to agreement, it never slams the door on negotiations. The South African government always keeps one or two objections on the table, but never rejects the principle of a settlement. When Pretoria rejects one proposal, it raises a counterproposal to be considered. SWAPO raises its share of obstacles as well. Negotiations have never reached the point where all the legitimate concerns of both sides have been addressed, where each Contact Group member has been satisfied that a final package was in place, where SWAPO has accepted such a package, and where the only remaining barrier to a settlement has been South Africa's refusal to go along. Moreover, with the change in American administrations, sanctions became less of an option for the Contact Group and the United Nations. Officials of the Reagan administration made clear early on that they opposed such sanctions, and in March 1981 President Reagan said: "Can we abandon [South Africa,] a country that has stood beside us in every war we've ever fought, a country that strategically is essential to the Free World in its production of minerals we all must have. . . ?"[4]

In February 1982 the Reagan administration acted on its distaste for such sanctions in relaxing U.S. compliance with the U.N. arms embargo against South Africa.

Neither political nor military options to prolonged negotiations have worked out for the parties or mediators; all are locked in seemingly endless talks. It would be a mistake to conclude, however, that the negotiations have been fruitless. Talks have seldom bogged down over "shape-of-the-table" trivia, and the participants have focused on the central, substantive issues, and have made real progress toward resolving them.

The Issues

One constant concern for both sides in the talks is who will have predominant influence in Namibia during elections. A recurring subissue is whether the United Nations or South Africa will administer the territory and run elections, and which one will have the more visible and authoritative presence. South African government representatives argue that to turn the territory over to the United Nations is to bias the elections in SWAPO's favor. The problem is one of perception. In the eyes of South African officials, the United Nations cannot impartially monitor elections, given that the U.N. General Assembly has recognized SWAPO as the sole representative of the people of Namibia and has granted SWAPO permanent-observer status.[5] Even though U.N. representatives in the Namibia negotiations have established great personal credibility with South African officials, and even though they have been eloquent in affirming the United Nations' neutrality, one can see why the South African government would suspect U.N. impartiality. If the United States finds it difficult to remain objective in a dispute involving national independence and human rights, the United Nations has even greater problems. Contact Group representatives at the United Nations, living daily with the reality of the U.N. as a peacekeeping organization, often had trouble accepting that South African perceptions could be quite different from their own.

SWAPO, on the other hand, argues that if South Africa continues to administer and police the territory as it always has, the elections will be biased in favor of the pro-South African parties. Both sides apparently doubt that suitable transition arrangements can be devised so as to assure a genuinely free and fair election. Whatever happens, whatever combination of a U.N. and South African presence is finally agreed to, a message will be sent to the electorate concerning who holds power in the territory. In which case, both South

Africa and SWAPO wonder if voters will vote their preference, or if they will be intimidated into voting for
the seeming victor in the negotiations.

This concern has translated into extended bargaining over a variety of issues: the size of U.N. and
South African forces, the location of South African
troops, the pace at which South African troops will be
withdrawn, and the future of the paramilitary Namibian
forces established by South Africa.   What will happen to
the South African police force in Namibia, and will
there be a U.N. police force?   Will the United Nations'
special representative or South Africa's administrator-
general govern the territory and run elections?   How
much of the apartheid structure will have to be dis-
mantled before elections take place?   Even after agreements seemingly have been reached on many of these
points, South Africa repeatedly has questioned the
advisability of a U.N. role during the transition, and
whether a more neutral party might be found to keep the
peace and monitor elections.

A second set of issues arising from the fundamental
question of who wields power in Namibia during the transition concerns SWAPO forces.   If South Africa is wary
about accepting a U.N. presence in Namibia during elections, it is adamant that SWAPO itself will not gain
through negotiations a position of greater influence in
Namibia than the nationalist movement has won on the
battlefield. At the same time, the aim of the negotiations is to achieve SWAPO's stated goal--independence
with majority rule in Namibia.   And the history of
decolonization in Africa argues that the nationalist
movement that has fought for independence stands the
best chance of winning elections.

South Africa thus has sought to minimize SWAPO's
military presence in Namibia during the transition,
while the mediators have sought to assure that SWAPO
members are free to participate and campaign in elections.   A number of questions have had to be dealt with.
What will be the provisions for the return of exiles to
participate in elections?   What about SWAPO dissidents
being detained in African countries?   Will SWAPO armed
forces be allowed to enter Namibia and establish bases
there?   Or will the U.N. monitor SWAPO bases?   What will
prevent SWAPO troops from intimidating voters, especially in the northern part of Namibia where half the
population--and SWAPO's popular base--is located?

Although negotiations have focused mostly on
arrangements for the transition to independence and
majority rule, the question of postindependence security, both for Namibia's white minority and for the new
nation's neighbors, also have been a persistent issue.
Will the elected constituent assembly be free to write
whatever constitution it desires, or will there be some
advance agreement on human rights?   Will the settlement

stipulate that South Africa can no longer assist insurgents in Angola, and that an independent Namibia will not provide bases for the African National Congress's (ANC's) antiapartheid forces? When will South Africa's separate claim to the port of Walvis Bay be settled?

Perhaps no agreements in the Namibia negotiations can be considered final, because so many issues seem to have been resolved only to be reopened later by one of the parties. Nevertheless, fairly solid agreements appear to be holding on a number of the major issues.[6] All but 1,500 South African troops are to be withdrawn gradually from Namibia before the elections. The remaining 1,500 are to be confined to two northern bases, with U.N. monitors. Namibia's paramilitary forces are to be disbanded, and a 7,500-man UNTAG force--comprised of troops from Yugoslavia, Panama, Bangladesh, Finland, Sudan, Togo, and Malaysia[7]-- installed alongside U.N. police monitors and a U.N. civilian contingent responsible for elections. The U.N. special representative and the administrator-general are to supervise the transition and elections jointly. SWAPO will gain no bases in Namibia, but its members can return unarmed to the territory to participate in elections. All exiles can return freely, and all political prisoners are to be released. SWAPO bases in neighboring countries are to be monitored by U.N. troops. The settlement will include nine agreed provisions concerning the drafting of a constitution, including a stipulation that a two-thirds vote of the constituent assembly is needed for approval, and that the constitution will include a bill of rights "consistent with the Universal Declaration of human rights," separation of powers, and an independent judiciary. The status of Walvis Bay is to be negotiated between South Africa and Namibia after independence.

Successes in the Negotiations

Failure to achieve a settlement in Namibia after more than seven years of mediation should not obscure the fact that talks have been conducted with great skill and creativity. Chief strategists of the mediation-- U.N. ambassadors Andrew Young and Donald McHenry during the Carter administration, Assistant Secretary for African Affairs Chester Crocker, and Frank Wisner, deputy assistant secretary during the Reagan administration--have pioneered strategies that not only have served these negotiations well, but will become models for mediating in the future.

Multilateral Mediation

The Namibia talks are a unique instance of collaborative mediation. From the outset, the Contact
Group members have conducted negotiations jointly. The
United States took the lead in organizing the Contact
Group and most frequently speaks publicly for it, but
this has by no means been a solo American effort bolstered by only a show of Western solidarity. With a
very few exceptions, which will be discussed later,
Contact Group representatives have met to formulate each
initiative and have then cleared their decisions with
their capitals. Frequently, Contact Group ambassadors
in South Africa and in key African states have submitted
assessments of the negotiations to their capitals, with
their recommendations on how the talks should proceed.
The Namibian negotiations have been collaborative
out of necessity as well as choice. The only leverage
mediators hold with a militarily powerful South Africa
is the threat of effective international sanctions
should South Africa block a settlement. That threat
will not be credible unless those Western countries that
have the veto in the U.N. Security Council and are major
trading partners of South Africa agree to form a united
front.
This collaboration has additional virtues. It
serves to correct the tendency of a lone mediator to
side with one faction in such a way that his efforts
become counterproductive. Often, a favored faction
concludes that it does not have to compromise because it
has the backing of a powerful ally; of course, the
less-favored faction loses all confidence in the mediator. As negotiations over Lebanon and El Salvador
demonstrate, this becomes particularly problematic when
the United States seeks to mediate a conflict involving
Soviet-backed factions. General tenets of American
foreign policy as well as domestic politics push the
United States toward supporting the anti-Soviet faction,
even when that faction lacks popular support and poses
major barriers to a settlement, and even when the
continuation of the conflict furthers Soviet rather than
American interests. In the Contact Group, by contrast,
some representatives have always been more inclined to
press SWAPO to make concessions to South Africa, and
others have always had the opposite inclination. The
Contact Group has been able to select representatives
for particular missions on the basis of their credibility with either South Africa or SWAPO. For example, the
British representative, Sir James Murray, was selected
in August 1979 to present to South Africa the new
proposal for a demilitarized zone on the Namibia/Angola
border.
Collaboration at times has slowed negotiations. It
is not easy to secure agreement on a single strategy

among five capitals. However, there are compensating
advantages. With more perspectives being brought to
bear on every problem, the Contact Group has been more
innovative than single mediators. It has been able to
critique its own efforts and to avoid the lone mediator's tendency to stick to a failing strategy either
because of bureaucratic inertia or because the credibility of a political leader is perceived to be on the
line.

Just as important as the concerted efforts of the
Contact Group members is their cooperation with key
African countries. These are the Front-line African
states--Tanzania, Zambia, Botswana, Mozambique, Angola,
and Zimbabwe--and the largest and wealthiest African
state, Nigeria. The Contact Group has discussed most of
its initiatives with representatives of these countries,
and the African leaders frequently meet to discuss and
propose initiatives of their own; they are responsible
for securing concessions from SWAPO.

Coordination with all these African countries,
rather than only one or two, is critical. The Front-
line states have functioned as a unit on a number of
issues over the years--on the struggles for independence
in Mozambique, Angola, and Zimbabwe, in the Zimbabwe
negotiations, and in regional economic coordination.
Nigeria maintains a strong interest in southern African
issues, and from time to time uses its economic leverage
to promote solutions. In the Namibia negotiations,
Angola plays the pivotal role. SWAPO's bases are in
Angola, and as the target of South Africa's raids,
Angola has the greatest direct interest in seeing the
conflict resolved. Angolan leaders have often proposed
pragmatic, innovative solutions to problems. Mozambique
also has occasionally taken the lead in promoting progress. As Portugal's other former southern African
colony, Mozambique has the closest relationship of all
Front-line states to Angola. Mozambique itself recently
served as a base for a nationalist movement, the
Zimbabwe African National Union (ZANU), and was instrumental in achieving a Zimbabwe settlement. Angola,
Mozambique, and Zimbabwe, having recently gone through
nationalist conflicts and decolonization, make well-
informed suggestions on proposals for Namibia's transition to independence. In 1984 Zambia convened direct
talks between South Africa and SWAPO.

Apart from these particular advantages in the
Namibian mediation effort, cooperation with the key
countries in the region has advantages that would hold
for other mediation efforts. One great advantage is the
urgency that countries of the region attach to securing
a settlement. As the introductory chapter of this book
points out, the first concern of an outside mediator is
seldom simply to resolve the conflict. For the Western
members of the Contact Group, the primary interests

include improvement of their relations in Africa and
countering Soviet influence in the region. For the
African states, however, a settlement based on independence with majority rule for Namibia is the central
concern. For the Contact Group, the Namibian conflict
is a distant one posing no direct threat to their security. For the Front-line, the conflict threatens security and undermines economic development. They are the
most persistent participants in the talks, demanding
progress when Contact Group members become dispirited or
distracted. Front-line representatives are often the
most pragmatic and innovative negotiators, offering
solutions when the more distant Contact Group members
and the more immediately involved parties to the conflict are reluctant to risk their other interests by
suggesting compromises. For example, it was Angola that
proposed the formula for internal party participation
that was essential to the 1981 Geneva talks. And Angola
opposed immediate sanctions against South Africa when
these talks failed to produce a settlement.

Constant involvement in the negotiations by
regional leaders corrects two tendencies among outside
mediators: the currying of favor by being "more African
than the Africans," and, conversely, viewing the conflict largely in East-West terms. When some Western
negotiators have winced at making concessions to the
white supremacist regime in South Africa for fear of how
African countries might react, the Front-line leaders
have urged the concessions because they promoted a
settlement based on majority rule. The inclusion of
internal parties in negotiations is one example. When
some Western negotiators have approached a problem in a
purely East-West context, Front-line leaders have sought
to bring negotiations back to the far more complex
regional realities. African leaders have attempted, for
example, to explain to the United States Angola's security needs for Cuban troops and have sought practical
solutions to the problems created by America's linkage
of a Namibia settlement to Cuban troop withdrawal from
Angola. In 1984, for example, President Kaunda proposed
that SWAPO accept a non-U.N. peacekeeping force in
return for South Africa's agreeing to drop the Cuban
troop linkage.

Leading strategists in the Namibian negotiations
have been skillful not only in initiating and sustaining
a collaborative effort, but also in continuing talks
despite frequent setbacks and stalemates. Of particular
importance was the Reagan administration's decision to
continue U.S. leadership in a mediation effort begun by
the Carter administration, and that did not fit so
easily into the new administration's priorities. Were
not the mediators so persistent, South Africa could
grant Namibia independence on South African terms--with
a Turnhalle constitution guaranteeing continued apart-

heid in the territory and a white supremacist government
dependent on Pretoria. Were the negotiations to collapse, the South African government could hope to win
Western acceptance of its continued dominance over
Namibia by initiating cosmetic changes, as it hopes to
do by declaring independence for some of its African
homelands and by adopting a superficially multiracial
constitution. By persisting in the mediation effort,
the Contact Group has kept alive the possibility of a
negotiated, internationally acceptable settlement. The
parties have discussed the spectrum of substantive
issues and have reached important understandings on
many. Progress has continued, even if it has been
incremental at times and suffered some setbacks. In
these negotiations, as in most, the price of abandoning
diplomacy would be a serious political deterioration.

Placing the mediation process in a U.N. framework
has helped keep the Contact Group, the African states,
South Africa, and SWAPO locked into the effort. To
abandon negotiations would be to renege on formal commitments, ratified by Security Council resolutions. The
U.N. context has had other advantages as well. From
time to time, the U.N. secretary-general has been called
upon to submit proposals. The secretary-general or a
representative has at times taken over the negotiations,
giving them new life on occasions when the Contact Group
had reached an impasse. The U.N. context maintains a
certain standard for the ultimate outcome of the mediation. The United Nations took over from the League of
Nations a responsibility to see that the territory
receives independence with majority rule, and that basic
human rights are protected in the decolonization
process.

Rights for the White Minority

The Reagan administration added an important element to the Namibian negotiations when it insisted on
provisions to protect human rights--including the rights
of the white minority--as the Carter administration and
Britain insisted for Zimbabwe. Before the Reagan administration, the mediators focused on arranging for fair
elections for a constituent assembly. That assembly was
to determine the security provisions for the white
minority. With the change of administrations in the
United States, a reevaluation of the Namibian negotiations brought suggestions that the entire constitution
might be made part of a settlement package--as was the
case in Zimbabwe. Agreement was finally reached in
November 1981 on a less sweeping but significant pro-
posal--that two-thirds of the constituent assembly would
have to agree to the constitution, giving the minority
greater say, and that the constitution would include a

bill of rights, an independent judiciary, and other
important provisions to protect individual rights. Such
provisions have value not only in principle, but also
because they are essential to enable South African leaders to defend a Namibian settlement among their own constituents against charges that they have sold out the
whites.

An important element in any protection for the
minority is for Western mediators to back up constitutional provisions with pledges of assistance. This was
an issue throughout the Zimbabwe negotiations. Dominant
minorities do not trust constitutional pledges alone.
After all, they have not wielded power with great concern for the individual rights of the majority. Promises of substantial postindependence assistance by the
Western democratic nations, tied to an independent government's adherence to the settlement, can be critical.
And the aid itself can contribute directly to security
for the minority--either by providing a new government
with the means to purchase minority-held property at
fair-market prices if land reform is an issue, or by
enabling it to extend services and economic opportunities to the majority without having to deprive the
minority.

Although provisions for white security in Namibia
have been important in these negotiations, South Africa
has attached even greater significance to provisions for
its own security. Parallel with the Namibia negotiations, South Africa has pursued an attack-and-negotiate
policy in its relations with neighboring countries. The
South African military escalated its raids on southern
Angola and attacked the capitals of Mozambique and
Lesotho. South Africa increased its support for insurgents in Angola and Mozambique and took actions to
destabilize Zimbabwe's economy.

At the same time, Pretoria intensified its diplomatic efforts to obtain mutual-security agreements with
Angola and Mozambique. If they will prohibit the Afri-
can nationalist movements, SWAPO and the ANC, from oper-
ating out of their territories, South Africa offers to
curtail its raids and destabilization efforts. How far
South Africa will go in this approach remains unclear.
Zimbabwe has a clear policy of refusing bases to the
ANC, yet South Africa has trained and aided saboteurs
against Zimbabwe. In early 1984 South Africa and
Mozambique announced an agreement on mutual security.
South Africa has withdrawn its troops from southern
Angola, and a temporary ceasefire is in place, but the
arrangements include no commitment from South Africa to
halt its support to UNITA insurgents in Angola.

The South African government reportedly is split on
the question of mutual-security arrangements. Some
South African officials apparently believe surrounding
states pose a threat to South Africa not only by harbor-

ing anti-South African nationalist movements, but by the very nature of their governments. According to this view, the victories of nationalist movements in Zimbabwe, Angola, Mozambique, and possibly Namibia pose a threat to South Africa in the precedent they set and in the radical and antiapartheid governments whose leaders have spent more than a decade fighting white-minority rule. South African leaders holding this view would rather destabilize neighboring governments in the hopes of imposing compliant puppet regimes than establish a modus vivendi with the triumphant nationalist leaders.

The United States' approaches to the regional-security questions that are linked to the Namibia negotiations have differed in the Carter and Reagan administrations. Under President Carter, the United States joined the African states and other members of the United Nations in condemning South African raids into Angola. The Carter administration held that the cause of the Namibia conflict was South Africa's illegal occupation of the territory, and the source of violence inside South Africa was the white-supremacist apartheid system. South African attacks on neighboring countries in order to preserve this status quo were not regarded as legitimate self-defense. Rather, the United States during the Carter years sought to persuade South Africa's rulers that the future of the white minority could be made secure only by negotiating early, peaceful change, before it was too late. Escalating violence would only bring irreversible polarization.

The Reagan administration adopted a different approach to South Africa's regional destabilization. Pretoria's raids on neighboring countries were regarded as understandable reprisals for ANC and SWAPO infiltration from neighboring countries into South Africa and Namibia. Assistant Secretary Crocker told a Senate subcommittee:

> We categorically ,condemn all terrorist and other violent acts that either of these organizations [referring to the ANC and SWAPO] take to try to bring about change in Namibia and South Africa. . . . As we have repeatedly said in the Namibia/Angolan context, we believe the spiral of violence is a two-way street, and we deplore it. [8]

The Reagan administration refused to join in international condemnation of South African raids against its neighbors. In August 1981 the United States cast a lone veto against a U.N. resolution that condemned a major South African raid into Angola. Although other Contact Group members voted for the resolution or abstained, the

U.S. representative argued that the resolution was not
balanced in that it "placed the blame solely on South
Africa for the escalation of violence which plagues the
entire region." [9] The United States instead urged South
Africa's neighbors, particularly Mozambique, to establish a modus vivendi with Pretoria--to deny the ANC
bases in return for South African agreements to halt its
own raids and support for insurgents in neighboring
countries.

Representatives of the Reagan administration may
regard this policy as essential to establish a framework
for a Namibia settlement. Only if the South African
government is confident that radical neighbors will
respect the security of its borders, it may be argued,
will Pretoria accept Namibian elections that SWAPO
almost certainly will win. But the strategy is fraught
with dangers. As has been discussed, there are factions
within the South African government which oppose letting
radical neighbors live in peace even if they harbor no
antiapartheid movements. Should these factions prevail,
South Africa would not live up to its part of the bar-
gains which Reagan administration officials have sought
to arrange. Moreover, the United States places itself
in a position of justifying South African raids against
its neighbors and South African efforts to preserve an
unjust and internationally condemned order. As one
observer put it, American diplomats sometimes play along
with what essentially is a good-cop, bad-cop routine.
South Africa raids a neighboring capital, killing civilians in their homes. Then the Americans come around and
say that South Africa may be persuaded to stop such
raids if the invaded country will just give South Africa
what it wants--the right to enforce apartheid in peace.

Flaws in the Mediation

The chief Namibia mediators in both the Carter and
Reagan administrations have conducted the talks with
skill, imagination, and patience and have made real
progress toward agreement among the parties. The United
States, as lead mediator, also substantially altered its
negotiating strategy with the shift of administrations.
Similar flaws, however, in the mediating efforts of both
administrations have actually contributed to stalemate.
As Zartman and Touval point out in the introductory
chapter to this volume, a mediator frequently has purposes other than resolving a particular conflict. And
so it is in Namibia, where the United States' other
purposes have impeded a settlement. By examining these
other goals and the ways in which they have prevented
effective mediation, we may learn some valuable lessons.

U.S. Mediation and "Other Goals"

During the Reagan administration the United States' primary purpose in the Namibia negotiations apparently has been to secure the withdrawal of Cuban troops from Angola. The new administration early on made clear to other members of the Contact Group, the Front-line states, SWAPO, and South Africa that America's continued commitment to the Namibia negotiations was conditioned on linkage between a Namibia settlement and the withdrawal of Cuban troops from Angola.[10] Reagan administration officials attached great significance to the presence of Cuban troops in Angola; this much was clear, in any event, during Alexander Haig's confirmation hearings. Secretary-of-State-designate Haig told the Senate Foreign Relations Committee that because the United States had not stood up to the Cubans in Angola, Cuban troops had intervened in Ethiopia, and because the United States had offered no resistance in Ethiopia, the Soviet Union had gained influence in South Yemen. Thus, a long line of dominoes stretched from Angola to Ethiopia to the Middle East. Who knew where the next would fall? It was now the United States' responsibility to reverse the first of these Cuban/Soviet gains.[11]

For some in the Reagan administration, it makes little sense for the United States to be pursuing a Namibian settlement unless the withdrawal of Cuban troops from Angola can be secured at the same time. A settlement would result in SWAPO, a Soviet-backed nationalist movement, assuming power in Namibia. It would also make it more difficult for South Africa to aid UNITA, the insurgents in southern Angola who had been aided by the United States until Congress prohibited the assistance. Thus, a Namibian settlement without a Cuban troop-withdrawal from Angola is perceived by some Reagan administration officials as strengthening the Soviet hand in southern Africa at the expense of the United States, and as contributing to the radicalization of the region.

The primary goal of Carter administration negotiators was to take a firm stand against South Africa's illegal occupation of Namibia and the extension of apartheid to the territory--to distance the United States from South Africa in the eyes of the African states and the rest of the world. Indeed, officials directly involved in the talks assumed that South Africa was not negotiating seriously toward independence with majority rule for Namibia. They often referred to South Africa's "two-track" strategy: namely participating in the negotiations only to avoid U.N. sanctions and to buy time for its own apartheid-based internal settlement. South African proposals, reservations, and demands were thus greeted with skepticism. South African concerns about whether elections would be free and fair, or

whether individual rights would be protected after
independence were viewed as a means only of prolonging
the negotiations, postponing the day when South Africa
would have to say "yes" or "no" to a complete proposal
for a settlement. Ambassador McHenry stated at the
outset of the negotiations in 1977:   "They [South
African officials] are probably trying to do as many of
those things that are internationally acceptable as they
possibly can as a way of rationalizing the internal
settlement." [12]

It is impossible to be certain of the South African
government's purposes. What is clear is that skepticism
on the part of the mediators can become a self-fulfill-
ing prophecy. If the skepticism is undue, negotiators
will miss opportunities for a settlement. But if the
skepticism is warranted, the mediators' reluctance to
press ahead (as though all parties were acting in good
faith) prevents them from demonstrating clearly that the
fault for lack of progress lies with South Africa, not
with them.

Thus, lead negotiators for both the Carter and
Reagan administrations regarded the Namibia mediation
effort primarily as a crusade against an evil: Soviet
and Cuban intervention in southern Africa in the case of
the Reagan administration, South Africa's violation of
international law and human rights in the case of the
Carter administration. In the course of these crusades,
both administrations often lost sight of the United
States' main interest in Namibia: an early, negotiated
transition to independence based on majority rule and an
end to race discrimination.

Both administrations have failed to mediate as well
as they might have. Diverted by other concerns about
East-West competition or America's image as an opponent
of racial domination, the negotiators lost sight of the
most important goal--a settlement. A settlement in
Namibia would do more than anything else to reduce
Soviet influence in southern Africa, enhance America's
status in the region, and counter racial domination.

On the other hand, the United States did not make
this mistake in the Zimbabwe negotiations. The focus of
the negotiating effort was always on securing agreement
among the parties on the conditions for free and fair
elections and on a democratic constitution that would
guarantee individual rights, including the rights and
security of the white minority. The United States succeeded in Zimbabwe. It has yet to succeed in Namibia in
part because of this fundamental difference in emphasis.

Global and Regional Politics

Both Carter and Reagan administration officials
have recognized that the United States stands to gain

from its pursuit of a Namibian settlement. The negotiations are a means to extend U.S. influence in Africa. The United States works closely with leading African countries in the pursuit of an important African objective. If the negotiations are successful, the United States will have denied the Soviet Union an opportunity to increase its influence in the region.

However, the Carter and Reagan administration negotiating strategies have also been counterproductive according to these very terms. The Reagan administration's public emphasis on the withdrawal of Cuban troops from Angola was in concept flawed; it would lose points with African governments, complicate the timing and even the prospects of a settlement, and advertise American impotence over the years it would take to achieve that goal. And it would give Cuba and the Soviet Union an unnecessary veto over whether or not the United States succeeded in Namibia. The Carter administration's emphasis on distancing the United States from South Africa similarly failed to make the most of potential advantages in global and regional politics. The United States has two potential strengths in undertaking Namibia negotiations: to act as a successful mediator, and to show that America is unsympathetic to apartheid. The first has greater potential because it shows that the United States can help secure a goal that is of utmost importance to other countries in the region and, moreover, can do something the Soviet Union cannot. The second has more limited potential because the United States cannot offer the kind of military support to the opponents of apartheid that the Soviet Union can. To emphasize opposition to apartheid at the expense of negotiations therefore diminishes the force of American diplomacy.

The United States' strategy in the Zimbabwe negotiations, by contrast, made the most of potential gains for the mediator in terms of power politics. The United States' position in the ideological competition with the Soviet Union is bolstered when the United States focuses on a fair settlement above anything else and seeks to resolve conflicts by means of free and fair elections and an agreement to a democratic constitution. Moreover, it is evident to all sides that the United States and other Western countries can buttress a democratic settlement by extending the economic resources required by a newly enfranchised majority while providing financial compensation for the minority. The Soviet Union, in contrast, can offer only weapons to perpetuate a conflict that is costly to all sides.

The "Hurting Stalemate"

The stalemate in Namibia clearly hurts SWAPO and the surrounding African countries, financially as well as militarily. The task for the mediator is to assure that the stalemate hurts South Africa enough to counter-balance the prospect for South Africa of losing the territory. However, both the Reagan and Carter strategies have had the opposite impact. They have helped prevent the costs of stalemate from outweighing the risks to South Africa of a settlement.

Once the Reagan administration tied a Namibia settlement to Cuban troop withdrawal, Pretoria was enabled to reject a settlement until the Cuban troops departed --and to keep the United States on South Africa's side in the process. Moreover, the United States painted itself into a corner by denying itself the opportunity to compromise its proclaimed goal. If the Angolan government agrees to a withdrawal of half the Cuban troops, or to their withdrawal to the northern half of the country, South Africa has only to respond that such arrangements are not sufficient, that there must have to be total withdrawal of Cuban troops or there will be no settlement. Can the Reagan administration, having made such a public issue of the troop withdrawal, then say that something short of complete withdrawal is sufficient--that ten thousand Cuban troops in Angola, for example, is a reasonable compromise? Under the Reagan strategy, South Africa can avoid having to decide on Namibia because it can help assure that the Cuban troops will not leave Angola simply by continuing both its raids on southern Angola and its support of UNITA insurgents. Moreover, once the South African government has committed itself to the goal of Cuban troop withdrawal, its task in selling a Namibia settlement at home becomes more complicated. If it does not secure total withdrawal before the settlement is implemented, it is vulnerable to charges of having sold out. On the other hand, even a partial victory on the Cuban troop issue may make a settlement easier for the South African government to sell.

Reagan administration officials argue that the linkage of a Cuban troop withdrawal to South Africa's withdrawal from Namibia has introduced a needed symmetry into the negotiations: Both South Africa and South Africa's archenemy, the Soviet Union, would be perceived as retreating. However, underlying this apparent symmetry is a fundamental imbalance. Cuban troops withdraw across an ocean to Cuba, but South African troops withdraw across the border. South Africa underscores this asymmetry for Angola by its raids on Angola and support for UNITA insurgents, even though Cuban troops avoid engagement with both South African and UNITA forces.

Cuban troops are, first and foremost, Angola's insurance policy against another South African invasion aimed at toppling the Angolan government. In 1975, when South African troops marched to the outskirts of Angola's capital, Luanda, it was reportedly the Cuban troops that offered effective resistance.[13] Cuban troops never invaded Namibia, let alone South Africa, nor got closer than 100 kilometers to the border. If at the time of a Nambia settlement Angola expels all Cuban troops, it will have only its own forces for self-defense against the more powerful South African military. After years of constant bombardment by the South African military, it will take more than South African agreement to a Namibia settlement to imbue Angola with confidence in South Africa's intentions to live in peace with its neighbors. The time will be right to seek total Cuban troop withdrawal from Angola sometime after a Namibia settlement is implemented, when it becomes clear that South Africa will respect Namibia's independence and will not reoccupy the territory under some pretext.

Carter administration officials, in attempting to distance the United States from South Africa and its positions, found another means of enabling South Africa to stall without reaching a "hurting stalemate." United States negotiators, not wanting to appear overly eager to grant concessions whenever South Africa forwarded a new demand or questioned a proposal, would stall (sometimes for several months) before presenting a South African concern to the Africans--and even questioned African concessions to the South Africans. In short, South African proposals usually elicited unnecessarily prolonged haggling. The United States would entertain only part of the proposal, and only after South Africa conceded on a point that may or may not have moved negotiations forward. The point seemed to be to ensure that South Africa got nothing for free--that Pretoria gave something for every concession it got.

American negotiators contributed to stalemate, for example, in their handling of the issue of SWAPO bases. In March 1979 South Africa insisted that SWAPO not be granted bases in Namibia and that SWAPO's bases in Angola be monitored by the United Nations, as South Africa's bases in Namibia were to be. Reportedly, the Front-line states decided early to concede on both these points in order to maintain momentum in the negotiations. But U.S. negotiators were skeptical. They proposed another plan to Angola in July 1979: SWAPO would forgo bases in Namibia, but its bases in Angola would not be monitored by the United Nations. Instead, there would be a demilitarized zone (DMZ) along the Angola-South Africa border to prevent armed SWAPO infiltration during the transition. There was to be no progress in the talks until South Africa accepted "the principle of the DMZ," which it finally did in December 1979. The DMZ proposal raised many new questions, which came to be the focus of negotiations until the end of the Carter administration. For instance, would the U.N. contingent have to be expanded? Would various armed forces have bases in the DMZ, and, if so, how many? How would UNITA forces in the DMZ be treated? In May 1982 the Front-line states and SWAPO accepted U.N. monitoring of SWAPO bases in Angola, and the entire DMZ issue was quietly shelved.[14]

Delays in responding to South African concerns undermined the United States' ability to use sanctions to obtain a final Namibia settlement, even though the threat of sanctions was at the very heart of the Carter administration's strategy. Sanctions could not be effective unless all the Contact Group members--representing most of South Africa's major trading partners--were fully committed to implementing those sanctions. The record shows that, as a rule, European countries are far more reluctant than the United States to use trade restrictions as a tool of diplomacy. A solid Western commitment to employ sanctions over Namibia would be possible only under two circumstances. One, South Africa would have to reject a complete settlement package, which the Contact Group had agreed addressed all the legitimate concerns of both sides. Or, two, South Africa would have to demonstrate unabashed stalling when it was also clear the Contact Group and the Africans were making every effort to move forward expeditiously. But by the end of the Carter administration, the South African government was still voicing legitimate, fundamental concerns about assurances in the settlement proposals for free and fair elections, and the Contact Group still had not determined how forthcoming it should be in addressing those concerns. As often as South Africa raised new demands and resurrected old issues, the fact remains that it should not bear all the blame for the delays in the negotiations. American leaders in the negotiations never tried the tactic of dealing expeditiously with each new South African concern--granting the concessions that would not jeopardize the ultimate goals of independence, majority rule, fair elections, and the progress of the talks. Had they done so, they might have maneuvered South Africa into a corner where new demands would have been perceived by all as nothing more than attempts to stall. Instead, the Contact Group was often responsible for long delays, as on the issues of SWAPO bases and participation by internal Namibian parties in talks.

The strategies of both the Reagan and Carter administrations created rifts within the Contact Group and between the Contact Group and the African states, further undermining attempts to create a hurting stalemate for South Africa. The worst divisions have come over

the Reagan administration's linkage of a Namibia settlement to withdrawal of Cuban troops from Angola. The
African states have publicly condemned this approach.
When Vice-President Bush traveled in Africa, each leader
he met made a point of publicly criticizing the linkage,
and he made that linkage more open and explicit than it
had ever been before. [15] Some members of the Contact
Group have publicly disclaimed any association with the
linkage, [16] while others have quietly allowed the United
States to proceed unilaterally with this phase of the
negotiations.
     Although the Carter administration's approach did
not provoke such sharp, public differences between the
United States and its negotiating partners, there was
genuine concern when the anti-South African position of
U.S. negotiators appeared to be impeding business at
hand. At one point in 1980 when the Contact Group was
delaying its response to South African demands regarding
SWAPO bases, the Front-line states implored the United
Nations to take over the negotiations in the hope that
this would revive them. At other times, Contact Group
members felt frustrated with the United States' insistence that they all be taciturn in the face of South
Africa's concerns. Other members seemed fearful that
negotiations would prompt the United Nations to impose
premature sanctions. Others wanted to add to the pressure in favor of sanctions by expediting settlement on
the outstanding issues. This was the case in 1980 when
the U.N. Security Council agreed to meet in December for
the purpose of deciding on Namibia.
     In the Zimbabwe negotiations, by contrast, the
United States and Great Britain focused on the kind of
settlement they wanted, which forced the pace by creating stalemates that hurt both sides. In these negotiations, the mediators posited that concessions could be
granted to anyone--a Soviet-backed nationalist leader or
a white supremacist. Concessions would be proposed,
considered, and urged on the parties if it furthered a
settlement and did not jeopardize fair elections or a
democratic constitution. Both sides had to concede much
in this process. The nationalist leaders agreed to pay
fair-market value for any nationalized property and for
land redistribution, even though the white minority had
years before taken the best half of the land without
compensating Africans. White leaders agreed to abide by
the results of fair elections, even though this would
mean the end of their power and privilege.
     The United States and Britain were able to gain
such concessions and force the pace of negotiations in
part because both sides subscribed in principle to a
settlement based on democratic values. Once one side
accepted a clearly democratic set of proposals, it was
very difficult for the other side to reject them.
Negotiations based on democratic principles had another

practical advantage. There would not be an early
military solution to the Zimbabwe conflict, and all
sides knew it. No faction would willingly surrender
militarily to a government imposed from the outside, or
to a coalition of its rivals. But all were sufficiently
confident of their popular appeal to take their chances
in fair elections.

Many of these same conditions prevail in Namibia
today. Both SWAPO and South Africa subscribe in principle to a settlement based on democratic values, and
would come under great pressure worldwide if either
rejected fair, democratic proposals accepted by the
other. Neither side can see military victory around the
corner. With all the resources South Africa put into
the Namibia campaign, SWAPO may be winning by not los-
ing--but an African nationalist victory is much further
away than it was for ZAPU and ZANU when a Zimbabwe settlement was reached. Were the United States to focus
primarily on securing acceptance of a democratic settlement, instead of on combating the evils of Soviet and
Cuban intervention or South African violations of
international law and human rights, the strategy that
worked in Zimbabwe might work in Namibia. Its other
goals would be best served as well.

However, South Africa cannot view the prospect of
fair elections in Namibia in the same way that the white
minority viewed such a prospect for Zimbabwe. At the
time of the Zimbabwe settlement, a case could be made
that any of the candidates could win. White military
officers clearly hoped that Joshua Nkomo would gain
enough votes to form a coalition with other minority
parties, and thus would need the old Rhodesian armed
forces to keep him in power. South African officials
thought Bishop Muzorewa would win, and were shocked when
Zimbabwe's African electorate rejected a leader who had
reached an accommodation with the white minority. South
African officials probably have learned their lesson
from Zimbabwe. They undoubtedly have few illusions that
the leaders who collaborated with South African rule in
Namibia would win an election. They most certainly
expect victory to go to SWAPO.

Nevertheless, there are still good reasons for
South Africa to risk fair elections in Namibia. The new
government of the impoverished territory will be far
more dependent economically on South Africa than
Zimbabwe is. If Western countries negotiate a settlement successfully, Namibia will emerge with some political ties and significant assistance ties to the West
as well. An elected government in Namibia is bound to
be less radical than one that takes power by force after
several more years of struggle. Moreover, if South
Africa has decided that it has to relinquish Namibia
eventually, it is better to accept a Contact Group-
negotiated settlement. This commits the West to a

solution that provides for minority rights, improves
South Africa's relations with Western countries and its
own neighbors, and encourages outside countries to seek
peaceful solutions in southern Africa rather than simply
to leave South Africa's white minority to its fate.

The Mediator's Methods

The strategies employed by U.S. negotiators in the
Namibia negotiations have deprived it of a primary mediation tool: "the constant potential of joining in coalition with one side against the other." [17] Otherwise,
the United States would be in an excellent position in
Namibia to shift weight from one side to the other.
American negotiators clearly seek an outcome that favors
the African side: Namibian independence from South
Africa under majority rule. Yet they also are committed
to the protection of individual rights and have a stake
in providing for the security of the white minority.
Such an outcome assures them that Namibia will serve as
a constructive model for peaceful change in South Africa
itself.   Moreover, in the eyes of both the African
states and the South African leadership, the United
States and other Western countries have better economic
and political relations with South Africa than do other
members of the international community. The South African leadership identifies in particular with the United
States and looks to the United States, as the leader of
the Western world, to rescue South Africa from the "Communist onslaught."   The United States, therefore, has
great potential to shift weight from one side to the
other in the Namibia negotiations, with its shifts
determined by the relative cooperation of each party
vis-à-vis a democratic settlement.
    However, the Carter and Reagan administrations have
tilted them toward one side or the other from the outset
of their mediation efforts.   The Carter administration
could not credibly tilt toward Pretoria at any stage,
and, as we have noted, South African concessions were
greeted with skepticism.   The Reagan administration,
with its East-West preoccupation, could not credibly
tilt against the strongly anticommunist Pretoria regime
or in favor of Angola or SWAPO. President Reagan
asserted at the outset of his administration that South
Africa had been a constant ally, and proceeded to focus
on improving military relations with it.
    If U.S. negotiators were to focus their efforts
increasingly on obtaining an agreement on conditions for
fair elections and on assurances that the rights of the
white minority would be protected--as it did in
Zimbabwe--their ability to shift weight from one side to
the other would be enhanced.   In Zimbabwe, the United
States and Britain made clear that no side would have a

veto over fair elections. If the internal parties unilaterally accepted a democratic settlement, the mediators pointed out, they would lift sanctions and support
them.   If the African nationalist leaders unilaterally
accepted such a settlement, sanctions against the Smith/
Muzorewa regime would continue.

The United States' role as a communication channel
for the parties has also suffered. The overriding preoccupation of Reagan administration negotiators with
Cuban troops in Angola has hindered communication on
issues of greater importance to the principal parties
involved.   For example, in May 1984 President Kaunda
sponsored a meeting for South Africa, the Front-line,
and SWAPO and purposely did not invite the United
States.   The goal of the meeting was to find a way
around the Cuban troop issue--and the United States was
regarded as a definite hindrance.

Carter administration negotiators erred in their
attempts to be more African than the Africans, resulting
in a failure to communicate African flexibility. From
time to time, Front-line leaders would agree readily to
a South African demand in order to move along the negotiations. United States representatives would be called
in to convey the concession to South Africa, but would
not deliver the message. Chief U.S. negotiators would
doubt that the Africans had really meant to grant South
Africa a concession without getting something in return,
and would go to the African states with a counterproposal. For example, the Africans would be urged to give
South Africa only half of what it asked for, and then
only on the condition that South Africa give something
in return.   In the end, the Africans might finally succeed in conveying their concession to South Africa after
months of unnecessary delay.

The Front-line states and other members of the Contact Group often have been more effective as "formula-
tors"--more capable of innovative thinking--than has the
United States. American negotiators have attached great
importance to adhering to their positions against a
Cuban troop presence in Angola or against South Africa's
violations of international law and human rights. Other
participants in the negotiations have been more flexible, pragmatic, and innovative in dealing with these and
other issues. South Africa, for example, did not give
particular weight to the question of Cuban troops in
Angola until the United States made it a central concern. For South Africa, the key problem is not Cuban
troops in Angola, but SWAPO troops, and how to prevent
their armed infiltration across the border during elections. South Africa has been innovative in its approach
to this problem, demanding that SWAPO not be given bases
in Namibia during the elections but be allowed to return
only if unarmed, proposing that the United Nations monitor SWAPO's bases in Angola as it would South Africa's

bases in Namibia, and finally suggesting a ceasefire on the Angola/Namibia border. Similarly, the African states have been flexible and innovative in dealing with South Africa over Namibia. In response to South Africa's concern about SWAPO infiltration across the border, Angola proposed a demilitarized zone. Angola also accepted the South African proposal that the United Nations monitor SWAPO bases in Angola.

The Carter and Reagan administrations' crusades against one or the other of the parties to the negotiation has also undermined the critical ability of the United States to offer "side payments" to the parties to the negotiations. The Reagan administration cut Zimbabwe's assistance because Zimbabwe did not support the United States diplomatically on non-African issues, and therefore lacks credibility when it suggests that the United States will aid the radical government of Angola if Cuban troops leave.

Just as the Reagan administration could not credibly offer aid to a leftist African government with close ties to the Soviet Union, the Carter administration could not credibly offer aid to help compensate a white minority in Namibia for having given up power. The Carter administration explicitly stated that its assistance to the newly independent Zimbabwe was not to be used to fund purchases of white-owned land by the government. American officials did not wish to see scarce African aid resources allocated to an elite for the loss of property which it had taken from the Africans in the first place. Front-line leaders were not nearly so rigid about the allocation of American aid. Recognizing that whites would have to be granted some financial security if they were going to relinquish power, and recognizing that a newly independent state would not have the resources to both "buy them out" and provide basic services for the black majority, one of the Front-line leaders commented that the United States and other Western countries should in fact provide a financial "safety net" for Zimbabwe's white minority. "You take care of the whites," the leader asserted, "and we will take care of the blacks."

Prospects for a Settlement

At the time of this writing, in summer 1984, prospects for the settlement in Namibia have improved. South Africa and Angola have reached a temporary ceasefire, South Africa has withdrawn its troops from southern Angola, and a demilitarized zone has been established in their place. South Africa and Angola have announced their intention to build on this ceasefire toward a Namibia settlement.

In explaining the ceasefire, South African Prime Minister Botha has stated that the conflict in Namibia has

> exacted a heavy price--in material, in international condemnation and in the lives of our young men. . . . Can it be expected of South Africa to continue to bear this burden under circumstances where we do not claim sovereignty over the territory, where we are exposed to criticism from the internal parties of South-west Africa, where we are severely condemned by the West and where the United Nations is threatening us with enforcement measures? [18]

For the South African government, the time may be right for a settlement. The country is economically weak after several years of recession and little able to afford vast military expenditures. Having just won a white referendum on new constitutional proposals, the government is politically strong and perhaps capable of negotiating a settlement that is certain to be controversial among its Afrikaner constituents. Moreover, the time may be right for a Namibia settlement in South Africa's relations with the United States. The Reagan administration, with its policy of "constructive engagement" with the South African government, is probably offering South Africa the best proposal it could ever expect on Namibia. The outcome of the 1984 American elections is uncertain. The U.S. House of Representatives has passed a number of measures restricting economic relations with South Africa, measures that were endorsed by the Democratic presidential nominee, Walter Mondale: They require U.S. opposition to IMF loans to South Africa; prohibit new U.S. investment in South Africa; prohibit U.S. bank loans to the South African government; require American firms in South Africa to follow fair-employment practices; prohibit krugerrand sales in the United States; and restore restrictions on U.S. sales to the South African military and police. Thus, South Africa has never been offered more carrots by the United States, has never been so close to having the carrots taken away, and has never faced such a real threat that sticks will be used.

But a Namibia settlement is by no means inevitable. The South African government could allow just enough progress toward a settlement to enable the Reagan administration to claim diplomatic gains during the presidential election campaign, but not so much that South Africa will be committed to giving up the terri-

tory. South African leaders anticipate a Reagan victory
and have little fear that the Democratic sticks will be
used. It is critical, therefore, that the United States
force the pace of negotiations, taking advantage of what
opportunities exist for settlement. That will require
that the United States be flexible on extraneous issues
that have hampered progress in the negotiations--e.g.,
the withdrawal of Cuban troops from Angola--and focus on
the essentials: agreement on fair elections and on provisions for the security of the minority that will give
up power.

     Namibia negotiations demonstrate that preoccupa-
tions with global or regional politics or with ideology
can so bias American negotiators that their mediation
efforts actually become counterproductive. But the
success in Zimbabwe demonstrates that Americans' "bias"
in favor of fair, democratic elections and protection of
individual rights can facilitate negotiations. When
neither side is near winning militarily, elections offer
everyone a chance to compete peacefully rather than to
capitulate. When a privileged minority is being asked
to give up power, protections for individual rights
offer hope for personal security. A strategy that
emphasizes this American bias in favor of democratic
solutions serves other U.S. interests as well. It
enhances the United States' credibility and prestige
both in the region and globally. It emphasizes a
strength that the Soviet Union does not possess. And it
furthers basic American values.

Chapter 4: Notes

1.   For history of the Namibia negotiations, see I. William Zartman, Ripe for Resolution (New York: Oxford University Press, 1985).

2.   UNSC/PV 2082 (7/27/78).

3.   Zartman, op. cit.

4.   President Ronald Reagan, interview by Walter Cronkite, March 3, 1981.

5.   UNGA/R 2145 (XXI) (10/27/66).

6.   Allister Sparks, Washington Post, March 25, 1983.

7.   New York Times, September 1, 1983.

8.   Colin Legum, Africa Contemporary Record 1981-82, A-50.

9.   Washington Post, September 1, 1981.

10.   Speech by Secretary of State Alexander Haig in St. Louis, Missouri, May 29, 1981.

11.   Confirmation hearings for Alexander Haig, January 10, 1981, p. 147.

12.   Colin Legum, Africa Contemporary Record 1976-77, A-16.

13.   For example, Washington Post, January 6, 1982, notes that several South Africans were taken prisoner during the 1975 invasion, but only three Cubans were captured.

14.   Zartman, Ripe for Resolution; Colin Legum, Africa Contemporary Record 1979-80, B-748-49; and Fleur De Villiers, in Johannesburg Sunday Times, May 20, 1979.

15.   "A New Partnership with Africa," speech by Vice-President George Bush before the Kenya Chamber of Commerce, Nairobi, November 19, 1982. See also November 1982 New York Times reports on Bush visit to Africa for African reaction.

16.   New York Times, October 13, 1982. French Foreign Minister Claude Cheysson said France, Germany, and Canada told U.S. that linkage was "not acceptable."

17.   Introductory chapter.

18.   Washington Post, February 1, 1984.

5.
THE INDO-PAKISTANI CONFLICT: SOVIET MEDIATION AT TASHKENT, 1966

Thomas Perry Thornton

The focus of the persistent conflict between India and Pakistan, and especially of the 1965 war, is the dispute over Kashmir. The history is complicated and not relevant to the subject at hand. Briefly, the Pakistanis claim (correctly) that Kashmir[1] is an overwhelmingly Muslim area and should have been allowed to opt for Pakistan when the Subcontinent was partitioned in 1947. The Indians claim (equally correctly) that partition provided for the semisovereign rulers of the princely states to choose the country to which they would attach their realms. The Hindu ruler of Kashmir chose India. While the legalities of the matter are debated endlessly, the fact is that following the fighting between India and Pakistan from 1948 to 1949, India was left in possession of the largest and best parts of Kashmir. Pakistan held a thin strip in the west ("Azad" or "Free" Kashmir), and considerable land in the north that provides a direct link to China. While India officially claims all of Kashmir and disputes the Pakistani occupation of its part, it is in fact content with the present situation. And since India is much more powerful than

Thomas Perry Thornton is adjunct professor of Asian studies at SAIS while on leave from the U.S. Department of State. Mr. Thornton dealt previously with South Asia on the National Security Council staff. The views expressed in this chapter do not necessarily reflect the policies of the Department of State or of the United States government. Mr. Thornton wishes to express his appreciation to K. Shankar Bajpai, ambassador of India to the United States, and to Yuri Gankovsky, head of the Near and Middle East division of the Institute of Oriental Studies, Academy of Sciences, USSR, for his helpful comments.

Pakistan, the situation is not likely to change. That was not, however, quite so clear in 1965.

Although the origins and the merits of the dispute are murky, the importance of Kashmir to both sides had become tremendous by 1965. For Pakistan, the loss of Kashmir had undermined the nation's entire rationale-- the union of all the predominantly Muslim areas of the Subcontinent. For India, Kashmir was evidence of its meaning as a secular state, the homeland of Muslims and Hindus alike. Although neither of these claims would stand up to the closest logical scrutiny, each became critical for its proponents and Kashmir became a crucial symbol for each country.

Following the establishment of a ceasefire in 1949 monitored by U.N. forces, the Kashmir issue became a hardy perennial of the international scene. Attempts at mediation had petered out by the mid-1960s, and it had become a well-institutionalized dispute. There was a general assumption that things would continue indefinitely without exploding, thereby providing the two countries with a gratifying issue and allowing successive generations of U.N. observers a continuing, pleasant occupation.[2]

The Events of 1965

After Nehru's death in 1964 the new government of Lal Bahadur Shastri took several steps to alter the status quo within Indian-held Kashmir. Some of the largely symbolic differences that had continued to differentiate Kashmir from the other states of India were abolished, and the Pakistanis took this as a sign that their claim to Kashmir was about to be buried completely. Furthermore, following the Sino-Indian War of 1962, India had undertaken an ambitious military modernization program. Although Pakistan had always been inferior in military strength, the new Indian program--even though directed mainly at China--promised soon to create a situation in which Pakistan's military capabilities would be so far outclassed that a military challenge of India over Kashmir would be impossible. Thus, on two counts the Pakistanis had come to the conclusion that they must act soon.

There were other territorial disputes between India and Pakistan. One of these involved the Rann of Kutch, a remote desert area where the Indo-Pakistani border meets the Arabian Sea. In early 1965 a series of military engagements took place there, in which the Pakistanis enjoyed a superior strategic position and gave a good account of themselves against the Indians. After several weeks of sporadic fighting, the dispute was mediated by the British and submitted to a tripartite tribunal--a tempting precedent for the Pakistanis to apply to Kashmir.

Encouraged by the experience in Kutch and at the urging of Foreign Minister Bhutto, Pakistani President Ayub Khan sanctioned a series of guerrilla actions inside Indian-held Kashmir, designed to stimulate insurrection and force the issue into the international arena--perhaps along the lines that had proven successful in Algeria and West New Guinea. Serious guerrilla operations began in early August but were not notably successful in causing an uprising. They were, however, troublesome to the Indians, who reacted in late August by seizing territory and passes on the Pakistani side of the ceasefire line near Poonch, through which the guerrillas had been infiltrated. This involved the first combat by regular forces from both countries. The Pakistanis continued the spiral of escalation on September 1 by sending armored columns across the ceasefire line into the southern areas of Kashmir around Chhamb, threatening the Indian land access into Kashmir. The Indians were in a tactically disadvantageous position and decided to extend combat beyond the cease-fire line. On September 6 the Indian army moved across the recognized international boundary into Punjab, well to the south of Kashmir, and the war had undeniably begun. [3]

Fighting continued for several weeks, both in Kashmir and along the length of the Indo-Pakistani border. (The border of India and East Pakistan--now Bangladesh--remained quiet.) After three weeks of fighting, neither party had won a decisive victory, although the Pakistani army had pretty well run out of steam and, more important, spare parts. Each side had occupied territory belonging to the other. The Indians held a salient near the key Pakistani city of Lahore and each side had occupied desert country farther to the south on either side of the Sind-Rajasthan border. Inside Kashmir itself, the Pakistanis held on to the Chhamb salient while the Indians maintained control of the strategic passes at Haji Pir and other locations in the salient around Poonch. The war was indecisive, but the Indians were more able to pursue hostilities, and their threat to Lahore was more serious than anything the Pakistanis had achieved. Most significantly, the Indians had proved that Kashmir could not be wrested from them by force.

From the very outbreak of the fighting, there had been calls for a ceasefire from all sides, including a series of unanimous and increasingly peremptory U.N. Security Council resolutions. Both the situation on the ground and the force of international opinion, therefore, pressured the parties to accede on September 20 to a U.N. demand for a ceasefire. The conflict came to an end following a dramatic session of the Security Council on September 22.

The U.N. demand for withdrawal had gone unheeded, but with minor exceptions the ceasefire was effective. Although war had never officially been declared, a state of hostilities continued, and something had to be done to separate the forces so that fighting would not resume. In addition, a formula had to be found for restoring the territorial status quo ante or some other mutually acceptable arrangement, and to repair the abnormal situation brought about by the fighting. The time was ripe for outside efforts to bring about a more formal kind of peace.

Waiting for a Mediator

Britain should have had pride of place as a mediator since both India and Pakistan were members of the Commonwealth, but the Indians believed that the British favored Pakistan. The United States was the dominant global power and had had close ties with Pakistan and India, but it was disqualified on several grounds. Both countries were bitter with Washington for cutting off aid during the fighting. Pakistan felt that the United States should have stood by its ally; India believed that the war would not have occurred at all but for the supply of American weapons to Pakistan. Both sides were still offended by Lyndon Johnson's cancelation of invitations to Ayub and Shastri earlier in the year. The United Nations would have been a logical instrument, but the Pakistanis believed it to be too much under American influence while the Indians probably feared that it would reopen the Kashmir issue and attempt to impose a solution. There was no viable nonaligned mechanism at the time and, in any case, Pakistan was not a member of the movement.

Only a year or so before, the Soviet Union would not even have been considered as a mediator. Khrushchev had lavished attention on India and been hostile toward Pakistan because of the latter's close cooperation with the United States. By 1965, however, Khrushchev was gone and South Asia was one of several areas where the new leadership sought a more balanced policy approach and a generally lower posture. The Indo-Soviet relationship, while remaining warm, inevitably felt the impact. On the other hand, the Soviets had become concerned over the burgeoning Sino-Pakistani relationship and made some tentative overtures to Pakistan. Ayub's visit to Moscow in April 1965 was a landmark in Soviet-Pakistani relations and contrasted sharply with the Johnson rebuff. The personal contact established between Ayub and the Soviet leadership was to play a useful role in facilitating the Tashkent Conference and its outcome. [4]

To the delight of Rawalpindi (and the dismay of Delhi), the Soviets took a neutral posture in the Rann of Kutch affair and moved away from their traditional pro-Indian position on Kashmir during Shastri's May 1965 visit to Moscow. All during the September conflict, the Soviets avoided taking sides. The Soviet Union, therefore, emerged as the only party capable of bringing the two sides together. India still enjoyed enough of a preference to feel secure, and Pakistan was sufficiently intrigued with the opening that the Soviets had offered. [5]

The Soviet Union had ample reason to become involved in the situation, having an understandable desire to restore stability in an area very close to its southern borders. (The fact of geographic proximity was a recurring theme in Soviets statements.) [6] Furthermore, it was deeply concerned about the Chinese role in South Asia. Peking had issued an ultimatum on September 8 to India as a means of exerting pressure on behalf of Pakistan. It was later withdrawn, but the specter of Chinese intervention still loomed. Even short of that, continued Indo-Pakistani hostilities would benefit the Chinese interest. Chinese intervention would also probably have triggered American support of India. [7] Lastly, the USSR was anxious to assert its voice in Asian affairs. Soviet propaganda stressed the theme that the USSR, as an Asian power, was a particularly suitable mediator, in contrast to the former colonial powers. [8] A successful mediation bid would enable the Soviets to step into the gap now left by the British and Americans in a critical part of Asia.

The USSR had never before offered to mediate a dispute between two other countries. The possibility scarcely arose in those terms among Communist countries and it was only in very recent times that the Soviets had established themselves as a respected international actor. The stakes were sufficiently high and the risks sufficiently low that Moscow decided to try its hand.

Even before the outbreak of widespread fighting, Kosygin had sent messages to Ayub and Shastri on September 4, noting Soviet concern over a dangerous situation near its borders and offering Soviet good offices if both sides so desired; Tass statements on September 8 and 12 publicized the offer. Then, on September 17, in the aftermath of the Chinese ultimatum, Kosygin reiterated his offer more forcefully and specifically, inviting Ayub and Shastri to come to Tashkent or some other suitable place in the Soviet Union "to establish direct contact with the aim of achieving agreement on the establishment of peace." He offered to attend personally, if Ayub and Shastri desired. [9] The Soviet offer was probably the least unattractive mediation possibility since it was couched in terms that promised little or no substantive Soviet involvement. Nevertheless, the

way to the conference was not easy. Shastri and Ayub
gave evasive replies. While both needed some formula
for justifying compromises that they were too politically weak to sell at home, they also feared that they
might come under pressure to make concessions that
neither could afford under any circumstances. The brink
on which they were tottering was not inviting; the
uncertainties of stepping back were also unattractive.

Some six weeks passed following the ceasefire
without forward movement. Secretary-General U Thant
appointed a personal representative to back up U.N.
appeals for a settlement, but to no avail. All of the
outside powers (except, of course, China) urged both
sides to come to the negotiating table, and the United
States especially pressed Ayub to accept the Soviet
offer. The British and American abdication reflected
not only their own inability to work with the parties,
but also a general disillusionment with the Indo-
Pakistani situation and desire to wash their hands of
it. In effect, they were now resigned to permitting the
Soviets a major role in the affairs of South Asia.
Under this combination of internal and external pressures, Ayub and Shastri agreed to meet at Tashkent in
the Uzbek SSR, with Kosygin acting as host. The
announcement was made on December 9. [10]

Issues and Interests

The three parties to the Tashkent meeting had a
variety of objectives. Ayub Khan faced a grim domestic
situation, having begun a costly war that he could not
win. He needed some movement on Kashmir to show that
his country's sacrifices had not been in vain. Shastri
was in a more enviable political position but had to
take account of aroused nationalism within India. He
needed to gather the fruits of perceived victory by
ensuring that the Kashmir issue was handled in a way
that precluded further Pakistani agitation. Kosygin
sought to use the conference to enhance the Soviet
Union's position as an Asian power and to defuse a
situation that the Chinese could exploit.

The most critical set of problems were those relating to the aftermath of the war, notably the disengagement of troops confronting each other at close range and
securing the withdrawal of forces to the prewar boundaries. [11] The Pakistani positions around Chhamb and,
especially, the Indian occupation of the Haji Pir Pass
were the real bones of contention. Shastri may have
realized that he would have to yield Haji Pir ultimately, but he had made fairly strong public commitments
to keep the passes as long as there was any threat from
Pakistan. Related to this was the need to exfiltrate
any Pakistani guerrillas still inside Kashmir. The

Indians saw this as a Pakistani responsibility and linked it to territorial withdrawal. Shastri's reported attempt to have Indian holdings inside Pakistan treated separately from the Kashmir positions was evidently a failed effort to gather additional bargaining chips. [12]

Ayub, on the other hand, was fully prepared for a withdrawal to the original borders and he resolutely opposed Indian retention of Haji Pir. His reported attempts to hold on to the Chhamb salient were hardly serious. He was silent on the issues of the guerrillas, for whom he disclaimed responsibility, and with Kosygin's support he argued that expelling them was up to the Indians. Overall, while the Indians were in a stronger position on the territorial issues, they were politically at a disadvantage since the U.N. resolutions had specifically called for total withdrawal.

There were also a number of secondary issues to be dealt with that had emerged from the war; several of these had much deeper roots.

-- Each side had seized merchant shipping of the other at the beginning of the war. Cargoes were being held and their return had to be negotiated. Nayar estimates that the Pakistanis held about ten times as much as the Indians. [13]

-- Diplomatic representation had been reduced at the beginning of hostilities; if a semblance of normal relations was to be restored, high commissioners (the Commonwealth equivalent of ambassadors) had to return to their posts.

-- The Indians had interdicted flights between Pakistan's two wings. Restoration of overflights was critical for Pakistan, economically and politically.

-- Each side held substantial numbers of prisoners of war.

-- There were numerous displaced persons who had either fled from the fighting, or (in the East) Hindus who had fled Pakistan out of fear that they would be victimized.

-- Vitriolic propaganda was at a high level between the two countries and cultural relations were frozen.

-- According to one source, Ayub hoped to explore the possibility of mutual troop reductions. [14]

-- The Indians had raised publicly a batch of broader issues in Indo-Pakistani relations but these were not related to the war and probably never got much attention. [15]

-- Finally there was the question of machinery for implementing whatever agreements were made, and (Ayub's idea) a framework for further meetings to deal with Kashmir and other issues. [16]

Aside from the question of withdrawal, the focus of the negotiation was on two points that underlay the war and the situation out of which it grew. The first was Kashmir. Ayub sought an outcome for the negotiations that would at most lead to the cession of Kashmir to Pakistan or, more realistically, ensure that the issue remained one of international concern. His main demand at Tashkent was for "negotiations" on the future status of Kashmir, leading to a "just and honorable settlement." His initial insistence on a formal agenda for the meeting grew out of this need. Shastri had no intention of yielding anything on Kashmir and only after considerable suasion was he prepared even to have the issue "discussed" between himself and Ayub. "Negotiation," especially with Soviet involvement, was out of the question and "Kashmir" as an agenda item was intolerable. Possession being at least nine points of international law, Shastri was in a nearly unassailable position on this score.

What Shastri sought was insurance that Pakistan could never again launch a war on India over Kashmir or anything else. His attempt to hold on to the strategic passes was a tactical move in that direction, but his main effort was devoted to gaining Pakistani agreement to the long-standing Indian proposal for a no-war pact between the two countries. It was only in that context, he asserted, that he would be willing to yield the passes. For Ayub, acceptance of a no-war pact would be tantamount to abandoning any effective claim to Kashmir since India would hardly make concessions peacefully. Ayub asserted that a no-war pact would be possible only in the context of a Kashmir settlement.

Conceptually, there were two sorts of problems at stake, and two possible levels of negotiations that might interact. Kashmir and the other long-standing issues can be viewed as a continuing problem that had been "mediated" sporadically by the United States, the United Kingdom, and the United Nations since 1948. It would have been possible to use the Tashkent meeting to address this broad range of problems and seek a comprehensive settlement of Indo-Pakistani antagonism. The war and its aftermath had focused international attention on the overall problem and could have provided the "hurting stalemate" that would bring the two sides to see the futility of continued antagonism and made them willing to reach a comprehensive settlement. [17]

Alternatively, of course, it was possible to focus on the narrow issue and simply use the Tashkent meeting to sort out the aftermath of the war and reestablish the

status quo ante of mid-summer 1965. The two sets of
issues could not, however, be completely disentangled,
since the three key problems to be addressed at Tash-
kent--withdrawal, Kashmir, and the no-war pact--were
closely related; the latter two were derivative of the
first. Ideally, the pressures brought about by the war
should have been used as a means of creating positive
feedback into the older problems. It soon became clear,
however, that this was not going to happen; indeed, the
long-standing bitternesses would feed back negatively
into the more immediate set of problems and raise doubts
that even these could be solved. The traditional disputes were too difficult and the underlying problems too
complicated to allow easy solutions. The war had not
"hurt" either side enough to force a reconsideration of
fundamental positions, and the chances were further
diminished by the fact that there was no ongoing mediation effort devoted to the broader issues into which the
Tashkent effort could be related. The potential for a
creative entwining of the two levels never materialized;
Ayub's call for a Kashmir settlement and Shastri's
demand for a no-war pact became obstacles rather than
bridges to understanding.

It emerged from this that India and Pakistan each
needed an agreement, but only if it met certain conditions. Failure to agree was less dangerous than acceptance of an agreement that would result in political
disaster at home. The Soviets, on the other hand, were
interested in an agreement for its own sake and had no
particular concern about its substance. Failure, for
Kosygin, would result if the conference generated high
expectations and then broke up without reaching an
agreement.

All concerned, therefore, were careful not be
become overly committed in public to a successful outcome. Of all the participants, not to mention outside
observers, only the Soviets were fairly optimistic.
Even they, however, hedged their bets carefully by
defining their role in the meetings in a way that
removed responsibility of failure from them by setting
the tone for the negotiations with a healthy mixture of
modest expectations and optimism.[18]   Objectives and
criteria for success were stated only in the broadest
terms for a peace process, rather than in any specific
product.

Kosygin's Role

The negotiations began in something of a procedural
vacuum, and the nature of the Soviet offer had precluded
any preliminary Soviet role in dealing with substantive
matters or even an agenda. There is no indication that
the Soviets ever specified in any detail just what

Kosygin's role at the meetings would be or how they would be organized. The Soviet offer was cast in terms of "good offices" (<u>dobriye</u> <u>uslugy</u>) which, according to the authoritative Soviet source are "various measures intended to establish communications links between the disputing parties in order to facilitate discussion between them or other peaceful measures to regulate the dispute." The purveyor of good offices does not seek to influence the substance of the discussions. [19] The Soviets underlined the contrast between this approach and the arbitration by which "imperialist" powers seek to involve themselves as judges in a dispute and thereby advance their own national interest at the expense of the parties.

We do not know what expectations Shastri and Ayub had of Kosygin personally, as opposed to their general understanding of the meaning of Soviet involvement. Kosygin had great prestige through his role in Soviet policy, but no special personal authority in the matters at hand nor in the tactics of diplomacy or international conciliation. Foreign Minister Gromyko and a large staff were very active in their tactical support of Kosygin, but he did not seem to be too dependent on them. In any event, once the few basic issues at dispute were mastered, the need for detailed knowledge was less important than the ability to build bridges between contending viewpoints. This must have been something that Kosygin excelled in after years of dealing with the baronies of the Soviet government and economy.

Kosygin came across as a colorless man, a trait which stood him in good stead as the long-term number-two man in the Moscow hierarchy and fitted in well with the image that the Soviets wanted to project at Tashkent. (Khrushchev, or even Brezhnev, could never have played the low-key role that Kosygin did.) The characteristic that was most commonly noted by observers at Tashkent was his persistence and stamina. He simply kept going for hours on end and, perhaps, wore Shastri and Ayub down through the dogged persistence that is a hallmark of the Soviet negotiating technique.

The Negotiating Process

The first two days of the Tashkent Conference were taken up with the customary formalities. Ayub and Shastri arrived separately on January 3, 1966, and were each met by Kosygin. The formal opening took place on the afternoon of January 4, following a luncheon hosted by Kosygin. The opening statements were muted. Kosygin spoke evenhandedly of the problems and opportunities before the conference; Shastri and Ayub set forth their

versions of the issues in moderate terms. Kosygin had
reportedly urged them to avoid mention of Kashmir. [20]
  The serious business of the meeting appears to have
taken place in two phases, at the beginning and at the
end, with an arid period in between. Initial difficulties over the agenda were addressed in a series of
mostly bilateral meetings on January 5 and 6. Ayub
sought to have a specific agenda heading for Kashmir to
demonstrate that the Indians had been forced to negotiate the issue. Shastri firmly resisted this and was, at
most, willing to have a loose, two-point agenda that
provided for discussions on amity and friendship between
India and Pakistan, and questions arising out of the
recent conflict. Kosygin reportedly offered to become
involved on January 5, but was discouraged in this by
Shastri since the conference had not yet become bogged
down. By the following day, however, Kosygin was seen
to take a hand directly, and American reporters surmised
that he had already become involved in making policy
suggestions. (Soviet spokesmen downplayed Kosygin's
interventions and maintained that he had become involved
in meetings only when specifically asked to by Shastri
or Ayub.)
  Kosygin approached the agenda issue both substan-
tively and procedurally. He pointed out to Ayub that
concentration on Kashmir would simply mean a rapid
breakdown of the talks. Reciprocally, he pointed out to
Shastri that the matter could not be completely ignored
in the light of Ayub's domestic political situation. [21]
In terms of procedure, he recommended that the development of an agenda and, apparently, initial discussions
on Kashmir be taken up in separate meetings of the
Indian and Pakistani foreign ministers, where Gromyko
could be involved as necessary. For Ayub, this arrangement was something of a godsend since Foreign Minister
Bhutto had clearly come to Tashkent with the objective
of wrecking the meetings. Shastri, too, was probably
glad to have the opportunity for private talks, and on
the first day the two already had excluded the foreign
ministers from their meetings. Ayub and Shastri
apparently shared Kosygin's view that a formal agenda
would unnecessarily limit their private meetings, [22] so
Kosygin's proposal provided both with a means of avoiding a sterile discussion of the agenda; it also provided
the foreign ministers with something to keep them busy
and out of the way. And, of course, they might be able
to come up with something useful. The foreign ministers' exact terms of reference (if there ever were any)
are not clear and nothing positive came of the meetings,
but they did serve the purpose of permitting the Ayub-
Shastri discussions to move forward. The two leaders
discussed Kashmir in broad terms but there is no evidence that anything was achieved beyond the restatement
of familiar positions. The question of an agenda also

died a quiet death, and on January 7 Ayub and Shastri simply decided to do without one.

According to Pravda on January 7, the early discussions also involved another procedural matter--whether it would be better to begin with broader or narrower topics. Kosygin had foreshadowed his position in his opening statement to the conference when he said that the task of the meeting was not to solve the major problems of the Indo-Pakistani relationship but to make progress toward their solution by improving mutual understanding and overcoming disputes that impeded progress. [23] His handling of the agenda matter also reflected an early judgment that the meeting could be best facilitated by postponing the more contentious, profound, and ultimately unnegotiable questions and dealing first with lesser problems. This is, of course, a traditional mediation technique and in theory leads through a series of confidence-building agreements on minor topics to a positive approach to the more fundamental issues at stake. At least as often, however, it is impossible to generate even the minimum amount of trust and goodwill needed to settle minor issues when major differences between the two parties are unresolved. Presumably, such lesser issues as the return of prisoners and property left over from the fighting and old standbys such as water use and boundary disputes could have been resolved by the foreign ministers, thereby helping Ayub and Shastri in their discussion of larger issues. For this to have worked, however, the foreign ministers' meetings would have to have been a useful negotiating forum and there would have to have been at least some tentative progress in the talks at the Ayub-Shastri level, since confidence-building has to go two ways. Unfortunately, neither of these conditions obtained.

The foreign ministers' meeting, which could have been very useful, foundered early on. Swaran Singh reportedly did attempt to address minor issues in the way proposed by Kosygin, but had little success.[24] Bhutto, however, had come to Tashkent with the objective of winning--if not for Pakistan then for his own political ambitions. This meant building upon his virtuoso performance at the United Nations in September by being visibly and vocally intransigent on the Kashmir issue. The foreign ministers' forum was thus totally futile, and critics of Bhutto maintain that his performance there cost Pakistan any chances that it might have had for some progress on Kashmir.[25] If any progress was to be made, it would have to be at the highest levels without much help from the foreign ministers.[26]

The situation was not improved when, on January 6, the Chinese government sent an ominous note to the Indians.[27] It did not set forth any ultimatum or commit the Chinese (or the Pakistanis) to any particular course of action, but it was widely interpreted as encouraging the Pakistanis to stand firm and break up the meeting if they wished.

The next two days of the conference, January 7 and 8, saw little forward movement. The foreign ministers were at loggerheads. Shastri and Ayub began to turn their attention to the issues of withdrawal of troops and the no-war pact, but the discussions were sterile and the two leaders did not even meet on January 8. Kosygin apparently also decided to pull back during this period, and restraint at this point made sense in order to maximize the effectiveness of interventions later when matters became more pressing. During this middle period, the principal burden on the Soviet side appears to have been carried by Gromyko, who was dealing with the foreign ministers. [28] The only output from these days was the exchange of drafts of a communique between the Indians and the Pakistanis, none of which won acceptance. [29] Swaran Singh then suggested that Gromyko try to produce a draft, but given the glacial situation--procedurally and substantively--the Soviet foreign minister could not have turned to his task with much optimism, and when it was circulated on the morning of January 9, it fared poorly.

Most observers agree that the evening of January 8 and the following morning constituted the crisis in the meeting. The Pakistanis, despairing of an even minimally acceptable outcome, announced abruptly that they would leave Tashkent on January 11, regardless of whether any agreement had been reached. The press coverage became extremely pessimistic, suggesting that the best that could be hoped for would be a communique, not an agreement. [30] Even _Pravda_ tempered its optimism on January 9 as the Soviets began to distance themselves from the proceedings, reminding everybody that they were only the purveyors of good offices and had no substantive responsibility. The facts of the situation warranted such pessimism. The nonnegotiation of Kashmir was hardly a substantive triumph, and two days of discussion of the no-war pact and withdrawal issues had been sterile. It was clear by this time that the many lesser issues could be resolved only if there were some broad agreement on the basic matters.

Under these unpromising circumstances, Kosygin apparently decided that it was time for him to reenter the fray. He became extremely active on the afternoon of January 9 and into the late hours of the night, extending what _Pravda_ (January 10) called "active and creative help." He shuttled back and forth between Ayub and Shastri, seeking out the views of each, conveying them to the other, and complementing them with suggestions based on his conversations. In surveying the three related issues of Kashmir, withdrawal, and the no-war pact, Kosygin apparently came to the conclusion

that the potential for mutual reinforcement among them
had evaporated, if, indeed, it had ever existed at all.
There is no evidence that Kosygin sought to bring out
positive elements among the three and thereby enhance
the depth, if not the scope, of the settlement, or that
he tried his hand at reformulations of basic issues that
might be more acceptable to the parties. The three
major issues became mutually limiting and the momentum
of the negotiation shifted toward finding the minimum
essential movement on each of them. The prospects of
success were so dim and the sense of crisis so high that
all parties were prepared to settle for procedural
rather than substantive steps in these difficult areas.
By doing so, however, a significant procedural result
was obtained and progress on specific pressing issues
was made possible. By abandoning a futile search for a
maximum outcome, Kosygin ensured that the critical
momentum was not lost.

Kosygin had been able to extract from Shastri the
minimum on the Kashmir issue (an acknowledgment that the
matter had been discussed), and had convinced Ayub that
he would have to settle for that. Unable to give much
support to Ayub on his principal desideratum, Kosygin
could hardly put much weight behind Shastri's demand for
a no-war pact, or even, according to one observer, a
friendship treaty. He did use the same argument here on
Ayub that he had used on Shastri over Kashmir--that Ayub
would have to make some gesture if Shastri were to be
able to sell a final agreement when he got back to
Delhi. This was the thorniest issue at the conference
and provided the greatest challenge for a successful
endgame for Kosygin. Much of the crisis atmosphere of
January 8 may have resulted from the fact that Shastri
and Ayub had made substantial progress in handling the
problem, only to have Bhutto try to undermine their
efforts. According to several sources, this led to a
sharp contretemps between Gromyko and Bhutto in which
the latter was told not to try to win at the conference
table what Pakistan had been unable to win on the battlefield.[31] Kosygin dealt with the problem by proposing
that Pakistan simply reiterate the commitment that it
had undertaken when it joined the United Nations, not to
use force for the settlement of disputes. G. W. Choudhury believes that the compromise actually was suggested
by Ayub and was then sold to Shastri by Kosygin.[32]
Whatever the case, much effort and skill were involved,
and Kosygin's handling of the issue was probably his
greatest accomplishment at Tashkent.

In dealing with the withdrawal question, which
Shastri sought to make contingent on conclusion of a
no-war pact, Kosygin remained firm throughout, pointing
out that the Soviets had supported the U.N. call for
total withdrawal and could not deviate from that position. He reportedly told Shastri that if the negotia-

tions broke down because India was unwilling to comply
with the U.N. Security Council's demand for a complete
withdrawal, the Soviet Union would not be able to protect India from adverse U.N. action. In the face of
this scarcely veiled threat, Shastri had little alternative but to agree that the old boundaries, both along
the Kashmir ceasefire line and along the recognized
international border, would be restored. Kosygin may
have also provided the wording that took care of the
problem of the Pakistani infiltrators within Kashmir by
suggesting that both sides agree to "withdrawal of all
armed personnel to pre-August 5 lines." The Indians
could claim that Pakistan had agreed to withdraw the
infiltrators; the Pakistanis were satisfied with the
formulation since it could be interpreted as only
referring to the overall withdrawal. (Pakistan did not
admit that any of its forces were inside Kashmir as
infiltrators.) This was an elegantly simple solution to
what had appeared to be an intractable problem, and the
issue simply faded away. After the conference the
Indians announced that the Pakistani government had
passed the word for the infiltrators to withdraw;
according to a senior Indian government official, the
question had been moot all along since the infiltrators
had left almost all of the Indian-held Kashmir well
before the Tashkent meeting. [33]

By the early hours of January 10, Kosygin's strenuous efforts had brought about agreement on all of the
key issues and successfully wrapped them into an acceptable package. [34] All that was left to do on the morning
of January 10 was to exchange further drafts "to fill in
some blanks." [35] The various lesser issues covered in
the final declaration were disposed of in haste once the
major issues had been taken care of. The press corps,
which had been predicting failure, was summoned and
informed to its amazement that a declaration (not, to be
sure, an "agreement") had been worked out and there
would be a signing ceremony in the afternoon. (The text
of the declaration is appended.) Kosygin participated
in the ceremony as a "witness." The appropriate fes-
tivities were held in the evening, and shortly after
midnight, Shastri died suddenly of a heart attack. His
body was returned to Delhi for cremation on January 11
and Ayub returned to a sorely troubled Pakistan.

Kosygin's Tactics

The relatively successful outcome of the Tashkent
Conference was a considerable achievement for Kosygin
and, so, raises the question of what particular mediation techniques he (and Gromyko) brought to bear.

First, the Soviets were both careful and skillful
in managing the public relations of the conference.

Despite the glare of publicity and the presence of
numerous foreign reporters, the Soviets ensured that the
meetings were held in strict privacy and the press
briefings from the Soviet spokesmen were masterpieces of
noninformation. The Pakistanis, and particularly the
Indians, were much more active in playing the press for
domestic effect, but that was something over which the
Soviets had no control. [36]
     The Soviets were relentlessly optimistic throughout
the proceedings, except for some wavering toward the
end. [37] The Soviet media kept up a constant drumfire of
propaganda, claiming that the prospects for settlement
were bright but were being undermined by imperialists--
especially the Western correspondents at Tashkent--who
were preaching gloom and doom as a way of undermining
the Soviet peace effort so that the imperialists could
continue their "divide and rule" tactics for dominating
South Asia. [38] (Overall, the Soviets maintained that the
Kashmir problem was a residue of imperialism and was
being exploited by the imperialists to strengthen their
position in South Asia. The former charge was true
enough, but claims that the West opposed a settlement
were transparently false even by Soviet standards.)
     This pervasive, if sometimes contrived, sense of
optimism was pressed equally on the participants in
private. Kosygin made clear that if the rewards of
success would accrue primarily to Shastri and Ayub, so
would the blame for failure. He steadily built up the
equity that each side had in a successful outcome and,
equally, brought home to them the burden that each bore
in the eyes of the world for ensuring success. In addition, by skillful maneuvering, Kosygin also brought at
least Ayub to the point where the Pakistani leader felt
that failure to reach an accommodation would be an
affront to Soviet hospitality and a shabby repayment for
all of the personal effort that Kosygin had put into the
negotiation. [39]
     A further general principle of Kosygin was absolute
neutrality. Neither during the conference nor after-
ward, when the euphoria had worn off, was there ever any
suggestion from any of the participants that Kosygin had
favored one side over the other, or supported one side's
point of view against the other. (Bhutto, of course,
would later claim that Ayub had yielded to Kosygin's
persuasion too easily, but that is a different matter.)
Kosygin's approach was reflected faithfully in the
external signs of evenhandedness at the conference--an
equal number of pictures of Ayub and Shastri on the
streets; equal press coverage; painfully balanced refer-
ences to each in Soviet speeches; and ritualistic alter-
nation of which name was mentioned first. [40]
     As noted earlier, the Soviet role in the proceed-
ings was almost always minimized. The Soviets insisted
that they avoid all interference in substantive matters

and simply limit themselves to promoting the success of
the conference.[41] Since the Soviet interest was a successful outcome of the negotiation rather than any specific substance, there is some weight to these claims.
Also, of course, they knew that they had taken on a
difficult problem; by keeping distance from the substance, they insulated themselves somewhat against
failure.

Kosygin, of course, introduced the two parties and
made himself available for whatever use they might want
to make of him. He presented himself not as a purveyor
of ideas but as a channel for the exchange of ideas.[42]
When carrying an unwelcome idea, he was careful to
disassociate himself from it so that a rejection would
not reflect on him and undermine his acceptability.[43]
Ayub reportedly was eager for Kosygin to take a more
active part in the negotiations because of Pakistan's
desire to internationalize its disputes with India as
much as possible.[44] The Indians were chary of this and,
when the Pakistanis claimed during the conference that
the Soviets were "mediating," Indian spokesmen sharply
refuted the claim. In fact, of course, while Kosygin's
actions remained fairly near the bottom of the spectrum
that runs from good offices through mediation to arbitration, he quickly became more than a communications
channel. He expressed his readiness to offer ideas, but
only if asked by both the parties--a useful posture in
that it forced the parties to agree on at least one
thing (that is, agreement to ask), making the mediator's
contributions weightier.

Toward the end of the conference, Kosygin's role
grew to the point where it was difficult to distinguish
procedure from substance (and, in a sense, in this particular meeting, procedure was much of the substance).
Even then, Kosygin's most crucial action, the preparation of a compromise draft, was taken only at the
request of the parties and after he had gone through
considerable effort in getting suggestions from the two
sides and exchanging them. If Kosygin's formal role at
the Tashkent Conference is somewhat ambiguous, it is
still more difficult to ascertain just how he performed
tactically. When Kosygin chose to step out of his
"communicator" role to make procedural suggestions, when
and how he actually became a substantive party to the
talks himself, were probably crucial determinants.

Kosygin's greatest assets were Shastri and Ayub
themselves. In contrast to some of their advisors and
to public opinion, both wanted a settlement and had a
statesmanlike vision of peace. He was also fortunate in
that he was working against an extremely favorable
international background. Soviet propaganda notwith-
standing, all significant external forces except China
supported the Soviet initiative and made clear that they
expected Pakistan and India to restore the status quo,

if not work out a lasting settlement.   When Bhutto
visited Moscow in November 1965, Kosygin had been able
to tell him that the United States supported the Soviet
initiative, and President Johnson used a variety of
channels to get this point across with his inimitable
forcefulness.   Both parties were suffering economically
as a result of the war, and the suspended American aid
program was a healthy incentive to settlement,
especially for Pakistan.   Equally, each side knew that
it could expect no support from any quarter should the
hostilities resume, except perhaps from China, and even
that was a questionable advantage for Pakistan. [45]
     The Soviets benefited particularly from the back-
ground role of the United Nations, which was firmly on
record in support of a rapid settlement. [46] Should the
Tashkent Conference fail, the dispute would revert to
the Security Council where the Soviet position would
carry great weight, both because of its veto and the
influence it would have among the other permanent
members as the United Nation's virtual agent in the
matter.
     This background of international support was not
only useful in a general way to Kosygin; he was also
able to use it very specifically as leverage on the
parties when he moved out from his role as communicator
and sought to influence the course of the negotiations.
The most striking instance occurred when Kosygin told
Shastri that if India failed to withdraw in compliance
with the U.N. Security Council resolution, the Soviet
Union would be unable to use its veto to protect India
from adverse action by the Security Council. [47] This was
very heavy pressure indeed, because India could not
expect support from any other permanent member on this
point.   It was the Soviet veto that repeatedly had kept
the Security Council from backing Pakistan on the Kashmir issue.   It was also suspected at the time that the
Soviets may have threatened curtailment of their arms
supplies to India, although it seems unlikely that
Kosygin needed to or would have wanted to go that far
explicitly.
     Kosygin was no doubt equally blunt in dealing with
Ayub.   An Indian publication claims that the Soviets
exerted parallel pressure on Pakistan, threatening to
use their veto against Pakistan if the Tashkent meetings
broke up as a result of Pakistani intransigence. [48]
Kosygin is more credibly reported as saying that Pakistan would stand isolated in the world against the
Soviet Union, India, and the West, with only China at
its side, if it bore responsibility for breaking up the
conference (Times of India, January 11, 1966).   He was
also direct in pointing out to Ayub that the Pakistanis
should be forthcoming on such issues as the no-war pact
because the accomplishment of troop withdrawals was more
important to them than to the Indians. [49]   Certainly

Gromyko's blunt rebuff of Bhutto (see above) indicated
Soviet readiness to step on toes if that was needed.
    On the positive side, there is little indication
that the Soviets sought to provide any incentives or
side-payments to bring about agreement. Despite his
interest in a successful outcome, Kosygin never
approached the other parties as a suitor. Brines
suggests that Kosygin may have offered arms supply as an
inducement for cooperation,[50] and some Pakistanis at
least believe that he promised Ayub to be more neutral
on the Kashmir issue. Neither of these points is
intrinsically unlikely and at least a continuation of
Soviet military assistance to India was implicit when
Kosygin suggested that Shastri should be less concerned
about provisions for the exfiltration of Pakistani
guerrillas inside Kashmir and more concerned about
maintaining a strong military capability. He is also
reported to have said that obtaining a no-war pact was
less critical since the Soviet Union would throw its
support behind India if the Pakistanis were again to
break the peace.[51] Except for this last point (which is
itself vague enough) there is nothing in these various
inducements that went much beyond what the Soviet Union
was already doing or hoped to do on the Subcontinent.
Inducements are after all commitments, and despite their
newfound influence in South Asia, the Soviets probably
did not wish to assume further commitments in that
unsettled area. In any event, they did not need to as
long as they were willing to settle for a minimum
satisfactory outcome of the negotiation.
    Given our restricted knowledge of just what went on
in the Tashkent discussions and the self-interested,
fragmentary, and sometime contradictory reports that we
do have, we cannot say with full confidence what kind of
pressures and inducements Kosygin brought to bear, and
we can be even less certain of the means and intensity
with which he did so. Observers assume that Kosygin
must have twisted arms rather sharply toward the end of
the conference because the case seemed such a difficult
one and victory was snatched so unexpectedly out of
defeat. Millar and Kapur, for instance, can find no
other rational explanation for the agreement finally
reached except pressure from Kosygin.[52] Not surprisingly, the participants are at great pains to show that
Kosygin did not apply pressure; Swaran Singh, for
instance, told the Indian parliament that it would be
wrong to suspect any such thing,[53] and most other
official and semiofficial writers take the same line.
An astute Indian journalist at Tashkent pointed to
Kosygin's ability to make Shastri and Ayub aware of the
wider repercussions of total failure rather than using
direct threats (Times of India, January 11, 1966).
Despite flashes of iron will, Kosygin was apparently
more at home in the role of cajoler, seeking to get each

side to see better the other's point of view. He was variously described as a "benevolent umpire," and a "friendly persuader." [54] Brecher assesses the situation about as well as possible, stating that it is not known "whether Shastri and Ayub reached agreement through persuasion or whether they yielded to cajolery and coercion, real or implied; probably all three elements were involved." [55]

Our knowledge of Kosygin's activities does not extend to an understanding of his microtactics as a mediator. We do not know, for example, whether he "held" concessions from either side and produced them at a time when they would have the greatest effect, or whether he simply transmitted them as they were made. Such evidence as there is implies the latter, although the closely intertwined discussions over the withdrawals and the no-war pact may have provided an opportunity for some creative mediatory efforts. We do know, however, that Kosygin was extremely skillful in the timing of his own intervention--seeing that things got off to a reasonable start, withdrawing for a time, and then intervening forcefully to ensure a successful outcome.

Whatever the gaps in our knowledge, it is clear that Kosygin's instincts as a negotiator were sound and effective. The key to his approach is perhaps best seen in a comment recorded by Warren Unna in the Washington Post (January 8, 1966), in which Kosygin draws on his experience as an engineer and likens the negotiating process to the firm seating of a bolt. The bolt must be driven in hard, but it is important to turn it back a half-turn to prevent later brittleness.

Outcome and Aftermath

The outcome of the conference was a declaration that achieved the minimum required--the establishment of the status quo ante in Indo-Pakistani relations, notably the territorial provisions. It also contained some fine thoughts about improved relations between the two countries. However, the declaration was perhaps more notable for what it did not include:

-- The "no-war" pledge that Shastri had desired was lacking. The reference to nonuse of force was an embarrassment to Ayub and provided Shastri with something to show for his efforts. The Pakistanis were quick to point out, however, that they had done nothing more than restate the principles of the U.N. Charter.

-- There was no provision for amelioration of the Kashmir dispute, although the Pakistanis claimed a step forward in that Kashmir was discussed in the presence of the Soviets, who now admitted that there was, in fact, a

dispute. They also claimed that Kosygin had committed
himself to remain concerned with Kashmir, but the Indian
press spokesman carefully played that point down.[56]

-- There was no self-executing mechanism set up for
further discussions designed to improve the basic Indo-
Pakistani relationship. The provisions in the declaration for further meetings are vague; the one held in
March 1966 did not move the situation forward. The
Pakistanis sought to focus attention on the prospects of
further negotiations but Shastri downplayed this with
the Indian press. Ayub's attempt to set a time limit
for discussions on Kashmir was rejected by Shastri.[57]

It is interesting but profitless to speculate
whether there would have been a fuller realization of
the "Spirit of Tashkent" had Shastri not died. Ayub and
Shastri seem to have developed some personal rapport and
may well have intended to move toward a more fundamental
rapprochement between their two countries. Nayar suggests that after the signing, Shastri approached Ayub
with a proposal for some realignments in the Kashmir
ceasefire and its establishment as an international
boundary.[58] Bhutto's claims that Shastri and Ayub had,
with or without Kosygin's participation, reached secret
agreements, is almost certainly false. Bhutto never
"revealed" the substance of any such agreements although
he was often called upon to do so and had ample opportunity over the following decade of his life. Nothing in
the later actions of either party suggests that there
were such agreements.[59] Later, suggestions that there
must have been agreement on some side-payments, since
each party failed to get what it wanted, are also not
supported by the evidence.
The specific provisions of the declaration relating
to the aftermath of the war were generally carried out
with dispatch over the next several months. By late
spring, the status quo essentially had been restored
because it was in the interest of the parties to do so.
It was clear by then, however, that there would be
nothing significant accomplished beyond that. Hopes
that both sides had learned a lesson from the war and
would be more inclined to live in peace were not fulfilled. The peace that the declaration was supposed to
bring was a fragile one, and in less than six years much
the same war was fought again. In retrospect, the Tashkent Declaration looks somewhat like a midterm ceasefire
agreement.
Perhaps the reason for this dubious legacy lies in
the fact that the declaration failed in two crucial
respects. First, the basic issues, Kashmir and a lasting rapprochement between India and Pakistan, were
skirted. Second, because the agreement was one of
mutual deprivation rather than of mutual gain with

regard to longer-term objectives (i.e., neither side got
what it wanted for the long term but each got its minimum short-term requirement) it provided neither party
with an incentive to strengthen the shaky structure that
had been erected. Tashkent became an important factor
in Ayub's political downfall; had Shastri lived, he
would have faced major problems in selling the agreement
to the Indian parliament.

A good part of the problem lay in the fact that the
war itself had not produced a clear outcome. Neither
side came to the bargaining table as victor. India had
had the better of the fighting and was under less pressure than Pakistan. The declaration reflected this
reality proportionately. It is indicative of Ayub's
unhappiness with the outcome that he refused to give the
declaration greater status by allowing Kosygin to be a
signatory or by joining with India in registering the
document with the United Nations. [60]

The only clear winner at Tashkent was the Soviet
Union. It outflanked the Chinese and succeeded in
asserting a leading role in the politics of South Asia,
never again to be rivaled by any outside power, including the United States. The Soviet Union apparently made
no commitments to either party to do anything that it
was not already doing. Its relations with India
remained close and its attempts to cultivate Pakistan
continued for the rest of the decade. Both sides looked
to the Soviets to maintain a benevolent interest in the
Subcontinent. This was especially true for Pakistan,
which tends to look for outside support. Although the
Soviets certainly maintained and increased their interest in the region--generally in a responsible way until
the 1971 war--they took few specific actions to move the
process of reconciliation along. Initial indications of
a more evenhanded stance on Kashmir had no practical
results. Soviet inquiries about the possibility of
further high-level meetings, as envisioned in the
declaration, were later raised in Delhi (and probably
Islamabad) but not pressed. [61]

Perhaps the Soviets had expended their energy and
could not muster more in the cause. More likely,
though, they had learned at Tashkent--and saw reaffirmed
by the later behavior of India and Pakistan--that there
was only limited scope for further helpful involvement.
The Soviet vision of bringing peace to Asia became
increasingly identified with the establishment of an
Asian security system over which they could preside,
similar to the hopes that they then had for a European
security system. In such a context, the Kashmir problem
would become as irrelevant as Alsace-Lorraine or
Macedonia in their respective parts of Europe. The
Asian security proposal found few takers, however, for
the Soviets had overestimated their influence in Asia.

After nearly two decades, the Soviet performance in
Tashkent raises some serious questions. Did it lead to
an overestimation of the potential for Soviet influence
elsewhere in Asia? Was it only a glorified ceasefire
agreement? Was it even such a feat on its own terms?
Some observers believe that there was never any real
danger of a collapse of the negotiations. [62] In defense
of the agreement, there are not many negotiations that
can stand the rigorous test of time, and certainly to
those who remember the event from personal experience,
the Tashkent mediation was a frightening cliff-hanger
that dealt effectively with the most urgent problems it
faced. [63] At the time, praise was virtually unanimous.

The Soviets themselves, having played down their
role during the conference, began modestly to sound
their own trumpet once success was assured, and to take
a share of the credit in general terms. Interestingly,
Kosygin's personal role is hardly mentioned in the
Soviet media except in an article by the scholar-
journalist son of Anastas Mikoyan--a point Kremlin-
ologists may find interesting. The Indians and Pakistanis were much more effusive in their praise of the
Soviet role and of Kosygin's personal contribution. The
Indians especially went well beyond the dictates of
politeness to their host. [64] Foreign Minister Swaran
Singh observed that

> One cannot but recognize the tremendous
> contribution which was made by Mr. Kosygin,
> who not only sponsored the idea of the confer-
> ence but also, at all stages, particularly
> when difficulties arose, acted as a messenger
> of peace and helped resolve all obstacles. He
> did not propose, much less impose, any partic-
> ular solution. Yet without his good offices,
> the Tashkent Declaration could not have taken
> shape. [65]

The press was even more outspoken. The Calcutta
Statesman, on January 11 said flatly that the credit for
the agreement should go solely to Kosygin. The London
Times story on the signing carried as its main headline,
"Agreement a Triumph for Mr. Kosygin," and the Western
press corps in general agreed that the outcome was a
triumph for Soviet diplomacy, effected primarily through
Kosygin's skill. Western governments were also generous
in their praise of Kosygin and relieved that the danger
of a renewed war had been averted. Had Kosygin been a
citizen of another country, he would very likely have
won the 1966 Nobel Peace Prize. Given what passes for
peace in the world, he probably deserved it.

Appendix

TEXT OF INDIAN-PAKISTANI DECLARATION OF TASHKENT

The Prime Minister of India and the President of Paksistan, having met at Tashkent and having discussed the' existing relationship between India and Pakistan, hereby declare their firm resolve to restore normal and peaceful relations between their countries and to promote understanding and friendly relations between their peoples. They consider the attainment of these objectives of vital importance for the welfare of the 600 million people of India and Pakistan.

The Prime Minister of India and the President of Pakistan agree that both sides will exert all efforts to create good-neighborly relations between India and Pakistan in accordance with the United Nations charter.

They affirm their obligation under the Charter not to have recourse to force and to settle their disputes through peaceful means. They considered that the interests of peace in their region and particularly in the Indian-Pakistani subcontinent of the peoples of India and Pakistan, were not served by the continuance of tension between the two countries.

It was against this background that [the states of] Jammu and Kashmir was discussed, and each of the sides set forth its respective position.

The Prime Minister of India and the President of Pakistan have agreed that all armed personnel of the two countries shall be withdrawn not later than Feb. 25, 1966, to the positions they held prior to Aug. 5, 1965, and both sides shall observe the cease-fire terms on the cease-fire line.

The Prime Minister of India and the President of Pakistan have agreed that relations between India and Pakistan shall be based on the principle of non-interference in the internal affairs of each other.

The Prime Minister of India and the President of Pakistan have agreed that both sides will discourage any propaganda directed against the other country and will encourage propaganda which promotes the development of friendly relations between the two countries.

The Prime Minister of India and the President of Pakistan have agreed that the High Commissioner of India to Pakistan and the High Commissioner of Pakistan to India will return to their posts and that the normal functioning of diplomatic missions of both countries will be restored. Both Governments shall observe the Vienna Convention of 1961 on diplomatic intercourse.

The Prime Minister of India and the President of Pakistan have agreed to consider measures toward the restoration of economic and trade relations, communications as well as cultural exchanges between India and Pakistan and to take measures to implement the existing agreements between India and Pakistan.

The Prime Minister of India and the President of Pakistan have agreed that they will give instructions to their respective authorities to carry out the repatriation of prisoners of war.

The Prime Minister of India and the President of Pakistan have agreed that the sides will continue the discussion of questions relating to the problems of refugees and evictions of illegal immigrants.

They also agreed that both sides will create conditions which will prevent the exodus of people. They further agreed to discuss the return of property and assets taken over by either side in connection with the conflict.

The Prime Minister of India and the President of Pakistan have agreed that the sides will continue meetings both at the highest and at other levels on matters of direct concern to both countries. Both sides have recognized the need to set up joint Indian-Pakistani bodies which will report to their Governments in order to decide what further steps should be taken.

The Prime Minister of India and the President of Pakistan record their feelings of deep appreciation and gratitude to the leaders of the Soviet Union, the Soviet Government and personally to the chairman of the Council of Ministers of the U.S.S.R, for their constructive, friendly and noble part in bringing about the present meeting which has resulted in mutually satisfactory results.

They also express to the Government and friendly people of Uzbekistan their sincere gratitude for their overwhelming reception and generous hospitality.

They invite the chairman of the Council of Ministers of the U.S.S.R to witness this declaration.

THE PRIME MINISTER OF INDIA, LAL BAHADUR SHASTRI.

PRESIDENT OF PAKISTAN, MOHAMMAD AYUB KHAN.

Chapter 5: Notes

1.   The term "Kashmir" is neither geographically nor politically quite accurate; it is, however, convenient for the purposes of this study. For a much fuller definition see Josef Korbel, Danger in Kashmir, rev. ed. (Princeton: Princeton University Press, 1966), 5-8.

2.   For the general international context as it affected the issues discussed here, see William J. Barnds, India, Pakistan and the Great Powers (New York: Praeger Publishers, 1972).

3.   The most extensive account of the 1965 war and its political setting is Russell Brines, The Indo-Pakistan Conflict (London: Pall Mall Press, 1968).

4.   Robert J. Donaldson, Soviet Policy Toward India (Cambridge, Mass.: Harvard University Press, 1974) is the standard work and includes a discussion of the Tashkent period. Robert C. Horn, Soviet-Indian Relations: Issues and Influence (New York: Praeger Publishers, 1982), also contains useful observations, especially on p. 13. See also Charles B. MacLane, Soviet-Third World Relations, vol. 2 (London: Central Asian Research Center, 1973), 56 & 111. Ayub describes the meeting with Kosygin in his autobiography, Friends Not Masters (Lahore: Oxford University Press, 1967), 172-73.

5.   Brines, Indo-Pakistan Conflict, 261-63, probably overstates the degree of Soviet estrangement from India. Delhi was, however, genuinely concerned that Moscow might move still closer to Pakistan as a way of countering Chinese influence (Hindustan Times, January 5, 1966).

6.   Walter Lippmann (Washington Post, January 13, 1966) observed that the Soviets' success in mediating the dispute was a result of their geographic position, and contrasted this with the American practice of becoming excessively involved in problems far from home. It is not irrelevant that the American obsession with Vietnam was just beginning to build at the time.

7.   Good coverage of the Chinese role is provided by G. W. Choudhury, India, Pakistan, Bangladesh and the Major Powers: Politics of a Divided Subcontinent (New York: The Free Press, 1975) and Bhabani Sen Gupta, The Fulcrum of Asia (New York: Pegasus Press, 1970).

8.   See, e.g., Lev Stepanov, "The Indo-Pakistan Accord," New Times, no. 3 (1966): 3-4; and Zhukov's Pravda article of January 16, 1966, reprinted in Current Digest of the Soviet Press, pt. 3 (1966), 21-22.

9.   Texts of the Soviet messages are in Vneshnyaya politika sovetskogo soyuza, 1964-65 (Moscow: Izd. Pol. Lit., 1966), 321ff.

10.   M. S. Rajan, "The Tashkent Declaration," International Studies 8 (1966-67): 5-6. U.S. pressure was particularly important because of the role American aid played in the Pakistani and Indian economies at that time. For a good survey of the various international factors affecting India and Pakistan following the war see Christiane Tirimagni-Hurtig, "La fin de la guerre indo-pakistanaise de 1965," Revue francaise de science politique 24 (1974): 309-27.

11.   Michael Edwardes, "Tashkent and After," International Affairs (London) 42 (1966): 381, claims that the danger of a breakdown in the ceasefire was small. That, however, was not the commonly held belief at the time.

12.   Kuldip Nayar, an Indian reporter, was particularly close to Shastri, and his extensive writings on Tashkent are among the most detailed sources. He is not, of course, a disinterested observer. For Shastri's motivations on withdrawal and the course of discussions on that topic, see Nayar's India: The Critical Years (Delhi: Vikas, 1971), 242-43, 247, and his Between the Lines (Bombay: Allied Publishers, 1969), 116-17.

13.   Nayar, India, 245.

14.   Choudhury, India, Pakistan, Bangladesh, 50.

15.   Dev Sharma, Tashkent: The Fight for Peace (Varanasi: Gandhian Institute of Studies, 1966), 13, n.3.

16.   Washington Post, January 11, 1966, and S. Mikoyan, "Tashkentskaya konferentsiya," Mirovaya ekonomika i mezhdunarodniye otnosheniya, no. 2 (1966): 102.

17.   Rajan, "Tashkent Declaration," 6.

18.   Mikoyan, "Tashkentskaya konferentisiya," 100.

19.   Diplomaticheskiy slovar', vol. 1 (Moscow: Izd. Pol. Lit., 1971): 488.

20.   The account that follows is based on concurrent reports of the conference appearing in the Times of India and Hindustan Times, January 6-8, 1966, and on the chronologies provided by Sharma, Tashkent, and Lev Stepanov, Konflikt v indostane i soglasheniye v Tashkente (Moscow: Izd. Pol. Lit., 1966). We have only a very partial view of what happened at the Ayub-Shastri meetings, most of which were tête-à-tête. None of the principals published his recollections. Among high-level attendees, reminiscences have been written by two men with heavy political axes to grind: T. N. Kaul, who was then Indian ambassador in

Moscow, Diplomacy in Peace and War (New Delhi: Vikas, 1979), and Pakistani Air Marshal Mohammed Asghar Khan, The First Round: Indo-Pakistan War 1965 (Sahibabad: Vikas, 1979). A much more useful account is that of the (then) Indian Foreign Secretary, C. S. Jha, From Bandung to Tashkent: Glimpses of India's Foreign Policy (London: Sangam Books, Ltd., 1983). Professor G. W. Choudhury, a political scientist and member of the Pakistani cabinet under Yahya Khan, had access to the Pakistani record of the conference and published some of his findings in India, Pakistan, Bangladesh. Two Soviet academician-publicists, Mikoyan and Stepanov, also wrote shortly after the meeting and probably had fairly good access to the views of the Soviet delegation.

21.   Mikoyan, "Tashkentskaya konferentsiya," 102; Sharma, Tashkent, 21; and Asghar Khan, First Round, 119.

22.   P. Viswa Nathan, "Tashkent and After," Far Eastern Economic Review (January 20, 1966), 78, and Ram Gopal, Indo-Pakistan War and Peace (Lucknow, India: Pustak Kendra, 1965), 127.

23.   Choudhury, India, Pakistan, Bangladesh, 50, and A. N. Kosygin, K velikoy tseli--izbranniye rechi i shtaty (Moscow: Izd. Pol. Lit., 1979), 357.

24.   Nayar, India, 244.

25.   Choudhury, India, Pakistan, Bangladesh, 52. It is hard to see how the Indians would have yielded anything even had Bhutto been on his best behavior.

26.   There was also a parallel set of meetings between the Indian and Pakistani military commanders at Amritsar, but they were adjourned without taking any action.

27.   For the text, see Survey of the China Mainland Press, no. 3615 (January 12, 1966), 29-31.

28.   The precise course of events at this stage is not fully clear. While Jha's From Bandung to Tashkent is the fullest firsthand account, his dating of events is slightly at odds with other sources.

29.   Stepanov, Konflikt, 45.

30.   Stepanov, Konflikt, 48 and the Statesman, January 9, 1966.

31.   Nayar, India, 245-46; Kaul, Diplomacy, 165; Times of India, January 11, 1966; and Durga Das, India: From Curzon to Nehru and After (New York: John Day Co., 1970), 398.

32.   Choudhury, India, Pakistan, Bangladesh, 52.

33.   Personal communication from E. N. Mangat Rai, who in 1965–66 was chief secretary to the government of Kashmir.   Also Brines, Indo–Pakistan Conflict, 406; Nayar, Between the Lines, 116–17; and S. M. Burke, Pakistan's Foreign Policy: An Historical Analysis (London: Oxford University Press, 1973), 351.

34.   Brines, Indo–Pakistan Conflict, 407, asserts that Ayub created difficulties over the wording on Kashmir at the last moment.   There is no substantiation of this but it would hardly be surprising if the Pakistanis sought to salvage something at the last moment on this critical point.

35.   Kuldip Nayar, Distant Neighbors: A Tale of the Subcontinent (Delhi: Vikas, 1972), 123, asserts that the final draft had really been prepared by the Indian delegation and only a few changes were made by the Soviets.   This should be taken with some reservations for the Soviets are generally credited with putting the final draft together.

36.   Stepanov, in his New Times articles, suggests the extent of Soviet press management.   Shastri, however, knew that he faced an uphill battle at home to get parliamentary and public support for the concessions he would have to make at Tashkent. Thus he sought to win the support of the Indian press contingent at Tashkent by briefing them extensively on the course of the nego- tiations and even asking their opinions.   Although this Indian press material must be treated with care, it comprises the principal source of our knowledge of what went on at Tashkent.

37.   Stepanov, "Indo–Pakistan Accord," and Sen Gupta, Fulcrum of Asia, 227.

38.   A particularly virulent piece is by P. Kryukov, "Itogi tashkenta," Mezhdunarodnaya zhizn', no. 2 (1966): 3–5.

39.   Durga Das, Curzon to Nehru, 297; Asghar Khan, First Round, 120; and Louis DuPree, Further Reflections on the Second Kashmir War, American University Field Staff Reports, South Asia Series, vol. 10, no. 3: 9.

40.   Nayar, Between the Lines, 117.

41.   Stepanov, "Indo–Pakistan Accord," 6.

42.   Choudhury, India, Pakistan, Bangladesh, 51.

43.   Kaul, Diplomacy, 165; and Nayar, Between the Lines, 117.

44.   Zubeida Hasan, "Pakistan's Relations with the U.S.S.R. in the 1960s," World Today 25 (1969): 30.

45.   Rajan, "Tashkent Declaration," 8; Brines, Indo-Pakistan Conflict, 402; and Salmaan Taseer, Bhutto: A Political Biography (London: Ithaca Press, 1979), 66.

46.   Durga Das, Curzon to Nehru, 397-98.

47.   Nayar, India, 247; Times of India, January 11, 1966; and Krishan Bhatia, The Ordeal of Nationhood (New York: Atheneum, 1971), 153.

48.   Link (New Delhi), January 16, 1966. Link is scarcely a credible source and the assertion is questionable since the Soviets had frequently used their veto against Pakistani interests. Kosygin may well, of course, have held out the inducement of nonuse of the veto.

49.   Brines, Indo-Pakistan Conflict, 409.

50.   Brines, Indo-Pakistan Conflict, 409.

51.   Nayar, Distant Neighbors, 122.

52.   Harish Kapur, The Soviet Union and the Emerging Nations: A Case Study of Soviet Policy Towards India (London: Michael Joseph, Ltd., 1972), 94; and T. B. Millar "Der Streit um Kashmir," Europa-Archiv 21 (1966): 633.

53.   Hindustan Times, February 22, 1966.

54.   Rajan, "Tashkent Declaration," 9; Hindustan Times, January 11, 1966.

55.   Michael Brecher, Nehru's Mantle: The Politics of Succession in India (New York: Praeger, 1966), 190.

56.   Choudhury, India, Pakistan, Bangladesh, 53. The subcontinental and foreign press of January 11 (London Times, Pakistan Times, Times of India, Statesman, Hindustan Times) provide important coverage, including the significant press conference of the Indian press spokesman, C. S. Jha.

57.   Mikoyan, "Tashkentskaya konferentsiya," 102.

58.   Nayar, Between the Lines, 116.

59.   For Soviet denials, see Choudhury, India, Pakistan, Bangladesh, 54 and n.15; a Pakistani refutation of Bhutto's claims of secret deals can be found in "Bhutto and Tashkent: A Staff Study," Outlook 2 (Karachi, January 19, 1974): 6-10.

60.   Dietmar Rothermund, Indien und die Sowjetunion (Tubingen: Bohlau Verlag, 1968), 35.

61.   One of the few specific post-Tashkent initiatives dealt with the division of the waters of the Ganges; it came to naught, as would Jimmy Carter's proposals on the subject a decade later.   See Surjit Mansingh, India's Search for Power (New Delhi: Sage Publications, 1984), 200, and, more generally, chaps. 1 and 2 of Horn, Soviet- Indian Relations.   Mikoyan, "Tashkentskaya konferentsiya," illustrates best the more balanced treatment of the Kashmir issue in the Soviet writings of the time.

62.   Brecher, Nehru's Mantle, 256, n.2, citing a senior Indian civil servant; and New York Times, January 9, 1966.

63.   Bhatia, Ordeal of Nationhood, 154, says that Shastri feared resumption of fighting.

64.   They did not, however, give any support to the Soviet claim that the Asian venue of the conference was helpful.   While the Indians and Pakistanis no doubt appreciated the modest charms of Tashkent, they would hardly have felt more at home there than in Europe.   Soviet assertions to the contrary are of course frequent, underlining the Soviet claim to be an Asian power.   Cf. "Istoricheskaya tashkentskaya deklaratsiya," in Kommunist, no. 1 (1966): 40-41, and Mikoyan, "Tashkentskaya konferentsiya."

65.   Quoted by R. K. Jain, Soviet-South Asian Relations, 1947-1978, vol. 1 (Atlantic Highlands: Humanities Press, 1979), 101-02.

PART II

Mediation in Practice: Organizations

6.
THE ORGANIZATION OF AFRICAN UNITY AS MEDIATOR

Michael Wolfers

Among the fundamental principles to which member states of the Organization of African Unity (OAU) adhere is the "peaceful settlement of disputes by negotiation, mediation, conciliation or arbitration."[1]   In nearly two decades of practice since the OAU was founded in 1963, mediation shading into conciliation has been the preferred means of settlement. The institution has developed appropriate machinery, generally a select group of heads of state mandated to mediate between the leaders of disputing states. This ad hoc procedure has proved effective in a fairly narrow range of cases, and the significant exclusions from the process have led some commentators to speak of a general failure of the OAU.

In 1982-83 the OAU faced an exceptionally difficult situation, with most of its efforts stalemated by both an unresolved crisis over the former Spanish Sahara and the self-proclaimed independence of the Sahrawi Arab Democratic Republic (SADR). The difficulty faced by the OAU in handling a dispute between Algeria and Morocco (and their allied states) should not be allowed to obscure the positive role played by the institution in its early years, when the mere notion of independence in Africa was still called into question. The argument over the Sahara has hung between the principles of decolonization and self-determination; but at least the two concepts are now widely accepted in Africa, questioned only by the minority regime in South Africa --a state ineligible for OAU membership.

Michael Wolfers is a writer and former African correspondent for the Times (London). He is the author of Politics in the Organization of African Unity and Black Man's Burden Revisited.

It is ironic that a dispute between Algeria and
Morocco should bring the OAU to the brink of collapse,
because it was the war between those two countries in
October 1963 that led the OAU to establish a process for
mediating inter-African disputes, and partial success in
this instance helped to legitimate the OAU as the representative body for Africa as a whole. The brief North
African war of 1963 within a few months of the OAU's
establishment helped prevent the establishment of an
institution designed to assist in peaceful settlement of
disputes--namely the Commission of Mediation, Conciliation and Arbitration agreed upon in Article XIX of the
OAU's charter. The details of that commission had not
been agreed by May 1963. It was merely determined that
a separate protocol would be drawn up for approval by
the Assembly of Heads of State and Government and that
it would form an integral part of the charter itself.
The draft of the protocol was discussed at the
first Council of Ministers in Dakar in August 1963, but
its acceptance was deferred to the second council in
Lagos in February 1964, during which a committee of
experts met under the chairmanship of Dr. T. O. Elias,
then attorney general and minister of justice of
Nigeria.[2] A draft protocol was examined at the third
council in Cairo in July 1964 and approved by the
Assembly of Heads of State and Government.[3] Under this
protocol, signed on July 21, 1964, the commission was to
consist of twenty-one members elected by the assembly
for a term of five years and eligible for reelection,
with no state having more than one of its nationals on
the commission. The proposed modalities of the commission's jurisdiction over disputes between states where
all parties accepted jurisdiction do not warrant
detailed consideration here, as they were not put to the
test, but they adhere to the usual practice in international law--of negotiations between the parties on the
basis of friendly intervention by a mediating third
party with proposals for a solution.[4]
Administrative steps were taken to bring the commission into being; the first elections were held at the
second assembly in Accra in 1965, and the commission was
convened in Addis Ababa in December 1967 to establish
rules and procedures and to begin the preparation of a
regular budget. Commission places were filled in 1968
at the fifth assembly in Algiers, but at the assembly in
Addis Ababa the following year, voices were raised to
remove the commission's permanent status, and this
change took place in 1970 at the seventh assembly in
Addis Ababa.   Soon the OAU Secretariat was asked to
dispose of the commission's assets and the institution
fell into disuse, although it still has some support
from individual member states. Dr. Elias, one of the
experts most closely involved in designing the commission, saw it as an African parallel to the International

Court of Justice.[5]   Dr. Boutros Boutros-Ghali, the
Egyptian political scientist and diplomat, has argued
that African states prefer the flexible procedures of
diplomacy to the technicalities of traditional international law.[6] Some observers have suggested that the
commission was doomed from the start by delays in con-
stituting it; although the commission could have been
established quite rapidly had it been responsive to
African needs in the mid-1960s.

In the absence of the formal institutional machinery laid down in the charter and protocol, the OAU
developed informal procedures for mediation--namely an
extraordinary session of the Council of Ministers or ad
hoc mediation in small committees of heads of state.
Generally speaking, the OAU practices collective mediation (without arbitration) through the exertion of political pressures. Although OAU membership comprises
nations of varying size and influence, as sovereign
states represented by statesmen at high--often the
highest--level, they do have similar capabilities.

The significance of the hierarchical rank of the
mediator is apparent in the two preferred channels of
mediation: the extraordinary session and the ad hoc
committee, the former engaging mediators of ministerial
rank and the latter often engaging heads of state. The
charter allows for extraordinary sessions of the council
and of the assembly at the request of any member state
and with the approval of two-thirds of all members. In
the formative period of the OAU, from 1963 to 1965, the
council held as many emergency sessions as regular ones,
but the first extraordinary assembly in the OAU's history concerning recognition and acceptance of the
People's Republic of Angola did not occur until 1976.
The first six extraordinary councils discussed the differences between Algeria and Morocco; the mutiny in
Tanganyika; border conflict between Ethiopia and Somalia, and that between Kenya and Somalia; the Congolese
problem (discussed in Addis Ababa and again in New
York); the Accra summit and complaints of Ghana's
subversion of other countries; and the illegal declaration of independence in Rhodesia. A prominent but not
exclusive factor was territorial definition, although
the normative approach of the OAU was strongly indicated
in the charter principle of respect for the "territorial
integrity of each State" (Article 3) and in a resolution
passed by the first assembly in 1964, in which all member states pledged themselves "to respect the borders
existing on their achievement of national independence."[7]

The 1964 resolution was intended to minimize
disputes arising from boundary claims, and the norm was
so widely accepted that the need for extraordinary council meetings almost disappeared (the emergency sessions
of 1970 and 1973 were held to consider broader issues of
the Portuguese invasion of Guinea and of the African

response to the Middle East war situation). In instances where potential parties sought to challenge the norm on colonial boundaries, the OAU was unwilling or unable to act, and such parties expressed their views through another forum.

Faced with the spectacle of its members in disputes that had reached the level of open hostilities, the OAU sought to reduce the conflict to a level where the parties could at least engage in diplomacy leading to peaceful settlement. The member states, enjoying precarious and often newfound independence, thought it was undignified for them to be seen quarreling among themselves, and feared that any argument could provide a pretext for interference by outside powers (particularly the former colonial powers in Europe). For this reason, if outside powers were already deeply embroiled in a dispute, the OAU had little effective leverage to offer. OAU mediators were often unable to resolve disputes, but they could contain them, invoking the concept of pan-African unity. In the early extraordinary councils, the OAU appointed a seven-member commission to arrange a ceasefire between Algeria and Morocco, called upon Ethiopia and Somalia to agree to a ceasefire, asked Kenya and Somalia to refrain from provocative actions and propaganda, and appointed a commission to help end fighting in the Democratic Republic of Congo (now Zaire) and to normalize relations between it, Burundi and the Republic of Congo. These appeals were intended to reduce short-term conflict, although it was realized that settlement of the underlying dispute could be a long-term process. Indeed, disputes between Ethiopia and Somalia have been a recurring blight for the OAU, particularly since the OAU's permanent headquarters are in Ethiopia.

Although the OAU by its very existence has sought to project itself as the regulatory body for African affairs (in what the charter preamble calls "a larger unity transcending ethnic and national differences"), it has not been able to assert or exert exclusive jurisdiction. The OAU is a regional body within the U.N. system, and all OAU members are also U.N. members. The United Nations has the attraction of certain universalist principles which may be less constraining than the specific OAU norms, commands greater resources and a wider range of secretariat skills, and has an experience in peacekeeping activities that the OAU lacks. (The OAU attempt to establish a peacekeeping force in Chad in 1982 was an interesting experiment, but a practical and political failure.)[8] It is remarkable, however, to what extent the OAU has been preferred to the United Nations for specifically African problems, and to what degree African members of the United Nations have sought to coordinate their own demands and actions within the wider body.

This trend in favor of the OAU was manifest in the 1963 dispute between Algeria and Morocco, which set many precedents for the OAU response to conflicts and approach to the role of mediator. War broke out on October 14, 1963, over territory that had been disputed on the basis of precolonial frontiers. King Hassan II of Morocco had reached a secret agreement with the provisional government of the Algerian Republic in 1961 to settle the issue by negotiation after Algerian independence, but negotiations did not take place, and relations between the two countries worsened. Emperor Haile Selassie of Ethiopia, to whose government the provisional OAU secretariat had been entrusted, sought to mediate, and Modibo Keita, the president of Mali, invited the leaders of Morocco and Algeria to meet in Bamako. A joint communique in Bamako on October 30, 1963, called for a ceasefire from midnight on November 1 and for an extraordinary meeting of the OAU Council to set up a commission to study the question and to make settlement proposals.

The formal opening of the extraordinary session of the council took place in Addis Ababa on November 15, 1963, and its substantive work began on November 16 with opening statements made on behalf of Morocco and Algeria; the ministers who spoke for both countries supported the aim of the OAU to contain African problems.[9] Time was available during the weekend for informal lobbying outside council sessions and, in particular, to take soundings about the membership of the commission. Before the member countries were announced, the chairman of the council explained:

> We have been guided by the desire to set up this Commission in such a way that it will be able to bring the two parties into accord; since its role will be conciliatory, it must enjoy the confidence of both sides. That is why we felt we ought to avoid debating this question and proceed with the necessary consultations, particularly between the principal parties, in order to submit a list of names drawn up by common agreement.

Ethiopia and Mali, which had been involved in previous attempts to damp down the dispute, were among the seven countries chosen, along with Ivory Coast, Nigeria, Senegal, Sudan, and Tanganyika.

The task of the ad hoc commission was, in accordance with the Bamako communique, to study the problem to determine responsibility for hostilities, and submit proposals for a settlement. The commission met in Abidjan and in Bamako, and in February 1964 the council recommended direct contacts between the ad hoc commission and the ceasefire commission. The mediators did not attempt to apportion blame or to determine the final outcome. Rather, they coaxed the two parties to withdraw their troops and to form a bilateral agreement on various aspects of the contention.[10] Further reports were made to the council in 1965 and 1966, and the ad hoc commission adjourned in 1967; Algeria and Morocco were left alone to continue bilateral negotiations. The conflict was formally concluded at the assembly in Rabat in 1972 when Hassan, speaking for Morocco and on behalf of President Houari Boumedienne of Algeria, asked for the file on the dispute to be closed. The two leaders signed final agreements at the closing session on June 15, 1972.

In this instance, Algeria had turned to the OAU, while Morocco (which at first had been inclined to look to the United Nations) did so with greater reluctance. Also, the extraordinary session of the council invoked what its resolution called "the imperative need of settling all differences between African States by peaceful means and within a strictly African framework." The essential feature was the involvement of other African states in creating an environment for bilateral negotiations, albeit slowly, and without taking the places of the diplomats of the disputing parties. The ad hoc commission represented a mix of Anglophone and Francophone states with members from the various regions of the continent. The OAU had an interest in mediating this dispute because it would have risked losing the credibility it was beginning to establish. The OAU assisted by providing channels of communication between parties which sought an alternative to fighting. Zartman states that "the OAU succeeded in stopping the war because the rest of Africa was more deeply committed to unity than to either belligerent, and because an armistice fit in with both Morocco's goal (to bring the unsettled border to Algeria's attention) and Algeria's aims (to end the war that it was losing)."[11] Although the OAU's ad hoc commission comprised seven African states--all of which had particular or potential interests in Algeria and Morocco--it appears the commission was a single actor in this instance and the bilateral dispute had little impact on other countries.

Conversely, the limitations on the OAU's power to mediate were apparent in the example of the Democratic Republic of the Congo, where the OAU's ad hoc commission was formed in response to an invitation from the two Congos and Burundi for a "fact-finding and goodwill mission to their countries."[12] The Congo crisis not only antedated the foundation of the OAU, but, more significant, combined internal conflict with external intervention, including intervention by non-African states. Despite the complexities and international

ramifications, the United Nations encouraged the OAU to
take responsibility for finding--or at least for helping
to find--a peaceful solution to this dispute.[13]

In September 1964, when an extraordinary session
was held in Addis Ababa on the Congolese problems, the
Malian and Algerian leaders expressed concern about the
repercussions of the Congo's internal crises on other
African countries. Moise Tshombe, who had been appointed prime minister of Congo in July, was eager to
win pan-African support because his position was
threatened by various rebellions--although he relied
heavily on mercenary forces even in the face of adverse
African opinion. At the extraordinary session he asked
for African troops to be stationed in areas where he
commanded support, leaving his own forces free to operate in areas of continuing rebellion. But this level of
commitment went well beyond what the African states were
willing to show for Tshombe. The OAU proposed instead
that the ad hoc commission encourage national reconciliation. Tshombe's delegation accepted the general thrust
of the resolution but abstained in the vote, apparently
because the resolution provided no troops, nor did it
condemn the rebellion.[14]

The ad hoc commission held several meetings in
Africa and even sent a delegation to Washington to lobby
the U.S. Department of State but its various contacts
became entangled with the cataclysmic events of November
24, 1964, when Belgian paratroopers were transported in
U.S. military aircraft to Stanleyville for the proposed
rescue of European civilians. The intervention provoked
a massacre and caused differences to widen both within
Africa and between Africa and outside powers. One
result was that the forum again shifted to the U.N.
Security Council. The Security Council session held
from December 9 to December 30 concluded with a resolution (199) that endorsed the OAU as a regional organization whose principal role was to settle African disputes. Although the resolution was seen to encourage
African diplomacy, the debate assumed that because
African disputes involved complex issues which went
beyond the continent of Africa, both the OAU and the
U.N. would inevitably be involved.

During the New York debates, the OAU council held
its fourth extraordinary session (also in New York) from
December 16 to December 21 and renewed the mandate of
the OAU commission. The ad hoc commission met in
Nairobi on January 29 and 30, 1965, and formed a subcommittee to visit Congo (Zaire), Congo Brazzaville, and
Burundi, with the aim of normalizing relations among the
three countries. Although the OAU's task was one, just
barely, of mediating, the hierarchical rank of the mediator became an important factor. The subcommittee at
the ministerial level planned an itinerary of visits for
all interested parties, but in the event, the principal

participants from Ghana, Guinea, and Nigeria, as well as a Kenyan rapporteur, were whittled down in number and status. Ghana failed to send a representative to the various meetings en route, and when the Nigerian minister, Nuhu Bamalli, fell ill, the Guinean minister, Louis Lansana Beavogui, decided that his country should also be represented by someone of ambassadorial rank. The subcommittee's purpose was to prepare for higher-level visits by the ad hoc commission. These plans were gradually overtaken by events, but the effectiveness of the subcommittee was hampered by the fairly low status of its members and thus their limited access to leaders. The hierarchy was implicit in the original composition of the ad hoc commission in September 1964. It was composed not merely of named member states but of states "placed under the effective chairmanship of H.E. Jomo Kenyatta, Prime Minister of Kenya," as the council resolution phrased it. The mediating committee comprised ministerial representatives with one designated senior statesman—in later years heads of state were more likely to be involved collectively in the mediating committee.

Although the Accra assembly in October 1965 took the view that the OAU had emerged successful and strengthened by its handling of the Congolese question, the outcome was obscured by a change of regime in Congo: Tshombe was dismissed as prime minister on October 13 and Mobutu seized power on November 24, 1965. With its international ramifications, especially after the Belgian paratroop landings, the Congolese problem was too big for the OAU to handle. In Immanuel Wallerstein's view:

> While the ability of the OAU to mediate disputes within its ranks in the family is one of the proud boasts of the Secretariat and is formally true in the sense that no other mediating agency such as the U.N. has been involved, the second Congo crisis illustrated the fact that in substantive terms the OAU is not politically in a position to keep non-African powers from being deeply involved in internal African affairs.[15]

The OAU continued to watch over Congolese affairs; it assisted in the withdrawal of mercenaries from Africa, but did not mediate the intra-African aspects.

In the late 1960s the most persistent problem in Africa was that of civil war in Nigeria, which divided that country and in some measure the rest of Africa as well—particularly after four African states (Tanzania, Gabon, Ivory Coast, and Zambia) had recognized Biafra.

Because secession was the issue, the OAU could not
envisage a mediating role, although its consultative
procedure does illuminate the way in which collective
African influence is exerted. At the fourth assembly in
Kinshasa in 1967 the OAU established a consultative
committee of six heads of state with a mandate "to the
Head of the Federal Government of Nigeria to assure him
of the Assembly's desire for the territorial integrity,
unity and peace of Nigeria." [16] The committee members
were involved in various negotiations that brought
Nigerian and Biafran representatives together, but they
did so in such a way as to throw the weight of OAU support almost entirely on Nigeria's side. Nigeria treated
the issue as an internal question, as did statesmen who
were temperamentally unwilling to condone secession.[17]
The consultative committee comprised the heads of state
of Cameroon, Congo (Kinshasa), Ethiopia, Ghana, Liberia,
and Niger--leaders whose governments were particularly
apprehensive of ethnic secession dangers within their
own countries.

In contrast to the OAU's handling of the Congolese
problem in the mid-1960s, the consultations on Nigeria
were conducted at the highest level, with much depending
on Haile Selassie's participation as chairman of the
consultative committee. Although the other African
presidents took a keen interest in their task and the
presidents of Cameroon and Niger (as close neighbors of
Nigeria) had additional bilateral concerns to consider,
such as the movement of refugees and the impact on
crossborder trade, it was Haile Selassie's prestige that
enabled him to entice high-level Nigerian and Biafran
delegations to discussions in Addis Ababa in August
1968. Such discussions, held under Haile Selassie's
chairmanship, were in the end abortive, as the emperor
made clear in his own report to the consultative
committee:

> The absence of the leading personalities to
> the conflict had contributed to the state of
> affairs whereby each side repeats historical
> incident, accusing the other of much atroci-
> ties. In this context what have been pre-
> sented as peace proposals, be it in public or
> camera, were, on the one hand, accusations and
> on the other proposals which have not
> varied.[18]

The hierarchical factor was again at play, only in
reverse, because the consultative committee was operating at a higher level than the representatives sent by
the parties to the discussions. It proved almost impossible to secure the direct participation of either prin-

cipal, Yakubu Gowon of Nigeria or Odumegwu Ojukwu of secessionist Biafra, after the Niamey meeting of July 1968. Similarly, when the consultative committee organized discussions in Monrovia, Liberia, in April 1969 the members of the consultative committee outranked the leaders of the delegations from the two parties in dispute, and the meeting produced only the bromide communique that "reconciliation, peace and unity may be restored to Nigeria." Although the task of consultation had been entrusted to African statesmen, they were closely advised by the OAU permanent officials, notably Diallo Telli, the then administrative secretary-general, who appears to have pressed for a fairly rigid interpretation of the institution's antisecession stance.

The Nigeria-Biafra conflict was bitter and prolonged and attracted enormous attention worldwide. Even if the OAU did not offer a mediating role, other political forces did attempt to provide mediation--whether on such limited aspects as relief food supplies or on the fundamental points of difference between the secessionist element and the federal majority. Among those who appeared to offer mediation were the pope and his advisors; Arnold Smith, secretary-general of the Commonwealth Secretariat; John Volkmar and Adam Curle on behalf of the Society of Friends (Quakers); and the International Committee of the Red Cross, whose role is discussed in Chapter 8. [19] The concerns of these and similar agencies were largely humanitarian. However, at an early stage of the civil war the Biafran party appeared to be looking toward Britain as a possible mediator. Britain, as the former colonial power, was expected to have a bias toward Nigeria, its colonial "creation," but was also thought to exercise potential leverage in the conflict because it was Nigeria's traditional and possibly major arms supplier. (As the war progressed Nigeria purchased arms from the Soviet Union; Nigeria's diverse sources were only one factor that ruled out Britain as the appropriate mediator.) Because the OAU was engaged in the problem from mid-1967, at least in a technical sense, the United Nations was able to remain in the background.

In the example of Nigeria there were numerous offers of mediation but no obvious mediator, with the corollary that no mediation offer was successful. It was fairly obvious that Biafra could not win an acceptable position through negotiation and, so, relied on military power to sustain resistance to Nigeria's authority. For the secessionists, the effective choice was between surrender and military defeat; unwilling to do the former, they succumbed to the latter. Neither party could offer relevant concessions except on relatively minor questions of relief supplies to the affected civilian population. There existed no visible bilateral resolution toward which a mediator could work.

In attempting to define what institutional power the OAU has to provide mediation, it may be helpful to mention, albeit briefly, some further long-standing issues that lie outside the OAU's mediating abilities. The OAU was not effective during the Middle East war in 1967, although the conflict did affect Egypt, one of the OAU's founding members. The OAU played almost no part in resolving the civil war in Sudan, which ended in agreement between the Sudanese parties in March 1972. The OAU could not respond to the invasions of Angola in 1975 and thereafter initiated by South Africa and Zaire.

*   *   *

On the Middle East question, a broad resolution of the eighth assembly in Addis Ababa in 1971 enabled President Moktar Ould Daddah of Mauritania, then chairman of the OAU, to consult with heads of state so that their influence could be used to support S.C. Resolution 242 of November 22, 1967 (withdrawal of foreign troops from all Arab territories occupied since June 5, 1967).[20] In earlier years the OAU had tended to avoid the Middle East issue, and the 1971 resolution showed a stronger-than-usual concern with Egypt's plight. The outcome was a committee of ten African heads of state; a subcommittee of four of these visited Israel and Egypt. But their visits, and the overall OAU action, did not give the OAU a role as a mediator; the whole process was one, instead, of regional support for the main U.N. line of policy and action.[21]

The Sudan settlement was particularly interesting: Here was an agreement between representatives of the southern and northern regions of Sudan to end their civil war, reached during discussions in Addis Ababa and through the good offices of the emperor of Ethiopia but not through OAU machinery or under an OAU umbrella. Before successful discussions could take place, many outside diplomatic elements were engaged in opening up channels of communication between the parties, which ranged from British radicals to Italian priests (a curious side-effect of the pope's visit to Uganda in 1969 was that a Communist member of the Sudan government was able to have informal contact with Sudanese political exiles in Kampala). But for the final settlement, the key outside institution was the World Council of Churches, acting either directly or through the All-Africa Council of Churches. The World Council of Churches paid for European-based representatives of the Southern Sudan Liberation movement to travel to Africa in order to confer with southern Sudanese leaders. It was these contacts between political and military personalities on the southern side, who had not previously been in close contact, that paved the way for negotiations in Addis Ababa.[22]

The conflict in Sudan was, again, an internal question (like that in Nigeria); it could have been taken to the OAU only by the Sudanese government. Unlike Nigeria, the parties did consider a compromise in the form of autonomy for southern Sudan--a solution that was not construed as secession and that did not make a military outcome inevitable. Both sides had reached a point where they wanted to give up fighting (although to this day some military leaders who had been on the southern side in the civil war deny having been asked their views, or having supported the position taken at Addis Ababa). The practical contributions to be made by the mediator lay in establishing a mutually acceptable center for negotiation and in forming a cohesive delegation on the southern side that would be a credible representative of southern opinion. The Sudanese war had reached a "hurting stalemate" and the channels of communication were crucial.

In the Angola case, the OAU was unable to function as a mediator even though it had tried during the years of armed struggle to conciliate the radically opposed nationalist forces of the MPLA (Peoples' Movement for the Liberation of Angola) with regionalist elements such as FNLA (National Liberation Front of Angola). This approach was continued in the twelfth assembly in Kampala in July 1975 through the creation of a ten-nation committee of inquiry. [23] The committee met in Kampala at the end of September and sent a mission to visit Angola in October. The mission reported later that month in favor of a government of national unity. Discussions continued in early November at an OAU Bureau meeting (one of the rare cases where that body was actually used for a major policy matter), and a meeting of the OAU Defense Commission was convoked. The Angola issue had already gone well beyond the remit of the committee of inquiry, and an invasion of Angola by South Africa, which was not an OAU member, as well as by the member-state Zaire, had internationalized the situation. Suggestions of an OAU peacekeeping force were made but not pursued. The difficulties Angola faced at independence, which were compounded by the United States' support for the South African invasion, presented a problem far more complex than the usual African family quarrel. MPLA's claims to political primacy were backed by military victory over invasion forces from the north and south of independent Angola's borders.

Mediation by the OAU is likely to be excluded where the dispute is internal to a particular state, where the dispute involves nonmember-states, where the dispute engages powers outside Africa, and where one of the parties is seeking to avoid compliance with the OAU acceptance of colonial boundaries and defense of the territorial integrity of member states. Mediation by the OAU is likely to come into play where two member states have resorted to force to back conflicting

claims, and where an appeal to the normative principles
offers a prospect of reducing the level of conflict to a
point where bilateral diplomacy can again operate.

Disputes between African states which erupt into
conflict are likely to involve territorial demands by
one party that are rejected or resisted by another. If
clearly defined boundaries are being transgressed, the
OAU response will likewise be clear and will support the
party whose boundaries have been infringed. If boundaries are not defined and the location of the boundary
itself is in dispute, the OAU response becomes more
delicate and difficult. The OAU does not have the
authority to define boundaries that were left unmarked
by the colonial powers era, but it will seek to help the
parties to agree upon a method by which to determine the
necessary boundary. The dispute between Ethiopia and
Somalia has been so recurrent and intractable because
there is no consensus as to whether territory or
boundaries are being disputed. Ethiopia sees the latter
and Somalia the former as the issue in dispute, and the
item can be inscribed on an OAU agenda and effectively
discussed only when the parties are willing for the sake
of debate to discuss the "border" question. Arguably,
Somalia turns to the OAU when it feels ready to seek a
"ceasefire" in the shooting war with Ethiopia. Further
complications arise when Somalia disclaims official
responsibility for hostile action in Ethiopia, or
invokes misgivings that its differences with Kenya and
Ethiopia (which date from before the OAU's foundation)
are not affected by the Cairo resolution of 1964, by
which member states pledged themselves "to respect the
borders existing on their achievement of national
independence."

Africa also encounters disputes between member
states which fall short of armed conflict but which
significantly inhibit relations between the parties and
may spill over to their neighbors and economic partners.
The OAU will try to patch up such quarrels in the interests of the wider unity mentioned earlier and to avoid
embarrassment for third parties. Attempts by commentators to construct typologies of African disputes encom-
passing the border conflicts of the early years of independence and the more varied disputes of later years are
largely unsuccessful.

Some commentators have defined the role of the OAU
committees by a fourfold categorization: inquiry and
consultation, arbitration, conciliation, and mediation.[24] This pattern is unsatisfactory and does not
easily encompass the variety of incidents that range
from the 1963 war between Algeria and Morocco, the
Congolese problem, the Nigerian civil war, and the
release of Guinean diplomats held in Ghana in 1966--just
some of the cases with which the OAU machinery has had

to deal. The OAU's responses have varied from effecting
temporary appeasements to conducting a prolonged study
of a particular question with proposals for a solution.
Another typology is based on gradations of violent and
nonviolent forms of foreign policy intervention, categorized largely by the instrument employed--from a
regular army to the public-opinion media. [25]   Yet
another, contrasting typology is based on underlying
causes of conflict rather than on the instrument: "Thus
conflicts are classified as to whether they are caused
by racial (or colonial), boundary or personality clashes
or external intervention in domestic disorders." [26] For
example, Zartman has examined Africa as a subordinate
state system in which "component members would collectively acquire greater power by individually giving up
some of their sovereignty to a bloc or group." [27] It was
in the interests of the African states in the system to
follow certain rules, and in doing so, to avoid the
weakness and vulnerability to outside pressures: Intra-
systemic solutions to problems were favored because
insecurity would be reduced if the African states
handled their own problems.

One difficulty in typifying African disputes is
that we are faced with a small sample of events, so it
becomes an almost whimsical exercise to identify some
characteristics as general while putting others aside as
specific to a particular occurrence. Zacher has made an
ambitious attempt to classify disputes within a single
framework, building on that to provide predictive indi-
cators. His main argument, based on observations of the
period 1963-77, discusses consensus and conflict in one
formula. [28]

A basic problem in prediction is that African
states are not monolithic powers which maintain consistent foreign policies and objectives over a long period
(Zacher confesses that his own analysis neglects the
religious factor of tension between Moslems and non-
Moslems in defining the coalition groups in Africa).
The reality of much of independent Africa is that policy
in some states is subject to the vagaries of small,
unrepresentative leadership groups. Over time significant variables may change. The religious factor, for
example, is an internal as well as an external variable.
Conflict in Chad has been, in part, due to uncertainties
that followed shifts between southern and northern leadership within the country, and the Moslem and Christian
balance in Uganda shifted under the military rule of Idi
Amin.

The political character of African states has been
changing in the nearly two decades since the OAU's
establishment: the near-demise of colonial-trained
political leaders, the advent of postindependence military cadres, and, in the late 1970s, the growing diver-
gence between countries of neocolonial dependence and

those of revolutionary independence, are some of the
more notable shifts. Such changes have helped determine
the OAU's role as a conservative agency established
merely to enforce rules, or as a body that will attempt
innovation. Rather than seeking to define the circumstances in which the OAU can mediate, it may be more
fruitful to examine how it mediates and through what
actors. The African states in the OAU have shown a
collective distaste for recourse to force, although the
OAU generally has been powerless to exercise significant
influence on fighting <u>inside</u> member states. Matthews
makes the succinct point:

> All in all, the OAU has exerted a favourable,
> though limited, influence on the attitude of
> states towards the use of force. <u>Normatively</u>,
> it has constituted a collective conscience
> that no African government can entirely afford
> to ignore; it has reinforced the general
> principle that resort to force is immoral, if
> not illegal. [29]

The OAU's power to mediate in African disputes is
not based primarily on the ability or personality of the
mediator--usually a small committee--but on the fact
that the mediator represents an association whose
approval is important to the parties and in whose work
the parties generally wish to participate. The OAU has
an institutional appeal for all African states, and few
states are willing to risk for long the collective
disapproval of all other African states. In speaking of
states in this context, we should be specific and say
that in the major policy debates, member states are
represented at the assembly by heads of state. The OAU
is a "club," and it is furthermore a winner's club. The
OAU is not an association of popular organizations and
political parties but one of individual statesmen, and
broadly speaking it does not look askance at those
statesmen, it does not ask for their credentials as
representatives of the interests of their peoples. The
prestige of the club is such that it is attractive even
to the wayward, and it is in the interests of the members to win back even the recalcitrant. The mystique of
the OAU is threatened if a particular statesman is seen
to be sulking outside (this psychological weapon has
been a powerful tool in the hands of Morocco's King
Hassan in his handling of the Saharan question).
A state may be represented at the assembly by a
delegate other than the head of state, but there is
substantial evidence to show that the delegation's power
in debate is weakened by the absence of the national
leader. For those African leaders who come to power

with limited international contacts, the OAU provides a context within which they can broaden their connections and thus consolidate their own status within the countries they rule.[30] OAU members may jib at the murder of Togo's Olympio, the accession of Zaire's Mobutu, Amin's seizure of power in Uganda, the overthrow of Nigeria's Gowon, and the killing of Liberia's Tolbert, but when the dust settles it is the new leaders who are sitting at the conference table. This fact makes all the more remarkable the reluctance of some members in 1982 to see the OAU chairmanship pass to Libya's Muammar Qaddafi. Only the combination of the chairmanship issue with disputes over the venue of the assembly, the membership of the SADR, and the seating of the Chadian delegation made it possible to abort the assembly scheduled for August in Tripoli. Despite the confusion of the Tripoli meetings, the necessary two-thirds quorum was almost reached, and many states were willing to participate on the simple proposition that the institution's survival was more important than any single divisive issue.

Although the members of the club have equal voting power, additional prestige is attached to some leaders, such as Haile Selassie in his day; also in the OAU's early days, certain connections (and rivalries) dating from colonial politics were significant in the exercise of influence. The charismatic standing of OAU leaders helps to explain why the extraordinary sessions at the ministerial level later gave way to ad hoc committees comprised of heads of state. Another commentator has noted that the "most successful method of conflict resolution in Africa has involved the intervention of heads of state or government who are widely respected and trusted by both parties to the dispute."[31]

The OAU has been ineffective in disputes involving non-African powers, which have no means or wish to participate directly in the OAU's work and are often more concerned with specific bilateral connections (the shifting alliances between the Soviet Union and the United States toward Ethiopia and Somalia are a case in point). High-level access to parties in dispute demands that the mediating body of statesmen possess similar capabilities. Collective rather than individual mediation is the order of the day, although in some instances one member of the ad hoc commission may be the most effective mediator by reason of individual prestige or relevant bilateral interests with both parties in dispute. Pressures on heads of state make it difficult to hold an extraordinary session, except in unusual circumstances. The compromise machinery that fulfills the necessary conditions for OAU mediation is the ad hoc commission of heads of state with a mandate from the membership as a whole.

When it becomes clear to the OAU that an ad hoc commission is needed to resolve a dispute, some care is

taken to designate the particular members. Some general
principles apply: select committees should normally
reflect the linguistic, regional, and cultural composition of the OAU, but not every ad hoc commission is a
miniature of the whole body. Preference, obviously, is
given to states whose leaders have some influence with
the leaders of the parties in dispute. The commission
that succeeded in 1975 in resolving territorial differences between Mali and Upper Volta comprised Togo,
Niger, Guinea, and Senegal, all of which are Francophone, West African states whose subregional alliances
were affected by the dispute. The countries comprising
the ad hoc commission formed in August 1976 to mediate
differences between Kenya and Uganda were almost
entirely drawn from the immediate area: Burundi,
Ethiopia, Rwanda, Sudan, Zaire, and Zambia. Because the
commissions work part of the time through secret diplomacy and private conversations, it is not possible to
pinpoint specific use of leverage, but one should note
the interdependence of the East and Central African
countries. Part of Kenya's economy is dependent on
transit trade through the port at Mombassa and the East
African railway system. Conversely, Sudan relies on
supply routes (at least to the southern region) through
Kenya and Uganda, and development projects in southern
Sudan can be seriously delayed by unrest in Kenya and
Uganda, particularly if this leads to border closures.
Examples of these local needs can be multiplied.   In
West Africa, for example, the major rivers sustain the
economies of more than one country.   Minor disputes
between two countries can delay large-scale projects
involving river utilization, e.g., transport and irri-
gation. Awareness of these realities prompt leaders in
coastal states to ensure goodwill among states in the
hinterland. Such states may also be suppliers of labor
for the activities of the more prosperous coastal
states. Of course, the commission should not be biased
toward one of the parties. If it is--as was the case
with the consultative committee on Nigeria--it is
disqualified as an effective mediator.

     In line with this implicit tactic of leverage
through economic influence, the ad hoc commissions
presiding over the more fundamental disputes usually
include Africa's larger powers, notably Algeria and
Nigeria--important oil-producing states that represent
both radical and conservative tendencies. But the OAU
has devised no set pattern for the formation of commissions. Instead, selective patterns are created to meet
particular cases. Selection of participants may be the
way to further develop the mediating role. Zartman's
conjecture on this point is that

African conflict management frequently operates through the mediation of other African
states outside the conflict subregion.   Its
operation does not depend on this characteristic, however, and future conflict management
could effectively evolve in a number of
directions: through the use of mediators from
other subregions, to strengthen continental
interaction; through mediators from within the
conflict subregion, to strengthen subregional
cohesion; or through mediators from within
non-subregional leadership blocs, to strength-
en their cohesion.   There are precedents for
all these patterns in the first 15 years of
independence. [32]

The OAU continues to change: In the late 1970s and
early 1980s the cohesion of the radical bloc was
strengthened by new political leaders from the Lusophone
countries who had devised coherent and concerted policy
approaches out of their experience with armed liberation
struggle.   Their experience makes them sensitive to
SADR's claims.   The reemergence of a radical group in
the OAU (after the jolt occasioned by the 1966 overthrow
of Ghana's Kwame Nkrumah) has brought a backlash from
the conservatives, a large minority within the OAU who
are at least able to prevent a two-thirds quorum
required for many purposes (it should be noted that
Article 28 of the charter requires only a simple
majority to admit a new member, but that a two-thirds
majority is required to decide the "important question"
of what constitutes a state).
     If the OAU wishes to succeed in its future mediat-
ing efforts, it must rely more on the institutional
appeal of the ad hoc commissions than on the personalities of certain leaders.   The OAU can boast few veteran
leaders who stand out for their individual merit and
prestige on a continent-wide scale.   Whatever view was
taken of the political values of a Haile Selassie, a
Jomo Kenyatta, or even a William Tubman, it was accepted
that they commanded attention by virtue of age and
experience in a continent where the wisdom of the aged
is still valued.   Among the founding fathers who spoke
in Addis Ababa in 1963, Felix Houphouet-Boigny of Ivory
Coast, Julius Nyerere of Tanzania, and Habib Bourguiba
of Tunisia were still in office at the end of 1984.
Leopold Senghor of Senegal and Ahmadou Ahidjo of
Cameroon had retired, and Milton Obote of Uganda was
back in office after a long spell of enforced exile, his
reputation tarnished by continuing violence in his country.   As age and wisdom become rarer and rarer in the
OAU, it should feel constrained to strengthen even more
its mediating commissions.   Instead of relying on indi-

vidual statesmen, they should turn to lower-ranking
diplomats and professionals.   The OAU Council, also,
should resume a more active role, and the assembly
should resuscitate the permanent commission, comprised
mainly of lawyers, first proposed in 1963 and 1964.   At
present, however, the collective spirit of the leaders'
club certainly looks awry.

Chapter 6: Notes

1.   This is the fourth of seven general principles in Article 3 of the OAU Charter, adopted in Addis Ababa on May 25, 1963. For a general discussion on the drafting of the OAU Charter, see Michael Wolfers, Politics in the Organization of African Unity (London: Methuen, 1976), which draws on the unpublished verbatim record, "Proceedings of the Summit Conference of Independent African States."

2.   T. O. Elias, "The Charter of the OAU," American Journal of International Law 59 (1965): 243-67.

3.   CM/Res. 42 (III).

4.   For a description of the suggested procedure, see T. O. Elias, "The Commission of Mediation, Conciliation and Arbitration of the OAU," British Yearbook of International Law 40 (1964): 336-54.

5.   Elias, "The Commission of Mediation, Conciliation and Arbitration."

6.   B. Boutros-Ghali, L'Organisation de l'Unité Africaine (Paris: Armand Colin, 1969) and Les difficultés institutionelles du panafricanisme (Geneva: Institut Universitaire de Hautes Etudes Internationales, 1971).

7.   AHG/Res. 16 (I). For a discussion of the broader issues of boundary questions, see African Boundary Problems, Carl Gosta Widstrand, ed. (Uppsala: The Scandinavian Institute of African Studies, 1969).

8.   For a comparative study, see Berhanykun Andemicael, Peaceful Settlement Among African States: Roles of the United Nations and the Organization of African Unity (New York: UNITAR, 1972).

9.   "Emergency Council of Ministers: Verbatim Report," unpublished.

10.   Andemicael, Peaceful Settlement Among African States, 8.

11.   I. William Zartman, International Relations in the New Africa (New Jersey: Prentice-Hall, 1966), 36.

12.   ECM/Res. 5 (III).

13.   For a summary account of OAU involvement in the Congolese problem during this time, see Wolfers, Politics in the OAU, 140-49. Another useful summary is provided by Andemicael, Peaceful Settlement Among African States, 20-30.

4.   See reports of Tshombe's press conference, C.R.I.S.P., Congo 1964 (Princeton: Princeton University Press, 1966), 473.

15.   Immanuel Wallerstein, "The Early Years of the OAU: The Search for Organizational Preeminence," International Organization 20 (166): 782.

16.   AHG/Res. 51 (IV). See also AHG/34, "Report of the OAU Consultative Committee on Nigeria" presented to the fifth assembly in Algiers in September 1968, which shows that the consultative committee consulted General Gowon concerning Nigeria's views before contacting Lieutenant-Colonel Ojukwu.

17.   For a summary account of OAU involvement in the Nigeria question, see John J. Stremlau, The International Politics of the Nigerian Civil War (Princeton: Princeton University Press, 1977), 82-106; 149-74 discusses the Commonwealth Secretariat's role, and 147 n.19 mentions the Quaker role.

18.   Annex VIJII to AHG/34 of September 1968.

19.   See Chapter 8, by David P. Forsythe, "Humanitarian Mediation by the International Committee of the Red Cross," in this book.

20.   AHG Res. 66 (VIII).

21.   For further discussion, see Yassin El-Ayouty, "The OAU and the Arab-Israeli Conflict: A Case of Mediation that Failed," in The Organization of African Unity After Ten Years, Yassin El-Ayouty, ed. (New York: Praeger, 1975), 189-212.

22.   Kodwo Ankrah, "In Pursuit of Peace in the Sudan," Study Encounter 25 8 (1972).

23.   The countries were Algeria, Burundi, Ghana, Kenya, Lesotho, Morocco, Niger, Somalia, Upper Volta, and Uganda.

24.   Mirlande Manigat, "L'Organisation de l'Unite Africaine," Revue Francaise de Science Politique 21 (1971): 382-401; and E. Kwan Kouassi, Les Rapports Entre L'Organisation des Nations Unies et l'Organisation de l'Unite Africaine (Brussels: Etablissements Emile Bruylant, 1978), 281-88.

25.   Zartman, International Relations in the New Africa, especially the table on p. 88.

26.   Robert O. Matthews, "Interstate Conflicts in Africa: A Review," International Organization 24 (1970): 336.

27.   I. William Zartman, "Africa as a Subordinate State System in International Relations," International Organization 21 (1967): 545.

28.   Mark W. Zacher, International Conflicts and Collective Security, 1946–77 (New York: Praeger, 1979), 17–28, 142.

29.   Matthews, "Interstate Conflicts in Africa," 352.

30.   Gamal Abdel Nasser said in the closed session debate: "We support the meeting every year, and in order to strengthen the contacts, in order to be acquainted with each other, and in order to strengthen the brotherhood in Africa."

31.   Matthews, "Interstate Conflicts in Africa," 353.

32.   Zartman, "Social and Political Trends in Africa in the 1980s," in Africa in the 1980s: A Continent in Crisis, Colin Legum et al., eds. (New York: McGraw-Hill, 1979), 92–93.

7.
THE ORGANIZATION OF AMERICAN STATES AS MEDIATOR

L. Ronald Scheman and John W. Ford

If one lesson is to be learned from the Organization of American States' (OAS) efforts to mediate disputes among its member states, it is that when procedures are informal, they work. The moment the framework becomes too rigid or formal, mediation falters.

This conclusion, and others documented in this chapter, emerge from the long-standing efforts of the American states to formalize a peace system based on mediation and arbitration. It began with a flurry of treaty-writing in the 1920s and 1930s, which produced eight major treaties on mediation, conciliation, and arbitration patterned after the Hague conferences of the early part of the century. The result was revealing. Only one dispute was ever submitted to the formal treaty procedures, that of Haiti and the Dominican Republic in 1937. [1]

Subsequently, an Inter-American Peace Committee was formed in response to a proposal by Haiti in 1940 without benefit of prior study or analysis. That committee, with no formal procedures or place in the

L. Ronald Scheman was assistant secretary for management in the Organization of American States. He is now counsel to the firm of Coudert Bros.

John W. Ford is a retired foreign service officer. He has served as a deputy U.S. representative to the OAS and as advisor to OAS Secretary-General Alejandro Orfila. He was also a member of the OAS Peace Committee and of the Committee of Seven, which obtained a ceasefire and troop-withdrawal agreement from El Salvador and Honduras during their conflict in 1979.

inter-American system but headed by a determined chairman, Ambassador Luis Quintanilla of Mexico, became the
main instrument of mediation and good offices over the
next decade. It successfully handled more than sixteen
cases with procedures that were tantamount to conciliation rather than simple mediation. Because it worked,
the nations decided to draft a statute for it. No
sooner had the formal procedures been inaugurated when
the committee began to fall into disuse. The nations
then decided to go further and incorporate the committee
into the Charter of the Organization of American States.
Since then it has not been used at all.
      The principal treaty governing mediation and
arbitration within the system, the 1948 Inter-American
Treaty on Pacific Settlement of Disputes (the Pact of
Bogota), unified all the previous arbitration and mediation treaties into one comprehensive document. Dubbed
one of the world's finest legal and worst political
documents, it has a major flaw: It has been virtually
ignored since it was signed. On the other hand, one
small, general clause in Article 7 of the Inter-American
Treaty of Reciprocal Assistance (Rio Treaty), which was
framed for purposes of collective security rather than
for resolving disputes, has opened the door to a wide
range of ad hoc mediation activities.
      In sum, virtually all of the successful mediation
efforts of the inter-American system succeeded because
of ad hoc arrangements, utilized by forceful personalities within a general framework which, to be sure,
encourages peaceful resolution of their conflicts.
Nations, like people, seem to resist rigid mechanisms
that try to predetermine their behavior or to impose
legalistic solutions on essentially political questions.
The way in which these mechanisms have evolved is an
important case study of international peacekeeping and
mediation.

The Role of the International Organization

      An international mediating organization, by its
nature, is qualitatively different from other actors.
First, it has a continuing presence, whether or not
there is a dispute. Second, it is a collective instrument and therefore more complex. Third, its principal
goal is a long-term one: to modify the behavior of
nations by restraining recourse to the use of force.
The establishment of an international organization for
mediation purposes is an a priori expression of a group
of nations' desire to resist pressures to use force and,
instead, to channel their grievances through other
instruments. The operation of such an organization--
being dependent upon the member nations--asserts that
accommodation is preferable to confrontation. This

preference, which works in different ways in various
regions of the world, has a firm foothold and a distinguished legacy in the Western Hemisphere.

In this context, an international mediating
organization cannot be viewed in isolation: It is part
of a process. A state's decision to accept mediation is
a careful calculation influenced by domestic and international factors. Consequently, the influence of an
international mediating agency is based on several components: (1) the ability to create an atmosphere and
network that render recourse to force detrimental to a
disputing nation's interests; (2) financial resources to
grant or withhold assistance, thereby increasing the
costs of violent conflict; (3) the presence of a forum
to air differences; and (4) an ability to mobilize an
international consensus capable of bringing pressure to
bear on the contestants at the time of the conflict.

The role of these four components in dispelling
fears, tracking rumors, and facilitating communication
falls squarely within the definition of mediation set
forth by Zartman and Touval in the introduction. Thus,
an international organization may be just as readily
judged by the times when it is not being used: Functioning somewhat as a court of last resort, such an
organization increases the likelihood of peaceful
resolution.

The importance of regional organization relates in
the first instance to the reality that violent disputes
occur, for the most part, among neighbors. We do not
find Ecuador and Yugoslavia or Bolivia or Burma in mor-
tal combat. Only where the interests of the superpowers
come into play does distance become submerged in ideological and power confrontations. The world is still
surprisingly parochial in its outlook. Nationalistic
feelings are expanding in ever-widening circles, but
they touch subregions first and more intensely before
they encompass the globe. This means, simply, that
regional experience is and will be relevant, that
regional disputes should be our main concern, and that
regional leverage on many levels is critical.

International economic leverage is most influential in the early stages of potential disputes.
Development loans or programs cannot take place, especially in border areas, where the potential for conflict
is high. The accommodations in the dispute among
Brazil, Paraguay, and Argentina over the use of the
Parana and de la Plata rivers in the late 1960s are an
important example. The OAS and the Inter-American
Development Bank helped lay the groundwork for large
hydroelectric installations, but the bank would not
finance them unless the countries resolved the disputes
capable of disrupting the venture. Here, financing
provided the needed leverage in inducing the countries
to accommodate their differences. [2]

Another vital component in mediation rests in human rights activities.[3] Certain mechanisms available to the international community throw an early spotlight on the behavior of regimes that reveal proclivities to use violence in dealing with international problems. These mechanisms also help establish an atmosphere that favors the selection of leaders who subscribe to the concept of the rule of law.

The development of multiple networks within the regional system is another factor that increases international leverage. Brazil, Venezuela, and Mexico are growing more important in inter-American dynamics as are the roles being played by the newly independent nations of the Caribbean. Networks utilizing nongovernmental organizations, professional societies, and commercial and cultural ties are generally far more influential in the regional context. The weight of adverse regional public opinion is frequently more burdensome to a wayward political leader than negative global reactions.

The argument against regional mediation holds that common backgrounds and cultures may not be conducive to impartiality--a quality more likely to be exerted from a distance.[4] This argument, however, actually supplements the importance of regional subsystems. As noted above, international organizations are valuable principally because they engender patterns of behavior among their member countries, even though members seek mediation from other sources outside the formal regional system in appropriate cases. For example, small groups of states within Latin America frequently play mediating roles outside the formal structure of the OAS. The Andean Group was a major player in resolving the Nicaraguan revolution in 1979; the other Central American states had a vital role in mediating the El Salvador-Honduras war of 1969. These are important examples, as are the appeals of Argentina and Chile to Great Britain and then to the pope in the Beagle Channel dispute. There is no inconsistency here. The central idea of the international mediating structure is that nations will not resort to force. They are encouraged to use any channels available, and, as we have noted, informal channels are frequently preferred. Secure in the knowledge that they have recourse to a larger forum if things get out of hand, disputing nations are thus encouraged to make other methods work.

The Inter-American Setting

In analyzing the functions of the American regional system in mediation, a thorough history is vital. The regional machinery has two purposes: (1) to circumscribe the use of U.S. power in the hemisphere, and (2) to devise ways to maintain peace among the

American states. [5] In applying its dispute-settlement
mechanisms, the inter-American system has been governed
by the overriding principle of nonintervention, the
guardian principle in Latin America's struggle with the
power dissymmetry in the hemisphere. Clauses in the OAS
Charter on nonintervention are the most comprehensive in
the world, far more detailed than those in the U.N.
Charter. These clauses, which were an intrinsic part of
Latin America's inter-American bargain with the United
States, and which also excluded the concept of a veto in
the hemispheric organization, make the OAS de facto the
mediating mechanism between the United States and Latin
America. [6] It also makes the Latin American members
circumspect about what they will allow the OAS to do and
the way the mediating machinery can be used. Given the
historical foundations for the Latin Americans' concern,
their perception is that the hemispheric organization is
vital in "maintaining peaceful relations between Latin
America and the United States" which "gives real content
to the existence of the system." [7] It is, in effect,
hegemony subjected to institutional discipline. The
argument that the OAS "was intended by the U.S. to
secure its preemptory authority against possible U.N.
involvement in inter-American affairs" [8] was firmly
refuted by several observers at the time of the OAS's
creation in 1948 and the fact that the United States
resisted the establishment of a regional system,
preferring a universal approach instead. [9]

A wide range of territorial and other disputes
within Latin America simmer in the midst of complex and
multifaceted foreign policies based on promoting
regional cooperation. In spite of the fact that most
Latin Americans have lived in interstate peace all of
their lives, there are many traditional rivalries in the
hemisphere. Ninety-four incidents have flared up from
these rivalries in the thirty-five years since 1947. Of
these, thirty-three cases, or 35 percent, were referred
to the regional system, in addition to eleven other
cases considered by the OAS, although not in the category of "traditional rivalries." Rather than being one
of the most peaceful areas of the world, as current
mythology assumes, the Institute for the Study of
International Peace has reported it as one of the most
incident-prone outside of the Middle East. [10]

Although many cases are not conclusively settled,
the hemisphere does not frequently go to war, or, to put
it in the reverse, the governments eagerly go to the
very brink of conflict and then seek a face-saving way
out. This, however, is not due to any "natural peaceful
instinct" in the Americas. Three closely related elements are, by and large, responsible. First is the
United States' attention to the area, especially in its
security considerations, after World War II. More
potential benefits could accrue to the nations by con-

centrating on strengthening relations with the United States rather than by fighting each other. Second, complementing this, the post-World War II era in the Americas was highlighted by the search for new ways of cooperation on a regional basis. Culminating in Brazilian President Juscelino Kubitchek's "Operationa Panamerica" and the Alliance for Progress, considerable pressures submerged parochial disputes in the prevailing cooperative atmosphere. Third, the OAS was present as a forum for the discussion of vexing issues. In short, during this period of history nations were finding ways to get along with each other, and arbitration machinery was in place and functioning.

Another major factor in the peace of the hemisphere has been the tendency of the three largest states--the United States, Brazil, and Mexico--to yield on most disputes in which they are involved. The emerging role of Brazil in the hemisphere and its policy of seeking to promote their national interests through accommodation rather than confrontation was a major influence. One has only to imagine what the hemisphere could be like if it were otherwise. The 1978 Amazon Pact among all countries bordering on the Amazon, the Itapu Agreement with Argentina and Paraguay on the use of the common river-basin waters, and the resolution of a long-standing border dispute with Venezuela in 1973 have been indicative of Brazil's policy. The observation of one commentator that Brazilian diplomacy, not U.S. policies, was principally responsible for the prevention of hostilities among Peru, Bolivia, and Chile in the late 1970s is significant.[11]

In the 1970s the prevailing thrust toward cooperation began to break down as expectations went unfulfilled, the United States' capabilities could not keep pace with its commitments, changes in technology, economics, and world politics eroded the traditional faith in common bonds, and the nations of the hemisphere, especially the larger ones, began to realize they had to rely on themselves to build their local economies, gain international markets, and defend their own interests.

This breakdown of postwar cooperation and the attrition of U.S. hegemony provided fertile soil for ideology-based conflicts, with far-reaching internal and external implications. Invasions across borders by dissenting groups of exiles--the prevalent form of conflict in the late 1940s and 1950s--took on new dimensions with the increased predominance of ideological issues. In addition, unresolved traditional disputes became more troublesome, such as the Argentine-Chile dispute over the Beagle Islands, the issue of Bolivia's access to the sea, the Peru-Ecuador flare-up over the Amazon territory in 1981, and the continuing Venezuela-Colombian tension over sea boundaries. The inter-

American system has more difficulty addressing these
kinds of issues directly, except as a "court of last
resort," if and when hostilities do break out. But its
presence helps create its own dynamics in the area, as
we will note below.

The Peacekeeping Machinery in the Inter-American System

Good offices, mediation, and attempts at arbitration have a long history in the Western Hemisphere.
Throughout the nineteenth century the European powers
were asked to play the mediating role in inter-American
disputes. With the rise of U.S. hegemony in the
hemisphere in the beginning of the twentieth century,
Bryce Wood notes that after 1910 "no Latin American
boundary controversy was settled by a European arbitration." [12] He observes that "it was no accident that
in the only . . . dispute terminated by arbitration
after 1910 the arbitrator was the Chief Justice of the
United States."
Attempts to formulate orderly and systematic
peacekeeping machinery for the Western Hemisphere began
with the First International Conference of the American
States (INCAS) in 1890. It was summoned by the United
States in part for the purposes of peacekeeping, but
primarily for commercial reasons. A general plan for
arbitration machinery was adopted at this meeting. It
was not until 1923 with the Gondra Treaty, however, that
the major advances toward systematic mediation began.
The 1929 Washington Conference on Conciliation and
Arbitration passed two major conventions, General
Treaties for Arbitration and Conciliation. However, the
exceptions were overwhelming. Of twenty signatories,
forty reservations were made for what nations considered
vital interests, mostly territorial issues. This began
a decade of feverish work on mediation, conciliation,
and arbitration in the 1930s with five treaties being
signed. The Inter-American Treaty of Pacific Settlement
(Pact of Bogota) was signed immediately after the war,
consolidating all these treaties. The Pact of Bogota
was supplemented by a number of subordinate protocols,
declarations, and agreements relating to nonintervention
and the nonrecognition of territory acquired by force. [13]
The antipathy of the Latin American governments
toward centralized mediating authorities was evident in
each treaty insofar as they consistently denied the governing board of the Pan American Union a role in mediating proceedings. This move was clearly designed to keep
the United States at bay and to avoid creating any mechanisms that might "strengthen the institutions of the
OAS for fear of strenthening the leverage of the U.S."[14]
The historical experience of this effort is
remarkable. All of these treaties, which were worked on

so diligently and all of which are still in force, were virtually ignored. The 1937 Haiti-Dominican dispute was the only conflict subjected to treaty procedures. Four other serious disputes at the time could have been submitted but were not: The Guatemalan-Honduras controversy of 1930; the Leticia controversy between Peru and Colombia in 1934, which was ultimately settled by the League of Nations; the Chaco War, which was then ongoing but was settled through ad hoc arbitration; and the Peru-Ecuador controversy of 1942, which was mediated but not in accordance with the 1929 General Treaty of Inter-American Arbitration. [15] It is an interesting commentary on the attitudes of that period that the failure of the countries to use the extant peacekeeping machinery led them to devise machinery that was more formal and compulsory, allowing no exceptions. The result was disastrous. In the debates of the Permanent Council of the OAS or in the meetings of consultation of ministers of foreign affairs today, hardly a single reference is made to the Pact of Bogota, no less to any of the individual treaties to which the states may be signatories. One of the few times the pact was recommended in a major dispute, the El Salvador-Honduras War of 1969, El Salvador responded by denouncing it.

On the other hand, the states continued to devise ingenious, nonobligatory instruments to serve their ends. The signing of the OAS Charter in 1948 seemed to signal an open season for interstate conflicts. These conflicts, predominantly involving exile activity in Central America and the Caribbean, were rooted, for the most part, in social turmoil and rivalries between democratic and dictatorial forces unleashed after World War II. The new inter-American system rose to the occasion immediately, but neither through the established peace treaties nor the recently signed Pact of Bogota. Instead, a series of informal mechanisms were employed to bring particular cases to the attention of the inter-American community and to create pressures on the contending parties. All of these were done either through the Inter-American Peace Committee or the Rio Treaty, which had been designed to supplement, not replace, the Pact of Bogota.

The regional focus of inter-American peacekeeping mechanisms was capped with the formation of the Organization of American States (OAS) in 1948. The three components of the system were the Inter-American Treaty of Reciprocal Assistance (Rio Treaty), signed in 1947, the Charter of the OAS (1948), and the Inter-American Treaty on Pacific Settlement (Pact of Bogota) (1948). Further steps to strengthen the system were taken in the 1960s and 1970s in the treaties of Tlatelolco and Ayacucho relating to control of nuclear weapons and arms limitation--treaties that were concluded outside of the formal OAS machinery.

The heart of the mechanism rests in articles 23 through 28 of the OAS Charter, the Pact of Bogota, and Article 7 of the Rio Treaty. In addition, articles 81 to 90 of the charter set forth the standards for the Inter-American Committee on Peaceful Settlement, a mutation of the old Inter-American Peace Committee.

The Pact of Bogota--the principal instrument for peaceful resolution of disputes--covers every kind of dispute except those within domestic jurisdiction or those already settled by treaty, judicial decision, or arbitral award. Its procedures include, first, good offices and mediation by a government or private citizen as agreed to by the parties (arts. 9-14). If this fails, it sets forth a procedure combining investigation and conciliation to be invoked immediately, under the authority of a commission of five members convoked by the OAS Council (arts. 15-30). Two members are to be chosen by each party and a fifth by agreement. They are charged with verifying the facts and with trying to bring the parties to a resolution within six months.

If this fails, the parties can agree to arbitration, which, if one party refuses, opens the option to the other party to invoke the jurisdiction of the International Court of Justice (ICJ) (arts. 21-49). If the dispute is a legal one, ICJ jurisdiction itself is the final arbiter of its jurisdiction. If a party refuses to cooperate, the OAS Council is given authority to set up the arbitration commission, and then the parties must arbitrate. If one party fails to carry out the award, the other may call for a meeting of consultation of ministers of foreign affairs "to agree upon appropriate measures to ensure the fulfillment of the judicial decision or arbitral award" (Art. 50). The document is as comprehensive as human ingenuity could devise. The absence of ratifications and use of the treaty, however, is vivid testimony that rigid and compulsory procedures make it "a good legal document . . . but a poor political one." [16]

When it was evident that ratifications of the Pact of Bogota would be slow, Brazil raised the question of its revision at the tenth INCAS in 1954 to make it more realistic. Mexico, which had been one of the principal architects of the treaty and already had ratified it, led in its defense, suggesting that instead of revising it precipitously, a better procedure would be to urge ratification by the states. The Mexican initiative was adopted unanimously, even though in the debate Argentina, Bolivia, Brazil, Colombia, and the United States favored at least a study of reasons for nonratification. As of 1982, thirteen countries have ratified the pact, ten of them without reservations.

While the Pact of Bogota was struggling to achieve a foothold, an unheralded group, the Inter-American Peace Committee, was on its way to the forefront of

inter-American peacekeeping. Established in 1940 by the
second meeting of consultation of ministers of foreign
affairs in Havana, shortly after the fall of France, the
committee had no statutes and few orientations. It was
approved with little concept of the important role it
was to play. The committee did not even report to the
OAS Council, although all members were representatives
of their governments, accredited to the Permanent
Council. Under the chairmanship of Ambassador Luis
Quintanilla of Mexico, it drafted its own statutes and
continued operating on its own authority, reporting only
to the periodic International Conferences of the
American States.[17]

Under the committee's original statutes, any
country, whether or not it was a party to a dispute,
could ask the committee to take action, and the
committee could request permission to go to any state
regardless of whether the state had agreed to the
committee's jurisdiction. John Dreier, U.S. ambassador
to the OAS during this period, comments that the very
informality and weakness of the committee might have
been its strength:

> It has made it clear that it has no authority
> to judge disputes or issue opinions upon the
> merits of a case presented to it. Nor is it
> authorized under the Havana Resolution to
> propose formulas of settlement or even to
> mediate between the parties. Far less does
> the Peace Committee have any authority to
> compel any government to act or refrain from
> acting as it chooses. Its only authority is
> moral. Yet the very weakness of the Inter-
> American Peace Committee has been the cause of
> its success in bringing together conflicting
> parties.[18]

Dreier goes on to explain that, "since the Committee has
no power to enforce any decision upon a government, it
is hard for any government to feel that its position is
endangered by coming before it."

Almost all of the cases referred to the OAS from
1948 to 1955 went to the peace committee, as will be
noted below. Because of its success, the tenth INCAS in
Caracas in 1954 which, recognizing the committee's growing importance, asked the council to prepare a formal
statute to govern its activities. That statute, when
finally approved in 1956, severely curtailed the powers
of the committee so that it could assume jurisdiction
only when both disputing states agreed; further, the
statute put a halt to the committee's ability to go
uninvited to trouble spots. Under the new statute: (1)

only a state party to the controversy could ask the
committee to act; and (2) the committee could proceed
only with the consent of the other party. "The effect
of the new change was that the Committee practically
ceased to function as an agent of conciliation, and the
report of the Committee noted that since the new statute
was put into effect, 'no case was submitted to it for
consultation.'" [19]
      In the committee's report to the second Special
Inter-American Conference (which drafted amendments to
the OAS Charter), it pointed out that

> This committee filled a gap left by the
> previous inter-American treaties, which did
> not establish any real organ for conciliation
> or mediation within the regional system. . . .
>
> The importance and usefulness of the Inter-
> American Peace Committee lie, above all, in
> the permanent character that stems from its
> composition by five members, elected by the
> Council of the Organization for periods of
> five years, which permits it to meet imme-
> diately in the event of a dispute between two
> states or a disturbance of the peace.
>
> This factor has justly been pointed out to be
> the primary condition for the efficacy of the
> procedures of conciliation. The agencies
> responsible for peacemaking or mediating
> action in a dispute should be permanent and
> not subject to a complicated process of lists
> or selection of the site and methods of colla-
> boration, so as to avoid all delay, however
> slight, in the work of restoring peace or of
> timely conciliation, before events take a
> sudden turn and possibly cause irreversible
> situations. . . .
>
> This importance and usefulness of the Inter-
> American Peace Committee to the American
> States emanates also from the flexibility of
> the recourse of conciliation and the possi-
> bility of dealing with situations marked by
> grave political tension, without the necessity
> of resorting to compulsory procedures that
> imply the application of measures in accor-
> dance with the treaties governing collective
> security. [20]

Referring to the new statutory provisions, it states:

> The provisions [of the new statute] leave the
> Committee in the position of not being able to
> initiate even taking cognizance of the matter
> until the consent of the parties directly
> concerned is obtained. This requirement of
> strict agreement prior to acting has caused an
> obvious decline in the number of cases studied
> by the Inter-American Peace Committee in the
> last few years. [21]

The report, interestingly, was signed by the United States, Argentina, Colombia, the Dominican Republic, and Nicaragua.

Two events ensued. The final nail was hammered in the coffin of the Inter-American Peace Committee when the nations decided to include the committee in the amendments to the OAS Charter in 1967 (arts. 81-90). Since then the committee has neither met on substantive issues nor handled any cases, although in 1971 the United States attempted, without success, to invoke its good offices in the tuna-fishing dispute with Ecuador. [22] The second was the reaction to this development, demonstrating the members' indomitable drive for informality and innovation. The OAS Council, acting provisionally as an organ of consultation, began to appoint ad hoc investigating committees doing essentially the same work but separate from the Inter-American Peace Committee. Thus, in the Costa Rica-Nicaragua dispute in 1955 and 1956, the Honduras-Nicaragua conflict in 1957 and 1958, and the Cuba-Panama issue in 1959, the Costa Rica-Honduras-Nicaragua conflict in 1959, and several others in the early 1960s, ad hoc investigating committees were sent to the trouble spot, regardless of the consent of the parties, to gather facts and report back to the council.

The Rio Treaty, created in 1947 at the ebb of support for the inter-American system, was ratified by all the original twenty-one members of the OAS. The new Caribbean members, except for Trinidad and Tobago, shied away from it. Recently, The Commonwealth of the Bahamas ratified it. Amendments updating the treaty were signed in 1975 and have been ratified by seven states. [23]

Authorizing action for the event of armed attack or "an aggression which is not an armed attack . . . or by any other fact or situation that might endanger the peace of the Americas," the treaty (arts. 6-7) gives rather broad powers to the meeting of consultation to take "all . . . necessary measures to . . . maintain inter-American peace and security." The treaty was drafted for collective-security purposes rather than as an instrument for mediation or maintenance of peace. However, Article 7 of the treaty specifies that

> in the case of a conflict between two or more American states . . . [The meeting of Consultation] shall take . . . all other necessary measures to reestablish or maintain inter-American peace and security and for the solution of the conflict by peaceful means.

This clause is the only reference to peaceful settlement of disputes in the midst of a text otherwise devoted exclusively to mutual assistance and common defense. It provided the alternative the governments needed.

In practice, the Rio Treaty has proved remarkably flexible. The ability of the Permanent Council of the OAS to act provisionally as an organ of consultation without actually summoning the foreign ministers has enabled the organization to respond expeditiously. In only eight of the forty-four disputes handled by the OAS have the ministers of foreign affairs been formally convened, two of which were for purposes of preparing amendments to the treaty. In ten cases the Permanent Council set itself up provisionally as a meeting of consultation and never called a full meeting because it resolved the issue before such a meeting was necessary. In almost every case in which the council acted in this manner, it appointed an informal, ad hoc committee to undertake investigations on the scene.

The treaty is about to undergo another radical change that may seriously impair its effectiveness. The July 1975 meeting to amend the treaty proposed that collective-security instruments be separated from peaceful solution of controversies inasmuch as they were two entirely different juridical situations; the proposal was quashed. [24] However, one new amendment did cast doubt on the future efficacy of the Rio Treaty in peacekeeping. A new Article 6 states that the assistance of an organ of consultation "may not be provided without the consent of that state." The clause is reminiscent of the one that sealed the fate of the Inter-American Peace Committee.

Operations of the Inter-American System

The inter-American system for mediating or arbitrating disputes is utilized as follows:

-- Central American and Caribbean disputes are more likely to wind up in the OAS;

-- Attacks by exile groups across borders tend to be referred to the OAS;

-- Most territorial or border disputes do not come to the OAS unless they break out into hostilities;

-- Disputes that break out into hostilities are submitted to the OAS machinery for the purpose of stopping the hostilities, both in South and Central America;

-- Serious disputes between smaller countries and the United States tend to be referred to the OAS.

Furthermore, the tendency to refer conflicts in their early stages to the international mechanism appears to be inversely proportional to the degree of national interests at stake and the size of the country. However, if the conflict escalates to open violence, the regional community generally insists on its jurisdiction, at first through the most informal machinery available.

Of the ninety-four incidents with a potential to erupt into conflict in the thirty-five years since the founding of the OAS, a third found their way into the inter-American machinery, and two-thirds were either resolved or were merely chronic flare-ups of ongoing rivalries, as evidenced by the repetition of incidents between Ecuador and Peru, Argentina and Chile, Costa Rica and Nicaragua, and Cuba and Dominican Republic, which, combined, account for more than a third of the total.

The thirty-three specific disputes referred to the OAS were part of a total of forty-four instances where the OAS' good offices were invoked. Various instruments of mediation were utilized in different periods. For the purposes of this analysis, three periods will be discussed: 1948 to 1956, during which the Inter-American Peace Committee was governed only by its own rules; 1956 to 1965, during which time the Inter-American Peace Committee began operating under a formal statute, until 1965 when the Dominican intervention took place. The last period under discussion is 1965 to date.

In the first eight years, 65 percent of the cases were presented to the Inter-American Peace Committee. In all, sixteen cases were considered under the peace committee, all prior to 1964; eighteen were handled under the Rio Treaty, both by the Permanent Council operating provisionally as an organ of consultation and in full meetings of consultation; and six cases were addressed under the charter. Four cases were considered by ad hoc procedures. The system has resorted to a diverse array of mechanisms, with little in the way of firm criteria distinguishing the applications.

The sixty-one cases that did not find their way to the inter-American system were predominantly territorial disputes in South America. The evidence is clear that the impact of the system on Central America and the Caribbean conflicts was far more profound than in South America. A majority of the interstate conflicts in Central America and the Caribbean came to the OAS, whereas only 13 percent of the disputes from South America were referred to the inter-American mechanism.[25]

Cases involving the United States were particularly interesting in that the smaller countries tended to petition the OAS with their intractable disputes with the United States, such as Ecuador's fishing claims in 1971 and the Panamanian claim regarding the canal. The larger countries, such as Mexico in the Chamizal dispute, relied on bilateral negotiations with the United States. Similarly, the United States decided that its major hemispheric problems should be aired before the hemispheric community during this period, mainly Cuba in 1962 and the Dominican Republic in 1965.

The cause of the dispute appears to be a major variable in determining the role and potential effectiveness of the international system. Border claims were disputed far less frequently--only 14 percent of the cases--than those in which such vital national interests were not at stake. Similarly, the machinery of the system was invoked in only 18 percent of conflicts identified as relating to natural resources. A far more important role was played in conflicts caused by the internationalization of internal power struggles, either by exiles or those involving ideological issues. Seventy-three percent of the cases relating to cross-border exile activity found their way into the inter-American system, as did 44 percent of the ideological problems. All major cases involving asylum in the early years of the system were referred to mediation machinery until the mass-asylum cases of Cubans in the Peruvian and Ecuadorean embassies in Havana in the 1980s.

The extent to which mediation procedures are used in the system depends a great deal upon the definition of mediation. Of the forty-four conflicts of specific OAS action in inter-American disputes, thirty-three of them could be categorized as disputes in which the organization was asked by one of the parties to try to tone down the conflict--mediation for management rather than resolution, according to Touval and Zartman's distinction. Twelve cases could be denominated as formal mediation in the sense that the organization played a clearly articulated role in reaching either a definitive conclusion or a point where the parties were willing to modify bellicose behavior and resume bilateral negotiations. Thus, insofar as the OAS makes its presence felt in trying to bring the parties to terms, it has been an active organization. However, most of the OAS's mediating energies were expended prior to 1965, and most of that dealt with conflicts between exiles fighting their own governments from across borders. In the thirty-four years between 1948 and 1982 the system was called upon forty-four times, of which, as we have noted above, thirty-three arose in the first seventeen years of its existence. In the seventeen years from 1965 to 1982, the OAS heard only eleven cases.

As the inter-American system strived to express itself through the most informal mechanisms available, different utilization patterns are revealed. It will be noted that in the 1948-55 period, almost all the cases went before the peace committee, of which half wound up in actual mediation. In no small measure the assertiveness of the committee during that period was attributed to the forceful leadership of two men: Luis Quintanilla of Mexico and Paul Draper of the United States. [26] In other cases, the Costa Rican claim of a Nicaraguan invasion in 1948 shortly after the Figueres regime came to power, a series of recriminations between the Dominican Republic and Haiti in 1950, the prelude to the Guatemalan revolution in 1954, and another Costa Rica-Nicaragua flare-up in 1955-56, the OAS Council acted provisionally as an organ of consultation, and so the formal meeting under the Rio Treaty was never held. The Inter-American Peace Committee and the OAS Council --acting provisionally--were the only mechanisms needed during this period of intense activity.

After the council adopted the restrictive statute on the Inter-American Peace Committee requiring both parties to a dispute to agree to the jurisdiction of the committee, only two more cases came before the committee under its statute. It undertook five other special investigations (under temporary authority granted by the fifth meeting of consultation in July 1959) on the causes of instability and human rights violations in the Caribbean, but that was the committee's last hurrah. [27]

The peace committee was predominantly used in the problem of exiles and ideological disputes. It was not asked to arbitrate territorial disputes in which other kinds of long-term issues were at stake--except for the Honduras-Nicaragua dispute in 1957 and the ICJ award in the same case in 1962. The reasons for the diminished use of all inter-American machinery after 1968 are not readily apparent except for the changing nature of the interstate conflicts in the Americas. Exile activity, which burgeoned in the post-World War II era, was predominantly directed against some of the old dictatorships. The leaders of these groups were, by nature, more sensitive to the pressures and ideals of the inter-American community. More recently, ideological disputes involving more vital national interests have

come more to the fore. In these sorts of disputes, the
countries apparently chose to tread more gingerly
because the cold war raised questions about the consis-
tency of international assistance with the principles of
self-determination and nonintervention. Of the six
major cases coming before the OAS after 1966, the peacekeeping provisions in the OAS Charter as distinct from
the Rio Treaty were used more frequently than ever
before, with ad hoc procedures continuing to be prevalent in the majority of cases. The major case during
this period was, of course, the El Salvador-Honduras
war, in which a variety of good offices, conciliation,
and mediation efforts were employed. This case will be
examined in more detail below.

The cases invoking the Rio Treaty before 1965
relied exclusively on informal procedures and ad hoc
investigating committees. The committees visited the
scene of the dispute and met directly with the governments involved. In five of the eight cases arbitrated
according to these procedures, more traditional mediation efforts took place, namely the Honduras-Nicaragua
dispute in 1957-58 over border violations, the Nicaragua
dispute with Costa Rica and Honduras over exile activity, the implementation of the terms of the ICJ award in
the Honduras-Nicaragua border dispute, the mutual accusations of exile activities between the Dominican Republic and Haiti in 1963 and, to a considerable extent,
efforts in the breakdown of Panama-U.S. communications
after the 1964 riots. More formal mediation was conducted either by the Inter-American Peace Committee
under its early rules or through ad hoc mechanisms. In
addition, all of these cases except one--the Bolivia-
Chile dispute over the Lauca River--involved the smaller
states of Central America or the Caribbean, and one, the
Panamanian dispute, involved the United States.

The nature of international arbitration machinery
has a great deal to do with the sort of cases submitted.
When parties first agree to accept the system, they know
there is a predetermined response: stop hostilities.
The question is, though, do American nations take steps
toward peaceful resolution of conflicts because of the
presence of the inter-American system, or have they
cooperated to build the system because they are pre-
disposed to such a command, "stop hostilities," in the
first place?

A brief history of peace and conflict would be
useful here. The fifty years prior to 1928 were peaceful ones for the Western Hemisphere. Few interstate
conflicts took place from 1879 (the War of the Pacific)
to 1929 and the initial rumblings of the Chaco War
between Bolivia and Chile. Peace was attributable in
part to the geography and population structure of
Central and South America; virtually no population
centers were near border areas, and transportation

facilities among the countries were quite poor. From 1929 until the outbreak of World War II, however, ten incidents, of which four constituted major conflicts, occurred in both South and Central America. [28]

When wars did break out during this period, the rudiments of the system were in place, but they were not used. As noted above, only the Dominican Republic-Haiti conflict was subjected to the procedures outlined in the inter-American treaties of this period. In all conflicts, however, mediation efforts were significant--nearly all of them ad hoc and outside the formal system. [29] In the ten disputes between 1925 and 1942, thirty-five different countries acted or attempted to act as intermediary. Jorge I. Dominguez examines eleven cases in Central America and two in South America after 1945. A total of sixty-three attempts at mediation were made in these thirteen disputes. [30]

We can observe from this that the tendency to seek peaceful solutions to disputes and to use informal mechanisms predates the OAS; in a sense, the OAS could be considered an expression of that predilection rather than the cause of it. Had that desire not been there, the OAS might not have worked at all. The system might also be described as an instrument expressly and consciously forged by the American states to give them time to find ways out of situations that otherwise could become unmanageable, with the clear reservation that if they, or any one of them, do not want to be helped, the system should not take it upon itself to interfere.

The record and the vigor of the nonintervention principle alongside the peacekeeping machinery, seem to affirm that the nations want a system to preclude hostilities, not necessarily resolve them--one which, like the policeman on the corner, will keep the contending parties at bay, but not enter the substance of their dispute. When the system limits itself to that role, it works. This is vital in determining whether the system holds lessons for other regions of the world or whether it is unique.

The dynamics and the mediating influences have worked differently in various situations. Three types of cases will be examined: mediation in open hostilities, preemptive mediation, and mediation in internal conflicts.

El Salvador-Honduras, 1969: Mediation
of Open Hostilities

Perhaps the most important direct mediation by the OAS occurred in the hostilities between El Salvador and Honduras in 1969, during which a ceasefire was achieved twelve days after the outbreak of hostilities on July 14, 1969.

The conflict was rooted in the economic and social problems afflicting both countries. Rural poverty, maldistribution of land, and growing population prompted a flow of Salvadorans into less-populated Honduras, which responded with legislation to stem the flow of refugees and establish a deportation program. [31]   A violent incident involving fans at the Soccer World Cup elimination in El Salvador caused diplomatic relations to be sundered on June 27, 1969. Immediate assistance in mediation was offered by the other Central American countries associated in the Organization of Central American States (ODECA), but Honduras appealed to the OAS on July 4, 1969, under procedures of both the charter and the Rio Treaty. [32]

The council met immediately, acting provisionally as the organ of consultation, and adopted a resolution expressing confidence in the ODECA mediation attempt and asking both parties to refrain from exacerbating the situation. Tensions continued to mount, however, which resulted in El Salvador's open attack on Honduras on July 14, 1969. [33] Meeting that night in its provisional capacity, the council dispatched a seven-member committee to the area with a broad frame of reference to help the parties reach a ceasefire. [34] The committee traveled immediately as Honduras bombed El Salvador, and 2,500 Salvadoran troops invaded Honduran territory. The council met again on July 15 and requested both parties to restore the situation to the status quo antebellum under Article 7 of the Rio Treaty.

The mediating committee (known as the Committee of Seven), chaired by Ambassador Sevilla Sacasa of Nicaragua, shuttled between the two countries and presented the governments with its own four-point plan on July 17. [35] The plan was aimed at stopping hostilities and assuring human rights protection, meticulously avoiding the substance of the claims. It called for (1) immediate ceasefire; (2) withdrawal of troops within seventy-two hours; (3) assurances of human rights protection from both governments; and (4) the placement of military observers to verify compliance. Inadequate communication between the capitals and the front lines plagued those mediators dealing with a reportedly uncooperative El Salvador. On July 18 when the deadline for acceptance passed without a Salvadoran response, the OAS Council proceeded to adopt a plan essentially identical to the committee's.

Continuing Salvadoran reluctance and armed action caused the council to summon the foreign ministers to a full meeting of the organ of consultation on July 26.[36] The foreign ministers were clearly determined to obtain acceptance of a plan for a ceasefire. They emphatically reminded both parties of their treaty commitments to renounce the use of force and not to honor any territorial gains made as a result of war. Two resolutions

were presented.   One sponsored by twelve countries
clearly pointed at El Salvador as the aggressor.   It
called for strict economic sanctions on El Salvador
unless it restored the status quo antebellum and opened
the door for other OAS members to come to the assistance
of Honduras.   A parallel resolution drafted by El Salvador sought to declare Honduras the aggressor.   When no
other member country endorsed the Salvadoran draft, the
mood of the nations was obvious, and El Salvador declared it would comply with the ceasefire and withdraw
from Honduras.   The final resolution of the July 26
meeting acknowledged the agreement of the parties to
submit their grievances to the procedures of the Pact of
Bogota.   The withdrawal was complete by August 3.
    Two mediation efforts were launched in the con-
flict.   The first included Guatemala, Costa Rica, and
Nicaragua--sister-states with El Salvador and Honduras
in the ODECA--and was initiated by the OAS, which took
up the matter on the appeal of Honduras.   Honduras considered itself the aggrieved party and felt it would
obtain more meaningful support from inter-American
public opinion so as to stem Salvadoran advances.
Because Honduras called for a meeting of consultation
and not for any specific mediation action, El Salvador
could not head off the proceedings.   (This important
procedural point relates to the debates that incessantly
rage around the issue of jurisdiction in the inter-
American system.   It also foreshadows the sorts of
impediments that the 1975 amendments to the Rio Treaty
could erect in mediation efforts.)
    The goals of the OAS mediators were clear and
limited: to establish a ceasefire and to obtain the
withdrawal of troops from occupied territories.   In
that, there was no hedging of bets and no question of
agreement on a complex agenda.   Although the parties
were formally kept apart, with the committee serving as
the principal communicating agent, the foreign affairs
ministers of both countries and their ambassadors met
regularly in OAS meetings.   This effort to bring the
actors together--almost in spite of themselves--was
central to the committee's success.
    The committee met its challenge aggressively.   It
submitted its own substantive proposals, communicating
the reactions to the disputing parties through its own
channels.   The committee then split up and relocated
half of its members to San Salvador, the other half to
Honduras to facilitate communication.   Most important, a
forceful and articulate chairman, Ambassador Sevilla
Sacasa of Nicaragua, understood the political and cultural environment of Honduras.   Consequently, the committee took a calculated risk of interpreting an ambiguous statement by the president of Honduras as a positive response.   On the evening of July 17 this provided
a breakthrough in the negotiations and set the tone for

the final agreement. [37] It was clear that the mediating committee viewed El Salvador as the aggressor and might have passed a resolution to that effect. It eventually abandoned that idea so as to maintain a policy of neutrality. As a mediating agency, the committee sought only to get the nations to agree to ceasefire and troop withdrawal.

Neither the committee nor the OAS was governed by a formal or precise agreement, complete with terms of reference. This, of course, turned out to be an advantage. The basic treaties give them, in effect, the a priori consent of the parties to assume jurisdiction. The range of action for the OAS is delimited by its charter and by the Rio Treaty, under which the meeting of consultation acted. Beyond that, no specific terms of reference, strategy, functions, or procedures were necessary.

The timing of the OAS's action on the Honduras-Salvadoran dispute has been described as coinciding with the exhaustion of financial resources and ammunition of the two countries, both of which were unprepared to fight an unplanned war. [38] The commitment of Honduras, which summoned the meeting of consultation, was made obvious by its initial acceptance of the four-point plan. For the Salvadorans, however, only the threat of OAS-mobilized economic sanctions worked to persuade them to agree to the terms submitted by the committee.

The major lever on the war-weary adversaries was the dual threat of economic sanctions and of assistance to Honduras in the event the terms were not met. The final agreement, reached twelve days after the conflict had started, was on the procedural issues of instituting the ceasefire and troop withdrawal. The agreement studiously avoided mentioning either the merits of the border issue or the conclusion of a peace treaty between the parties (which took another eleven years). The OAS had only one issue to address--regardless of the substance of the dispute--and that was to pressure the parties to resolve it peacefully.

After the ceasefire, developments demonstrated how volatile the clash was and how valuable a continuing institutional presence would be. [39] Border incidents continued--including overflights, airplane hijackings, and skirmishes--any of which could have resulted in a breakdown of the agreement if the OAS had not maintained its jurisdiction. In that sense, the mediating presence of the OAS continued to smooth over the small outbreaks for a considerable period of time until the major flare-up was considered under control and the duties were turned over to ODECA. A demilitarized zone was established around the disputed border. When further disputes arose, the demilitarized zone was widened. When armed conflict erupted again in 1976, the OAS immediately dispatched border patrols to separate the combatants.

Initiatives begun by newly elected Secretary-General Alejandro Orfila in 1976 resulted in the reinitiation of negotiations between the parties. Upon learning that he could not get a commercial flight from San Salvador to Tegucigalpa on his first visit to the two countries, Orfila requested permission for a special flight. Salvadoran Foreign Minister Borgonovo decided to accompany the secretary-general to the Honduran capital, where, meeting in the airport with his Honduran counterpart, the foundation was set for the signing of a mediation agreement on October 6, 1976.

El Salvador's denunciation of the Pact of Bogota on November 26, 1973, meant that an entirely new set of procedures had to be established. The provisions of the mediation agreement required the selection of a mediator by lot from among four names, two submitted by each country. All proceedings were to remain absolutely confidential, and the mediator was expressly forbidden to issue reports or make public statements. In another important provision, the parties agreed not to withdraw until mediation was completed. After that, if one party disapproved, the other could invoke ICJ jurisdiction.

Not much is known about this stage of the mediation because the negotiations were private. Communications were confidential, conducted first through Dr. Jose Luis Bustamante y Riveiro, an eminent octogenerian Peruvian jurist, who was chosen by lot and who soon brought the parties into direct nonpublic negotiation over the issues. The final agreement, signed on October 30, 1980, was followed by a ceremony at the OAS. [40] Much of the border was delimited, standards and procedures were outlined for delimiting the rest, and the parties agreed that the ICJ would rule on any differences.

Pre-emptive Mediation: Two Cases

The Case of Ecuador-Peru. The dispute between Ecuador and Peru exemplifies how international organizations can exercise moderating and mediating influences even when they are not immediately involved. In inter-American meetings Peru has long advocated that no single state should be permitted to bring a dispute before any inter-American body, and it has made reservations to that effect in most of the major treaties. That objection--designed to impede a unilateral Ecuadoran attempt to reopen an old dispute before the larger body--had a profound effect on the nature of the agreements reached among OAS members. [41]

The dispute involved 120,000 square miles of jungle between the Marañon-Amazon and Putumayo rivers, and several early attempts to resolve the issues ended

in failure. The king of Spain sought to arbitrate in
1904, and the United States tried to mediate in 1929,
1933, and 1936.   After skirmishes broke out on the
border in 1941, joint mediation was proffered by the
United States, Argentina, and Brazil. That same year,
the military attaches of the three countries met in Lima
to witness an agreement on the mutual pullback of
troops.   With the third meeting of consultation of
foreign ministers scheduled for Rio in 1942--shortly
after the bombing of Pearl Harbor--both governments were
convinced to sign a treaty on January 29, 1942; it was
ratified by both a month later. The final peace treaty
was guaranteed by four countries--the United States,
Argentina, Brazil, and Chile. One commentator at the
time noted that all the inter-American treaties--the
Gondra Pact, the General Treaties on Conciliation and
Arbitration--which had been ratified by the parties,
"were of no service in facilitating the settlement of
the controversy; as in the Chaco and Leticia affairs, it
was the [informal] inter-American intermediary efforts
that gave abundant evidence of . . . responsibility for
continental peace." [42]
     Relations between the two countries continued to
be plagued by flare-ups. In spite of the agreement,
Ecuador tried again and again to get the OAS to assert
its jurisdiction. The first attempt, in 1955, failed.
However, a 1981 flare-up in which several soldiers were
killed resulted in a meeting of consultation of foreign
affairs ministers.[43] The meeting issued a request for
action by the guarantors under the 1942 pact, thereby
inherently reaffirming the community's commitment to the
terms of the pact. Although Peru was satisfied with
this implicit reaffirmation, Ecuador was also pleased in
that it had succeeded in establishing the principle
that, should hostilities with Peru break out, recourse
to the larger hemispheric body was available.   The
predominant moderating influence in this case was the
stark fact of the availability of international
machinery. It greatly helped the governments to control
a highly emotional and volatile situation.

     Guatemala and Belize.   The role of the inter-
American system in claims relating to former British
colonies is of a qualitatively different nature than
those of other inter-American disputes; Argentina and
the Malvinas Islands, the Venezuelan claims to the
Esequibo region of Guyana, and the Guatemalan claims
regarding territory in Belize.   All disputes affect
vital national interests, and--as with the Malvinas in
1982--no one necessarily turns to the inter-American
system as a mediator.   The Argentines called upon the
system to demonstrate the solidarity of Latin American
nations in the face of a European power, as Guatemala
has tried to do in various ways on previous occasions.

In each case, Article 8 of the OAS Charter blocks membership for any new applicant as long as it has a territorial dispute with an OAS member.

Problems arising from these long, smoldering disputes were in evidence at the 1948 Bogota Conference, at which the OAS Charter was signed. Referring to a proposed Guatemalan resolution denouncing European colonies in America, U.S. Secretary of State George Marshall then stated:

> The policy of the United States of America in regard to European colonies in the Western Hemisphere has been one of opposition to the extension of such colonies or of European political influence in this Hemisphere. . . .
>
> With respect to the current disputes under discussion here, the Delegation of the United States would feel compelled to refrain from supporting any resolution which would appear to prejudge the conflicting claims of friendly nations. It is the hope of the United States Delegation that the interested parties will redouble their efforts to seek equitable solutions based on law and justice, and in conformity with our highest inter-American traditions and ideals. [44]

The Brazilian delegation declared, at the same time, that it considered an inter-American conference "not an appropriate forum for debating a question that affects the interests of countries outside the continent." [45]

The Guatemalan-Belize dispute is an important example because it demonstrates how the effectiveness of an international organization depends on its own direct actions and also its passive position as a place where parties can test the opinion of their fellow members. On several occasions Guatemala has notified the OAS of hostile British troop movements, but OAS opinion is increasingly opposed to hostile actions against Belize. [46] The issue--basically one of Guatemalan claims over Belize--has been discussed in reviewing the agenda items for the OAS General Assembly. [47] A lack of unequivocal support of the members for the Guatemalan claim, in contrast to the Malvinas situation, has been another type of moderating influence.

In 1972 Guatemala brought a draft resolution on a threat to peace to the second General Assembly of the OAS immediately after its secret negotiations with Great Britain had broken off. [48] Guatemala then asserted its claim to all of Belize, which caused Great Britain to

reinforce its local garrison. This prompted the Guate-
malans to call for a declaration of solidarity with
Guatemala, claiming the presence of an armed threat from
British forces in the territory.

Because the immediate flare-up was rooted in the
assertion of British troop reinforcements, the issue was
taken up immediately by the General Assembly, which was
chaired by Jose A. Mora, former secretary-general of the
OAS and then-foreign minister of Uruguay. He teamed
with Secretary-General Galo Plaza, and they offered
their good offices to the parties. They arranged for a
meeting in their presence between Dr. Roberto Herrera-
Ibarguen, minister of foreign affairs of Guatemala, and
the Earl of Cromer, British ambassador to the United
States, which Dr. Mora reported on in his meeting with
the General Assembly on April 21, 1972.[49] Citing the
desire of both governments to resume negotiations, Dr.
Mora affirmed the need of the organization to verify the
withdrawal of the troops and asked the OAS to accept the
British invitation to send an observer to Belize for
that purpose. The OAS General Assembly's final resolution established the precedent for an OAS presence in
the case--an issue which was contested by the new Caribbean members, Trinidad, Jamaica, and Barbados--and
directed the secretary-general to send the requested
observer.[50]

A Colombian general, dispatched to the area on May
1, 1972, had precise written instructions to keep the
mission completely nonpolitical.[51] He undertook the
mission with the acquiescence of the Guatemalan
government but was responsible solely to the OAS General
Assembly. His report to the Permanent Council on June
7, 1972, gave full details of the British troops and
affirmed that, in his opinion, the forces were not a
threat to the peace and security of Guatemala. Although
the legality of the OAS's action was contested by some
member states, it satisfied both Guatemala and Great
Britain, which responded to the OAS initiative and
allowed the observer to move decisively within a matter
of days. Within two months, the parties were able to
resume negotiations.

In this sense, the mediation was successful in
bringing the parties back to the negotiating table. But
the organization clearly avoided the role of a mediator
in the larger dispute, leaving the major issues unad-
dressed. Further flare-ups occurred in 1975 and 1977
prior to the independence of Belize in 1981 and again
after independence in 1982. The July 1975 flare-up was
again brought to the attention of the OAS Permanent
Council by Guatemala, but there was no request for
action.[52] Similarly, in late June 1977 rumors of
imminent independence for Belize caused a buildup of
Guatemalan troops and led to a parallel buildup by the
British in Belize. Guatemala's permanent representative

to the OAS again officially notified the Permanent
Council, and OAS officials acted informally to bring
Foreign Minister Molina Orantes of Guatemala together in
a secret session at OAS headquarters with the British
minister of state for foreign affairs, Edward Rowlands,
on July 6 and 7, 1977.[53] The talks allayed Guatemala's
fears and led both parties to undertake immediate measures to decrease the tension in the area.

The complexities of the issue continue. The
Inter-American Juridical Committee, which handles
juridical matters for the OAS, issued a declaration
supporting Guatemala.[54] On the other hand, the
Caribbean states are actively seeking to eliminate the
restrictions barring full OAS membership for Belize,
whose formal application for admission came two days
after its independence on September 21, 1981.[55] But, on
the initiative of the Belizean government, discussion of
Belize's application was temporarily postponed soon
after a vote of 24-1 to maintain it on the agenda. As a
result, the eleventh General Assembly in 1981 resolved
to restudy the question of Article 8 to the Charter,[56]
which could have important implications in the Belizean
case as well as in that of Venezuela's claims on Guyana.
The organization followed up this approach when Belize
was invited as an observer to the twelfth regular session of the General Assembly in 1982. In all cases, the
overwhelming approval of the member states to take cog-
nizance of the issue and not to support Guatemalan mili-
tancy conveys messages that would be difficult, if not
impossible, to do without the presence of the international machinery.

Mediation in Issues of Ideology: The Terrorist Wars

Can the international system deal with violence
resulting from pressures for internal political change?
If so, how? As noted above, when violence spills across
national borders through the activity of exiles, as it
did frequently during the 1950s, the OAS was able to
address international aspects of the issue. These
groups frequently advocated principles of democracy that
were consistent with and amenable to regionally applied
pressures. With communications and transportation getting to be more and more accessible, however, ideological elements (with power bases in other areas of the
world) are becoming more complex. As the availability
and easy transport of weapons from multiple sources
increases international implications, so does the difficulty of containing inter-American conflicts to the
hemisphere.

One result will be increasing tension in the
"rival" roles of regional and global international
organizations, especially the OAS and the United

Nations.   Because the Soviet Union's interests are
expressed predominantly in the United Nations, the issue
of alternative peacekeeping instruments on a regional
and global level has become an extension of the ideological battle.   It thus requires a separate examination, and may require a different type of mediation of
its own. [57]

Ideological conflicts in the Americas fall into
two categories: (1) ideological threats carried across
national borders, and (2) localized, domestic threats,
or so-called terrorist and guerrilla wars.

Beginning in 1964 with Brazil, followed by
Argentina, Uruguay, Venezuela, Colombia, Nicaragua, and
now El Salvador, the internal terrorist wars have not
been subject to the traditional precepts of international law.   Although distinctions between international
and civil wars are set forth in the U.N. Charter, little
is said about internal conflicts with obvious but complex linkages to other states.   The blurred lines are
not clarified either by the tendency of the parties to
such conflicts to use the rhetoric of international
law--without any relationship to the substance of the
dispute.

The precursor to these events was the 1954
revolution in Guatemala, followed by the 1960 revolution
in Cuba, the 1965 intervention in the Dominican Republic, and civil wars in Nicaragua and El Salvador in
recent years.   The United States was a major actor in
each of these disputes.   Mediation was not a factor in
the early cases.   It was tried briefly in 1954 when
Guatemala went to the Inter-American Peace Committee,
and a group of nations then asked the OAS to act under
the Rio Treaty.   But the action was too late; the Arbenz
government was overthrown before the matter could be
considered.   Because the cases involving Cuba were
defined as issues of collective security, this was
placed in a different context in the international
machinery.

The recent experiences of the inter-American
system, such as the situation of Nicaragua in 1979, are
noteworthy for the emergence of a new, informal mechanism: the Inter-American Commission on Human Rights.
Its report on Nicaragua's serious human rights violations was principally responsible for OAS action in the
seventeenth meeting of consultation; also important was
the direct action of the Andean nations, which sought a
direct mediating role of their own. [58] On the same human
rights grounds, the OAS Council moved to consider the
July 17, 1980, coup d'état in Bolivia at the behest of
Colombia, Ecuador, Peru, and Venezuela.   The OAS
"deplored" the coup, along with the United States and
Mexico, and the consequent violations of human rights,
asking the Inter-American Commission on Human Rights to
examine the situation. [59]

The commission might be used with greater frequency in these types of cases because of another "informal" mechanism--a clause in the new Inter-American Convention of Human Rights that allows the commission to "place itself at the disposition of the parties . . . with a view to reaching a friendly settlement." One interesting request initiated in September 1982 under this article came from the government of Nicaragua. It requested assistance from the commission in its politically sensitive difficulties with the Meskite Indians, authorizing the commission to make contact with the Meskitos and to devise a solution for their grievances.

The commission's potential may be best observed in its resolution of the seizure of the Dominican embassy by a guerrilla force in Bogota. On February 27, 1980, guerrillas from an organization called M-19 took more than fifty hostages during a reception at the Dominican Republic embassy. Their initial demands included a ransom of $50 million in return for the hostages and the release of more than 200 alleged political prisoners.[60] The Colombian government and the guerrilla group negotiated for four weeks without success. On April 1, in response to certain allegations by Amnesty International--the Colombian government formally asked the commission to undertake an on-site investigation of human rights violations in Colombia. Although the invitation referred exclusively to the commission's bilateral agreement with the government of Colombia, it was subsequently revealed that the invitation was insisted upon by the guerrillas.[61]

The commission delegation arrived in Bogota on April 21, meeting first with the president and the next day with the leaders of the guerrilla group inside the Dominican embassy. The commission firmly stated to both parties that its role had to correspond to the functions authorized under its jurisdiction, and that, accordingly, it would not be a mediator. However, regardless of the semantics, it would do whatever it could to find a solution to the problem within this context.

Within several days of their arrival, the delegation produced a written proposal outlining settlement terms. An exchange of letters between the commission and the government of Colombia, stating their mutual understanding, would constitute an agreement between those parties. The letters would thereupon be shown to the guerrillas, who would indicate their concurrence.

The letters verified that the Colombian government would authorize the commission to carry out an on-site investigation with full freedom to contact any alleged political prisoners being tried in the courts-marshall. The government also would agree to allow the commission to observe the courts-marshall to assure that they were being conducted in accordance with law, as well as to investigate any complaints in connection with the

trials, especially those in which "proof may have been
obtained by means that clearly violate human rights so
that if the violations were proven, the individuals
affected may challenge the validity of the verdict." [62]
The letter from the Colombian government concluded by
stating:

> The members of the Inter-American Commission
> on Human Rights may serve as guarantors vis-
> à-vis the individuals who took over the
> premises of the Embassy of the Dominican
> Republic, of the Government's strict compli-
> ance with all clauses of this letter which
> takes effect immediately as far as the
> executive is concerned.

The reply of the commission the following day
confirmed its willingness to accept the role outlined by
the government. When both of the communications were
sent to the guerrilla group, they replied with a letter
stating their understanding that the exchange of notes
between the Colombian government and the Human Rights
Commission "represents to us a full guarantee that our
comrades-in-arms being held prisoner, accused of crimes
of a political nature, will receive the protection of
your commission." [63]
This device of an exchange of letters was
important in enabling the commission to articulate the
needs of both parties without calling for direct
confrontation.
That the guerrillas sought to involve the Inter-
American Commission so as to guarantee fair trials and
gain greater international awareness of their plight was
clear from the start, although the terms they finally
accepted were substantially different from those originally proposed. The Colombian government also had good
reason to desire the commission's intervention. Cries
of human rights violations from private human rights
groups--strongly denied by the government--were embar-
rassing. [64] The commission's presence was thus regarded
as instrumental in repairing the damage done by the
reports. This motivation is clearly reflected in the
April 1 letter from Colombia's foreign affairs minister
to the chairman of the commission, in which he invited
the commission to come to Colombia, stating: "In particular, we wish to move ahead with the investigation
. . . as a result of the report of Amnesty International; it is our obligation to make the veracity of
these investigations clear. . . . We wish you to see
for yourselves the impartiality with which they were
conducted." [65] The decision of the Colombian government
is also thought to have been affected by the stalled

negotiations. The outcome enabled the Colombian government to defuse both the internationally sensitive hostage situation and the accusations of human rights violations without compromising its position against the
release of any political prisoners. For the guerrillas,
the compromise facilitated their safe conduct out of the
country and provided them with a face-saving device to
release the hostages without harm.

International machinery for mediation and concili-
ation--as reflected in the inter-American regional sys-
tem--seems most effective when the following conditions
are in place:

1.   an informal, noncompulsory negotiating
environment;

2.   contending parties can be separated in
order to gain time and avoid hostilities;

3.   the availability of nonthreatening and
flexible procedures;

4.   hostilities have already broken out;

5.   both parties have a fundamental respect
for the premises and principles of the OAS;
and

6.   any nation may place a "threat to peace"
on the agenda: Limiting international jurisdiction to cases in which the contending
parties both agree is equivalent to a veto
power and emasculates the leverage of international efforts.

The system's ability to respond credibly to outbreaks of violence is its most important source of leverage. In this way it can effectively mobilize international pressures when they are most needed. Its ability
to provide an immediate hearing to an aggrieved party,
to dispatch ad hoc observers to the scene of problems,
and to throw the spotlight on lawlessness and human
rights abuses make it a force in the internal decision-
making process of any country. Thus, it institutional-
izes the opportunity to resolve disputes. The reality
of the national political processes, with which it must
work, preclude it from being turned into a rigid
requirement.
    In contrast to traditional mediation, interna-
tional organization reflects the nations' desire for
pre-established machinery that will help avoid the
uncertainties of ad hoc arrangements in the heat of
conflict. In many cases, machinery motivates nations to

mediate their own conflicts. Thus, the international
machinery is most useful not for any action of its own,
but just because it exists. It is, in reality, a type
of safety net. The Brazilian foreign minister, comment-
ing on the Beagle Channel dispute between Argentina and
Chile, made the point that for such disputes, the
nations are grateful for the Rio Treaty and its provisions for the status quo antebellum. Costa Rica states
repeatedly that it owes its national existence to the
OAS since it has disbanded its internal army.

In the last analysis, there are no neat boxes into
which these cases can be placed. International machinery cannot be perceived apart from the governments that
vote on whether and how to use it. Its credibility is
highly sensitive to a fundamental international reality:
consensus among its members. The inability to act where
cleavage exists among member states, and its difficulties in the face of willful national leaders and ideological confrontations delineate its role.

But in all instances, regional networks play a
vital, if intangible, role in modifying the behavior of
nations. They gain time to marshal pressures and
influence national decision-making during the heat of
confrontation. And, while they may not be able to
resolve the underlying issues, they can influence events
so as to avoid escalation.

While there is still some way to go for the
agencies to become, in Yeats's words, "a center that
will hold," the experience of the inter-American
regional system has set clear and important signposts as
to what we must look for: an institutional base that
eliminates time-consuming scrambling in the heat of
conflict, a set of overriding principles rooted in the
status quo antebellum to remove any claim of legitimacy
from resort to force, a flexible mechanism which allows
room for improvisation according to the nature of the
grievances, and the firm political will of the strongest
members of the community to use and abide by the deliberations of the institution. Such an organization,
using this sort of framework, can be an important
instrument in eradicating some dangerous international
flashpoints.

Chapter 7: Notes

1.   The documentation relating to the observations in this
introductory overview is contained in the text below. For a
general review of the history of the inter-American system, see M.
Margaret Ball, The OAS in Transition (Durham: Duke University
Press, 1969); Ann Van Wynen Thomas and A. J. Thomas, Jr., The
Organization of American States (Dallas: Southern Methodist Univer-
sity Press, 1963); Charles G. Fenwick, The Organization of American
States (Washington D.C.: Kaufman, 1963); and the Inter-American
Institute of International Legal Studies, The Inter-American System
(New York: Oceana, 1966).

2.   Jorge I. Dominguez, "Ghosts from the Past,"
unpublished paper presented to the OAS (May 18, 1977). See, for
example, "U.S. Now Backing Guatemalan Loans" in New York Times,
October 10, 1982.

3.   For a discussion of the human rights issues in the
resolution of disputes see Kenneth R. Lee, "Peacekeeping and Human
Rights," University of Virginia Journal of International Law 22
(1982): 293-343.

4.   Joseph S. Nye, Peace in Parts (Boston: Little, Brown &
Co., 1971), 130. See Nye's arguments that "regional organizations
. . . contribute small but useful pieces to the puzzle of peace,"
with its capacity to "isolate" and thereby "contain" conflicts, at
p. 133.

5.   Richard J. Bloomfield, "The Inter-American System," in
The Future of the Inter-American System, Tom J. Farer, ed. (New
York: Praeger, 1979), 8. See also Ball, The OAS in Transition, 14,
15, 172, 584; Thomas, The OAS, 15, 157ff. An excellent general
discussion of the origins of the inter-American system is found in
Arthur P. Whitaker, The Western Hemisphere Idea (Ithaca: Cornell
University Press, 1954).

6.   C. Neale Ronning, Law and Politics in Inter-American
Diplomacy (New York: John Wiley & Sons, 1963), 64.

7.   Mary Jeanne Reid Martz, "OAS Reforms and the Future of
Pacific Settlement," Latin American Research Review 12 (1977): 177.

8.   Stephan M. Gorman, "Present Threats to Peace in South
America," Inter-American Economic Affairs 33 (1979): 69.

9.   Alberto Lleras Camargo, The Inter-American Way of Life
(Washington D.C.: Pan American Union, 1951), 6-7; Inis L. Claude,
"The OAS, the U.N., and the United States," International
Conciliation 547 (1964), 6; Aida Luisa Levin, The OAS and the U.N.
(New York: UNITAR, 1974), 4ff. See also Thomas, The OAS, 31.

10.   Report of the Stockholm International Peace Research Institute (SIPRI). Reported by United Press International, August 16, 1979. See also Washington Post, January 3, 1977, citing a Brookings Institution study of deployment of U.S. military forces since World War II. Of 215 instances cited, 55 were the result of incidents in the Western Hemisphere. See also El Tiempo (Bogota, Colombia), September 15, 1981, 68; New York Times, November 23, 1980; Miami Herald, March 26, 1981, 14.

11.   Gorman, "Present Threats to Peace in South America," 53, 66. See also Dominguez, "Ghosts from the Past," 14, 21, 25.

12.   Bryce Wood, The United States and Latin American Wars, 1932-1942 (New York: Columbia University Press, 1966), 7.

13.   A full listing of the treaties and conventions will be found in Inter-American Treaties and Conventions, Treaty Series No. 9 (Washington D.C.: Organization of American States, 1980); J. Lloyd Mecham, The U.S. and Inter-American Security: 1889-1960 (Austin: University of Texas Press, 1961).

14.   Nye, Peace in Parts, 6.

15.   Ball, The OAS in Transition, 430; Fenwick, The OAS, 196.

16.   Ball, The OAS in Transition, 427. See also John C. Dreier, The Organization of American States and the Hemisphere Crisis (New York: Harper and Row, 1962), 37.

17.   Fenwick, The OAS, 198, 203.

18.   Dreier, The OAS, 38.

19.   Fenwick, The OAS, 204.

20.   Report of the Inter-American Peace Committee to the Second Special Inter-American Conference, OEA/ Ser. L/III/II.11 (March 31, 1965), 2, 3, 6 (emphasis added).

21.   Report of the Inter-American Peace Committee, 7, 8, 14.

22.   Minutes of the Permanent Council of the OAS, OEA/Ser. G/CP-38/71 (January 29, 1971).

23.   As of June 1982, the amendments to the Rio Treaty were ratified by Brazil, Costa Rica, Dominican Republic, Guatemala, Haiti, Mexico, and the United States. Guatemala and the U.S. made reservations.

24.   This was the position of the Peruvian delegation. Martz, "OAS Reforms," 178.

25. Dominguez, "Ghosts from the Past," at 12 and 18, for further observations on this phenomenon. See also Wolf Grabendorff, "Interstate Conflict Behavior and Regional Potential for Conflict in Latin America," Journal of Interamerican Studies and World Affairs 24 (1982): 267-94.

26. Conversations with Ambassador John Dreier.

27. Resolution IV of the Fifth Meeting of Consultation of the Ministers of Foreign Affairs (August 1959). The special powers were specified as "temporary" until the 11th INCAS could take formal action.

28. All of these incidents are discussed in Mecham, The U.S. and Inter-American Security.

29. Wood, "How Wars End in Latin America," The Annals of the American Academy of Political and Social Science (November 1970), 42.

30. Jorge I. Dominguez, "Mice That Do Not Roar: Some Aspects of International Politics in the World's Periphery," International Organization 25 (1971): 193.

31. New York Times, July 16, 1969, 12; July 20, 1969, 16. See also L.T.G., "A Microcosmic View of the OAS: The Honduras-El Salvador Conflict," Virginia Law Review 57 (1971): 291-314.

32. Inter-American Treaty of Reciprocal Assistance: Applications, vol. II (Washington D.C.: Organization of American States, 1973), 269ff (hereafter referred to as Applications).

33. New York Times, July 15, 1969, 1. Final Report of the Mission of Military Observers Established by the Thirteenth Meeting of Consultation of Ministers of Foreign Affairs, OEA/Ser. G/CP-1205/81 (October 26, 1981), 34 (hereafter referred to as the Final Report of the Mission of Military Observers).

34. The terms of reference of the committee were not cast in terms of mediation. They were given a broad mandate to "study on the spot the situation that has arisen between Honduras and El Salvador and the events that have caused it and to report to the Council. . . ." Minutes of the Meeting of the Council of the OAS, July 14, 1969 (OEA/Doc. c-a-713); Applications, vol. II, 282; Reports of the Committee: Organization of American States, Report of the Committee of the Council, Doc. OEA/Ser. F/ II.13/7 (July 26, 1969) (hereafter, Report of the OAS Committee). Subsequent reports of the committee provide full details. These are: Second Report, Doc. 55, October 27, 1969; Third Report, Doc. 67, November 4, 1969; Fourth Report, Doc. 72, December 13, 1969; Fifth Report, Doc. 83, January 27, 1970; Sixth Report, Doc. 92, February 9, 1970; Seventh Report, Doc. 94, March 19, 1970.

35.   Applications, vol. II, 285, 290, 292, 295.

36.   Applications, vol. II, 322, 326, 329, 353; vol. III, 17; Final Report of the Mission of Military Observers, 35; New York Times, July 30, 1969, 1.

37.   These observations were based on interviews with members of the committee. See also Applications, vol. II, 291; OAS Doc. OEA/Ser. F/II.13/18 (July 29, 1969).

38.   Wood, "How Wars End in Latin America," 50; Fifth Report of the OAS Committee, OEA/Ser. F/II.13/83 (January 27, 1970), and Seventh Report of the OAS Committee, OEA Ser. F/II.13/94 (March 19, 1970); New York Times, July 18, 1969, 3; Washington Post, July 15, 1969, 14.

39.   New York Times, August 13, 1969, 18; November 14, 1969, 12; January 31, 1970, 13; February 8, 1970, 14.

40.   Applications, vol. III, pt. 2, 3; text of treaty is contained in Final Report on the Mission of Military Observers, 99.

41.   Martz, "OAS Reforms," 182.

42.   Mecham, The U.S. and Inter-American Security, 170; Wood, The U.S. and Latin American Wars, 255ff.

43.   OEA Doc./Ser. G/CP Acta 450/81 (January 28-29, 1981).

44.   Report of the U.S. Delegation to the Inter-American Conference for the Maintenance of Continental Peace and Security (Washington D.C.: U.S. Government Printing Office, 1948), 57, 88ff (hereafter, Report of U.S. Delegation).

45.   Report of U.S. Delegation, 86.

46.   OAS Doc. OEA/Ser. G/CP-1197/81, 24; OEA/Ser. P/AG/CP-297/81 (October 16, 1981).

47.   Report of the Preparatory Committee on the Draft Agenda for the Eleventh Regular Session of the General Assembly; OEA/Ser. P/AG/CP-297/81 (October 16, 1981).

48.   OEA/Ser. P/AG/Comm I/Doc. 5/72 (April 14, 1972); Washington Post; May 11, 1972, H51; New York Times, June 28, 1972, 2.

49.   OEA/Ser. P/AG/Acta 46/72 (April 21, 1972), 54-55.

50.   OEA/Ser. P/AG/Comm I/Acta 6/72 (April 20, 1972), 15, 29. See Res. 79 OASGA II-0/72 (April 21, 1972).

51.   OEA/Ser. G/CP/Acta 74/72, Anexo I (June 7, 1972), 3, 45ff.

52.   OEA/Ser. G/CP/Inf. 746/75 (November 9, 1975).

53.   New York Times, July 7, 1977, 6; OEA Ser. G/CP/Inf. 1162/77 (July 8, 1977).

54.   OEA/Ser. G/CP-935/79 (March 5, 1979). Cf. Seymour J. Rubin, "The Falklands (Malvinas), International Law, and the OAS," American Journal of International Law 76 (1982): 594.

55.   OEA/Ser. G/CP-1197/81 (October 2, 1981); OEA/Ser. G/CP/Acta 465/81 (September 23, 1981).

56.   AG Res. 541 (XI-O/81), Eleventh General Assembly (St. Lucia, December 1981).

57.   For a fuller discussion, see Levin, The OAS and the U.N.

58.   Report on the Situation of Human Rights in the Republic of Nicaragua, OEA/Ser. L/V/II.45, Doc. 16.

59.   OEA/CP-431/80 (July 24, 1980); OEA/CP-432/80 (July 25, 1980).

60.   Washington Post, February 28, 1980, 1.

61.   Washington Post, April 26, 1980, 22.

62.   Report on the Situation of Human Rights in the Republic of Colombia, OEA/Ser. L/V/II.53, Doc. 22 (June 30, 1981), 10 (hereafter Report on Colombia); Washington Post, April 22, 1980.

63.   Report on Colombia, 14.

64.   Washington Post, April 25, 1980, 30.

65.   Report on Colombia, 1. Sixteen negotiating sessions were held between February 27 and April 21. See Inter-American Commission on Human Rights, Diez Anos de Actividades, 1971-1981 (Washington D.C.: Organization of American States, 1982), 85.

8.
HUMANITARIAN MEDIATION BY THE INTERNATIONAL COMMITTEE OF THE RED CROSS

David P. Forsythe

The International Committee of the Red Cross (ICRC) is an independent, all-Swiss component of the International Red Cross. Over time this first of all Red Cross agencies has become the primary Red Cross actor in situations of political and armed conflict. Other agencies of the International Red Cross, such as the National Red Cross and the League of Red Cross, handle natural disasters and social work. The ICRC, in its role of representing the Red Cross network in political and armed conflict, disclaims any official role as a mediator. Nevertheless, in a number of ways the ICRC practices humanitarian mediation, even as it seeks to avoid political mediation. And at times humanitarian and political mediation become intertwined. Hence, it is appropriate to consider how the ICRC experience contributes to an understanding of mediation, while keeping in mind that the ICRC practices a unique form of mediation. [1]

At the outset it bears emphasizing that the ICRC eschews the label of mediator. Currently, the organization has no official policy on the subject. Its collective policymaking body, the assembly, has not pronounced an opinion on the matter, and neither its president nor any other member of its professional staff has articulated a policy in regard to mediation. When ICRC officials are asked about mediation they refer to a 1941

David P. Forsythe is professor of political science at the University of Nebraska at Lincoln. He has served as a consultant with the International Red Cross, and his book on the International Committee of the Red Cross is entitled <u>Humanitarian Politics</u> (Baltimore: The Johns Hopkins Press, 1977). He has written other books dealing with human rights and American foreign policy.

233

statement by Max Huber, the distinguished Swiss jurist and former ICRC president. That statement says, in effect, that the Red Cross has never been so adventurous as to interpose itself in political conflicts likely to endanger peace, nor between belligerents to get them to cease hostilities. Four reasons are given for this position. First, it is rare for a conflict to occur in which the only obstacle to peace is a neutral person or institution. Second, institutions already exist for the peaceful resolution of disputes--i.e., conciliation commissions, panels of arbitration, general-purpose international organizations, and the World Court. Third, the ICRC has no "political" influence to exert in the mediation process. Fourth, the ICRC often lacks knowledge of the overall situation needed for choosing the most opportune time and the most appropriate suggestions for successful mediation. [2]

Webster's New World Dictionary of the American Language, College Edition, defines mediation as: "intercession or friendly intervention, usually by consent or invitation, for settling differences between persons, nations, etc." Although a former ICRC official recently took exception to an academic who had presented the ICRC as a general mediator, if Webster's meaning is kept in mind, one can see that the ICRC practices what can be called "humanitarian" mediation. [3]

The "elastic clause" is a starting point for understanding the rules governing ICRC action. According to the statutes of the International Red Cross, the ICRC can take "any humanitarian initiative which comes within its role as a specifically neutral and independent institution and intermediary and [can consider] any question requiring examination by such an institution."[4] This so-called humanitarian right of initiative can lead, and indeed has led, to friendly intercession, usually by consent, for settling humanitarian differences between persons and nations. A few historical examples demonstrate the process.

In the Spanish civil war of the 1930s, which occurred when there was no treaty covering internal war, ICRC delegate Marcel Junod first tried to get the fighting parties to agree to stop shooting hostages. As he was in the country with the consent of the various authorities, he undertook an effort to resolve this humanitarian problem affecting both sides. This attempt to fashion an agreement failed. Later, however, Junod was able, again on his own initiative, to get the Republicans and Nationalists to agree to exchanges of prisoners--first involving Spaniards and then foreign combatants such as Russians and Germans. Junod, in effect, mediated these and other particular problems. He never sought to mediate the political problems at issue in the Spanish civil war such as who exercised authority. He and the other ICRC personnel restricted

themselves to such humanitarian or human rights issues
as prisoners, the sick and wounded, the missing, neutral
zones and emblems, and repatriation.   On these latter
issues the ICRC sought to resolve problems between
individuals and the authorities, and between the two
competing authorities themselves. [5]
    One can see the same process at work during World
War II. Despite the fact that considerable treaty law
had been developed by that time to protect the human
rights of sick and wounded combatants and prisoners of
war, the ICRC found the international law of war failed
to cover all humanitarian concerns. The ICRC tried to
fill these lacunae by, in effect, mediating the problems. For example, the ICRC took the initiative to
secure an agreement among the belligerents concerning
the naval transfer of prisoners of war, an agreement
involving advance notification of routes for ships
marked by the ICRC emblem. [6] The ICRC also was able to
obtain an agreement to treat some interned civilians
analogous to prisoners of war. Unfortunately, the ICRC
was not able to apply this agreement to the vast majority of interned civilians nor to negotiate its way into
German concentration camps.

ICRC Tasks

    In discussing humanitarian mediation by the ICRC,
one needs to recall a few points about the branch of
international law called humanitarian law, or human
rights in armed conflict, which affects the way in which
the ICRC protects and assists persons adversely affected
by political and armed conflict.
    One way to look at ICRC activity is to say that it
has conventional and extraconventional tasks. The term
"conventional" refers to treaties such as the Geneva
Convention of August 12, 1949, and its two additional
protocols in 1977. Under this conventional or treaty
law, the ICRC is given certain rights, and states are
obligated to carry out certain duties.
    The ICRC also acts outside the scope of this law
regulating armed conflict. In this sense, part of its
activity is extraconventional. Since World War II much
and perhaps most of ICRC activity has been directed
toward protecting and assisting political prisoners--
that is, persons detained by reason of political events
and not covered by the international law of armed
conflict. To a much lesser extent the ICRC has been
involved in other situations such as political hijackings and kidnappings.
    In the area of conventional tasks, the most spe-
cific mandate of legal authority to the ICRC concerns
visits to prisoners of war and detained civilians

protected in international armed conflict. The Third
Geneva Convention of 1949, Article 126, states:

> Representatives or delegates of the Protecting
> Powers [neutral states appointed by the bel-
> ligerents to help implement humanitarian law]
> shall have permission to go to all places of
> internment, imprisonment and labour, and shall
> have access to all premises occupied by pris-
> oners of war; they shall also be allowed to go
> the places of departure, passage and arrival
> of prisoners who are being transferred. They
> shall be able to interview the prisoners, and
> in particular the prisoners' representatives,
> without   witnesses,   either   personally   or
> through an interpreter.
>
>   . . .
>
> The delegates of the International Committee
> of the Red Cross shall enjoy the same preroga-
> tives.   The appointment of such delegates
> shall be submitted to the approval of the
> Power detaining the prisoners of war to be
> visited [emphasis added]. [7]

Similar language in the Fourth Geneva Convention
(Article 143) covers detained civilians. With regard,
therefore, to such persons in armed conflict, the ICRC,
according to law, does not need to engage initially in
mediation but may demand to see these protected persons.
In other words, detaining authorities are legally obligated to accept the offer of the ICRC to help authorities implement the law to which they have agreed. [8]
    In all other situations covered by the law of
armed conflict, including internal as well as international war, the ICRC is not given specific rights.
Rather, it is given the general right to offer its
services for humanitarian tasks.   Thus, beyond the
specific right to visit privately with persons who are
detained in international armed conflict, the ICRC must
negotiate to carry out its humanitarian tasks.   For
example, the ICRC must, in effect, mediate to change
detention policies. Although the Geneva Conventions and
Protocols require detaining authorities to meet certain
standards pertaining to hygiene, nutrition, medical and
religious services, the judicial system, repatriation,
communication, and so forth, the law is not self-
executing. There are always questions about how much is
enough, and whether security or the economic condition
makes legal standards moot.   Since the ICRC is not a
court, it must, in effect, mediate between detainee and

captor or sometimes between belligerents in order to secure the most humane conditions practicable.

The existence of humanitarian law does give the ICRC a legal standard to which it can appeal in this mediating process. From the ICRC's point of view, this is the most important contribution of the Geneva Conventions. Fighting parties do not usually appoint Protecting Powers (perhaps because they do not formally declare war); similarly, they do not usually contest the right of the ICRC to see detained persons. (North Vietnamese authorities constituted an exception to this pattern during the Vietnam War. More recently, the ICRC has been denied access to detainees in Afghanistan, the Ogaden, and Western Sahara.) But belligerents may give access to the ICRC but disagree with the ICRC regarding whether the legal standards have been met. It is in the ensuing mediation that appeals to humanitarian law can be helpful.

The ICRC does not have a legal foundation for its extraconventional activity, which primarily concerns political prisoners. In the 1970s and early 1980s the ICRC visited political prisoners in about forty countries every year. Because there is no international law covering these prisoners, the ICRC must exercise its right of initiative to gain access. Once in a position to mediate on behalf of detainees, it appeals to the unwritten moral standard of humanitarian norms supposedly adhered to by all civilized, responsible men and women. It appeals to what is reasonable, moral, just, or simply in accordance with what the ICRC has observed in comparable situations.

The normative basis for other ICRC extraconventional activity is amorphous. In the famous Zerka affair, involving the hijacking of three airplanes to the Jordianian desert in 1970, and in kidnappings by the Tupamaros, urban, left-wing guerrillas in Uruguay, the organization found it difficult not to be manipulated by the political actors, in part because of the absence of a normative basis to anchor its position. It is not, therefore, by accident that the ICRC has recently sought to keep involvement in extraconventional situations to an absolute and exceptional minimum. [9]

The ICRC's Mediation

The process of mediation can be broken down into four areas: (1) the initial reason for ICRC involvement in a situation; (2) the ICRC's mandate or terms of reference; (3) the actual mediation process of the ICRC; and (4) the result of ICRC activity. In each of these areas we will look at the conventional and extraconventional situations.

Conventional Mediation. The ICRC was the collective founding father of the first Geneva Convention in 1864. From the time it was organized, the ICRC has taken an interest in human rights in armed conflict. Parts of statutes of the International Red Cross reflect this central concern in defining the ICRC's role:

> to undertake the tasks incumbent on it under the Geneva Conventions, to work for the faithful application of these Conventions and to take cognizance of any complaints regarding alleged breaches of the humanitarian Conventions;
>
> to take action in its capacity as a neutral institution, especially in case of war, civil war or internal strife; to endeavour to ensure at all times that the military and civilian victims of such conflicts and of their direct results receive protection and assistance, and to serve, in humanitarian matters, as an intermediary between the parties;
>
> . . .
>
> to work for the continual improvement of humanitarian international law. . . .

Hence, for some 120 years the ICRC has concerned itself with human rights in war. This long history of distinguished service (the ICRC's founder, Henry Dunant, was the first winner of the Nobel Peace Prize and the ICRC recently received the U.N. prize for human rights) is reflected in its mention in the 1949 Geneva Conventions and 1977 Protocols, despite the fact that the ICRC is, from the Swiss juridical point of view, a private, Swiss association.

The essential point is that in principle the ICRC is almost universally regarded as having some role to play in wars. Its history and its standing in international law confirm it as a neutral humanitarian actor in armed conflicts.

However, two caveats about ICRC involvement in wars are warranted. First, while the ICRC is widely regarded as having a role to play in wars, in any particular war the ICRC may be unwelcome. Thus, some fighting parties, while not contesting the historical and legal position of the ICRC, protest its involvement in specific situations, based on the rationale that there is no armed conflict extant in the formal sense. Hence, the ICRC is rejected on technical grounds. Marxist states have frequently used this and other ration-

ales. For example, the Soviet Union has not agreed that
its troops are in an armed conflict in Afghanistan;
moreover, the Karmal government did not permit the ICRC
to operate in Afghanistan after the summer of 1980.
North Vietnamese authorities refused to allow ICRC
representatives to see detained U.S. military personnel.
The present government of Ethiopia refuses to admit that
it is engaged in an internal war in Eritrea and thus
refuses to allow ICRC access to that area from Ethiopian
territory.

An exception is Poland, which has permitted ICRC
visits to persons detained under the martial law
declared in December 1981. Like non-Marxist states,
which often reject ICRC intervention under the law of
armed conflict, Poland allowed the ICRC visitation
rights under its right of humanitarian initiative.
Israel in dealing with territories captured in 1967, and
Britain in dealing with Northern Ireland, have permitted
the ICRC to visit certain detainees but have argued that
the law of armed conflict does not apply. [11]

The second caveat pertains to rights and status
conferred on the ICRC at the diplomatic conference which
produced the 1977 Protocols to the Geneva Conventions.
That conference, greatly influenced by Third World
delegations and supported by Marxists, debated several
provisions pertaining to the ICRC. One such provision
involved the right of the ICRC to visit detainees in
internal wars. Another involved the right of the ICRC
to serve as an automatic substitute for Protecting
Powers if they are not appointed within a stated time.
Another involved the right of Red Cross agencies to
provide relief without the consent of the fighting parties. However, compared with the 1949 mandate, there
was no advance for the rights and status of the ICRC. [12]
Hence, while the ICRC is generally accepted in wars,
countries are not eager to expand its rights at the
expense of state prerogatives.

Extraconventional Mediation. The initial reason
for ICRC involvement in extraconventional situations is
more complex. First and most important, the ICRC has
undertaken a process similar to that in situations of
armed conflict with regard to political prisoners. That
is to say, the ICRC has perceived a need to try to protect in a limited way persons not protected in any other
way. It has manifested that concern over a period of
years. Now it is in a position to say to a detaining
authority: We have been accepted by numerous other
authorities for this job; we would like to enter your
area of control for the same humanitarian purposes.

The ICRC has been trying to help political prisoners for about sixty years. The work became more intensive and systematic in the 1950s, however, when colonial
situations in places like Kenya and Cyprus caught the
attention of the ICRC. Increasingly the ICRC noticed

that persons were treated as enemies of the ruling
authorities, yet were not covered by the law of armed
conflict. Thus, then the ICRC perceived that victims of
conflict could benefit from the presence of a humanitarian intermediary, it took the initiative to help them.
As efforts to protect political prisoners increased, the
ICRC tried to systematize its work and specify conditions triggering the exercise of its right of initiative. Moreover, the ICRC adopted the unofficial policy
of visiting regular prisoners in parts of the world
known to have recurring political prisoners so that it
would already have access to prisons at the time of the
next wave of political arrests. Nonetheless, it is
still a "judgment call" by the ICRC as to where it will
get involved. Factors affecting that decision include
reports of brutal treatment or inhumane conditions,
large-scale domestic strife or political instability,
and past patterns of political repression.[13]
     Also affecting the ICRC's judgment about initial
involvement with political prisoners is the prospect of
a successful reply. The ICRC does not always publish
information on this area. Thus, it is suspected that
the ICRC has not made direct approaches to authorities
in places like the Soviet Union and China during the
past few years because it anticipated a negative reaction and feared that such overtures might endanger
conventional actions in Afghanistan or Southeast Asia.
At the same time, the ICRC may be working on indirect
methods such as building better relations with country
Red Cross societies or ministries of health.
     The ICRC's initial involvement in other extracon-
ventional efforts almost defies categorization. In some
hijackings, countries with citizens or property involved
have asked for ICRC intervention. In some kidnappings,
family members, or sometimes National Red Cross societies have asked the ICRC to intervene. Since the ICRC
already has a full agenda working with political prisoners and situations of armed conflict, and has had
problems dealing with hijackings and kidnappings, it now
tries to restrict its involvement in extraconventional
mediation.[14] With hijackings, it has indicated officially that it will try to avoid becoming involved in
negotiations. With political kidnappings as well, the
ICRC has left mediation to governments and international
organizations. The reasons for this restrictive action
are based on Huber's 1941 mandate, a desire to do well
what it is already doing, and a desire to protect the
neutral image of the ICRC against efforts at political
manipulation.
     Thus, in the area of extraconventional activity,
the ICRC generally will be assertive in trying to get
into a situation where it can mediate between political
prisoners and their captors. Otherwise it will wait to
be asked and try to defer to other intermediaries con-

cerning negotiation. After all, individuals in political hijackings and kidnappings are not out of the line
of fire like prisoners of war; such individuals are the
weapons of combat. Hence there is less room for maneuvering without getting involved in factional and ideological politics.

Terms of Reference. When the ICRC mediates
between fighting parties or between protected persons
and ruling authorities in armed conflict, its terms of
reference are based on international law and the ICRC's
own traditions. For example, the right of private
visits with prisoners of war and interned civilians is
specified in the law. · When the ICRC conducts such a
visit and compiles a report on prisoners of war or
civilians interned by a foreign power, by ICRC tradition
that report goes both to the detaining power and to the
power whose national is detained. These reports, in
turn, can lead to further mediation by the ICRC between
belligerents with differing views as to whether legal
requirements have been met. No doubt, in these various
exchanges the ICRC delegates and officials sometimes
offer their views as to what is acceptable and what
needs improvement, or how changes can be made. It also
is known that the ICRC will sometimes not forward a complaint from one party to another if in the judgment of
the ICRC the complaint would be to no avail or would
exacerbate hostility.[15]   Nevertheless, the mandate of
the ICRC in armed conflict is basically established by
law and tradition. This fact accounts for one of the
reasons why the ICRC is an acceptable intermediary.
Belligerents know that the ICRC·will work with medical
and material relief, religious and psychological services, prisoner treatment and communication, observation
of trials, and personnel exchanges.

Some believe that humanitarian efforts lay the
foundation for political agreements--that humanitarian
mediation improves the chances for political mediation
by others. But this is difficult to prove. Argentina
in 1982 may have immediately offered to repatriate captured Britons, and the United Kingdom may have offered
to reciprocate; both of these acts may have been a signal for emphasis on negotiations. But there is no clear
indication that such humanitarian agreement helped
resolve the fundamental political issues in the Falklands crisis. The "spillover" effect of humanitarian
agreement remains an intriguing subject for speculation.

In dealing with political prisoners, the ICRC
tries to set its terms of reference on the basis of
tradition and by analogy to situations of armed conflict. The ICRC would like to visit all political
prisoners privately and regularly and see adequate
attention given to the same humanitarian values which
have been written into the Geneva Conventions and
Protocols. In the world as it is, however, the ICRC

manifests what might be called a floating mandate. Beyond a minimum floor, such as no visits with detaining officials present, it will take what detaining authorities will give, at least initially, and then strive to negotiate the terms of reference to standards of the Geneva Conventions.

Hence, the ICRC may accept some initial limitations on its scope of action. It may agree to see some political prisoners but not others simply because it permits some contact. In Rhodesia under Ian Smith, the ICRC worked with administrative detainees but not those convicted of a political crime. In the Republic of South Africa it was just the reverse. In some Latin American countries the ICRC has been denied access to certain military installations while being allowed into civilian prisons. And in some countries of Africa and Asia the ICRC will initially undertake a very restricted visit to demonstrate to authorities the nature of ICRC activity. Where reports suggest an extremely brutal situation for political prisoners, the ICRC will accept almost any limitation to get a foot in the door the first time. However, the ICRC insists on private visits. Thereafter it will insist on regular visits and seek to broaden its scope of activity over time.

In such cases the ICRC insists on progress in humanitarian matters as the price of its continued presence in a country. The ICRC knows that its presence gives detaining authorities the Red Cross "good housekeeping seal of approval." It also knows that some authorities may try to get that seal without making improvements in detention conditions. The ICRC therefore claims that it is alert to attempts by a shrewd detaining authority to limit its work to only marginal matters.

In extraconventional matters the ICRC has exercised its toughest stance only one time. It terminated visits in South Vietnam during the 1960s because of lack of progress. There have been some situations, as in Portuguese Mozambique, where the ICRC suspended its presence while negotiating an end to torture and mistreatment. But some observers are concerned that the ICRC sometimes becomes trapped in a "one more blanket" mentality, that is, bringing in more blankets to routine political prisoners in the regular jails while not gaining access to important political prisoners. The ICRC may not want to pull out because it is making some progress, but the detaining authorities continue to restrict the ICRC from ensuring that all torture and mistreatment cease. Trying to do the good it can, it is manipulated into routine matters while egregious situations continue beyond its purview. This question of the ICRC's appropriate terms of reference is a moral and political can of worms. One hopes that independent

studies in Argentina, Chile, and El Salvador will shed
light on this perplexing subject.

Process of Mediation

From the preceding discussion of initiation of
ICRC diplomacy and terms of reference, one can see under
what circumstances the ICRC gets involved. The specific
"how" of this humanitarian process depends on each situation. Elsewhere I have described the negotiating process used by the ICRC.[16] It might prove illustrative
here to recall some of the salient events from the
ICRC's involvement in the 1967 to 1970 Nigerian civil
war. Although no one situation perfectly captures the
process of ICRC mediation, the Nigerian case shows
certain recurring themes: the intertwining of humanitarian values and high politics; the mixing of international and national phenomena; and the complexity of
humanitarian mediation. [17]
During the first year or so of the war the ICRC
maintained a neutral image with both fighting parties;
it had access to both leaders, Gowon and Ojukwu, and it
acted without major problems. During this early period
Biafra linked Red Cross material assistance to high
politics, demanding that such assistance not be flown
into Biafra directly from Nigeria; the ICRC successfully
avoided major controversy over this symbolic issue by
flying food and medicine into Biafra on a small scale
from other territory, with a "fly at your own risk"
agreement negotiated with Lagos. After Biafra lost Port
Harcourt, however, the Nigerian blockade resulted in
greatly increased malnutrition in the secessionist
territory. The ICRC increased efforts to get relief
into Biafra even after the original flight agreement was
withdrawn by Lagos. But when the Nigerian air force
shot down an ICRC plane and thus challenged ICRC assertiveness, the ICRC was faced with a choice. It could
either remain assertive, flaunt the new Nigerian policy,
and perhaps damage its future utility in armed conflicts, or it could suspend flights, reduce its help to
starving civilians, and seek a new negotiated arrangement that would preserve its tradition of acting only
with the consent of both parties in a conflict. After a
brief period of public friction with Lagos, the ICRC
basically chose the second course.
In the Nigerian civil war, humanitarian relief was
inextricably linked with the basic political issues of
the war. Would Nigeria or Biafra set the terms for
relief entering the eastern region? Could Biafra use
relief flights to shield arms shipments? The authority
and power of each party was at issue, not just the
starving civilians in the east. The ICRC mediated the
issue as best it could, skirting the political dimen-

sions. Even when Lagos retracted its original "fly at your own risk" permission, the ICRC continued its flights because of private assurances from Nigerian officials. But ICRC flights created a glaring hole in the Nigerian blockade that the Lagos hawks finally decided to close. At that point the ICRC ceased its flirtation with being a revolutionary humanitarian actor and reverted to its more traditional style of acting only with the consent of the parties involved in the conflict. Since Biafra never agreed to relief under rules set by Nigeria, the ICRC did not play a major role during the final months of the war.

In this war, both parties saw humanitarian relief as a political subject of great importance. Thus, the ICRC found itself at the center of negotiations about the war. It was in touch with various governments involved and was itself the target of much diplomacy and many public relations campaigns. If at times the ICRC seemed to display a pro-Biafra slant, and if at times it seemed impervious to Nigerian sensitivities and interests, this war may have proven to be the anvil upon which a politically more sophisticated institution was hammered out. Current officials of the ICRC may be displaying the same dynamism and ingenuity displayed by the organization in the Nigerian conflict, but without the difficulties inherent in proceeding too far beyond a negotiated agreement.

Results

The Nigerian case study appropriately leads to a discussion of the results of ICRC mediation. That case study reminds us of two standards for the evaluation of ICRC activity whether conventional or extraconventional: (1) what did the ICRC help achieve in a particular situation; and (2) what did the ICRC achieve in reference to future needs?

According to some observers, the ICRC never achieves enough in a particular situation precisely because it desires future utility. ICRC neutrality and discretion keep it from being more effective. Since the ICRC usually will not publicly criticize a party, nor pressure a party into doing what it will not consent to, some regard the ICRC as politically naive and often ineffective.

ICRC operating philosophy is based on the position that the present and the future are important and that the ICRC can only be accurately evaluated according to both. It argues that history has demonstrated the need for a permanent organization able to perform the same humanitarian tasks in different situations. Moreover, the ICRC believes that history also shows a certain process in humanitarian standards. Even if one proceeds slowly according to the lowest common denominator among public authorities, the ICRC sees a growing body of international law and a line of diplomatic practice indicating some amelioration of the harshness of war and political conflict. While staying within the bounds of country consent can be frustrating--whether one is speaking of the Nigerian civil war or of Nazi concentration camps--the ICRC maintains that it has a useful and frequently successful function to perform in the world society--especially since other actors exist to pursue other paths in defense of human rights (Amnesty International, Joint Church Aid in the Nigerian war).

There are two sources of "evidence" according to which one can evaluate the position of the ICRC and its critics. One source is the diplomatic record of events. This record is, for the most part, locked within the archives of the ICRC, the restricted documents of states, and the memories of nonstate actors. In principle we do not have access to this material and those historians who do gain access may not ask the questions we are discussing.[18] Thus, we are left with the occasional leak to the press or the exceptional academic study based on direct observation and interviews with participants.[19] This first source of evidence is therefore quite small and probably indeterminate about the outcomes of ICRC mediation of humanitarian issues.

The second source of "evidence" is attitudinal: What do informed observers think of ICRC success, despite the actual record? Here again the body of evidence is not large. The International Red Cross itself made some effort during the 1970s to find out what government officials, Red Cross workers, and others thought of the various Red Cross agencies and programs.[20] This unscientific survey gave relatively high ratings to the ICRC and its work to protect the rights of prisoners of war and others. Perhaps the better indicator of respect for the ICRC is its actual involvement in armed conflict and situations of political detention. Respect by authorities seems to be very general, but permission given by Polish authorities to visit detainees there in 1982 may possibly indicate increased ICRC acceptability in Eastern Europe.

Elsewhere I have tried to compile a balance sheet of the accomplishments and failures of the ICRC in recent situations of internal war and situations of political detention.[21] There are both pluses and minuses, but my overall conclusion is that the human rights of war victims and political prisoners would be protected less well if the ICRC did not exist. As Telford Taylor noted, if it were not regarded as wrong to bomb military hospitals, they would be bombed all of the time instead of only some of the time.[22] The ICRC has had some success, and some is better than nothing.

Conclusion

In this chapter I have attempted to demonstrate that the ICRC does engage in humanitarian mediation even while trying to avoid more general political mediation. I also have reminded the reader of the two general areas of ICRC mediation: conventional and extraconventional. This distinction is most important in discussing the initiation and terms of reference of ICRC mediation. Because of the ICRC's long association with the Geneva Conventions for war victims, and now with the 1977 Protocols, it sees itself as having a role to play in armed conflict according to rules laid down in that law. This view is shared by most public authorities. With regard to extraconventional initiation and mandate, the ICRC's position is more flexible, and its effort on behalf of political prisoners is growing but less firmly established in the view of public authorities.

The overall process of ICRC mediation can be described in the abstract, but precise analysis requires a case-by-case study. The Nigerian study indicates a central point about the process of ICRC mediation: the organization usually acts only on the basis of the consent of those involved. Discretion and lack of public pressure characterizes its diplomacy. The few efforts to transcend consent have led retrospectively to a reaffirmation of the ICRC's traditional manner of operation.

In some ways ICRC humanitarian mediation seems similar to other types of mediation. Fundamentally, the ICRC does try to help ameliorate conflicts, leaving the primary responsibility for events to others. Its role as a humanitarian intermediary legitimizes its presence in conflicts. It has certain "carrots" which it can exchange for its presence in a conflict. It implicitly offers an improved image to a fighting or detaining authority. Once admitted to a territory, the ICRC gains a certain amount of leverage vis-a-vis interlocutors: it can threaten--implicitly or explicitly--to issue critical statements or to suspend or terminate its presence. While examples of public criticism, suspensions, and terminations can be found, it is difficult to determine how much the ICRC uses this leverage in day-to-day practice. The ICRC also is like other mediators in that it has an interest in certain types of solutions, not just in any agreement. Not only is it linked to the standards of the Geneva Conventions, but also it must protect its own image in the face of criticism that its minimum standards are too low. If the ICRC is in a country and serious human rights abuse subsequently occurs, the ICRC's own standing as a responsible humanitarian actor is damaged.

In other ways ICRC mediation is unique. Quite clearly, the ICRC does not threaten to join a coalition against one party. Concomitantly, impartiality is a necessary attribute of the ICRC for it to function as an intermediary. Of course, in the process of making an interpretation of what the Geneva Conventions or general human rights norms require, the ICRC can end up in one camp or another. For example, with regard to the Fourth Geneva Convention and territories captured by Israel in 1967, the ICRC could issue certain opinions concerning collective punishments and expulsions which are critical of Israel and supportive of Arab views. But the ICRC's position in these specific conflicts is the result of its concern for human rights as identified in the Fourth Geneva Convention and is not the result of political maneuvering with the Arabs to marshal pressure on Israel. The difference lies in the fundamental motivation of the parties or, if you will, in their calculated positioning. The ICRC also is different from other mediators in that at least some of the time it secures permission to involve itself in a conflict. However, an ICRC presence does not guarantee that the parties are interested in resolving or ameliorating the problems. They may simply wish to deflect criticism of their policies or improve their image. Finally, it can be noted that the ICRC concerns itself with secondary or tertiary issues. If the situation is armed conflict, then winning the conflict is primary; if the situation is one of political unrest, then stability or other political goals are paramount. Since the ICRC does not concern itself with the central political issues of the conflict and since it must be regarded as impartial in order to enter the conflict, possibilities for "humanitarian manipulation" may be limited. The "carrots" already identified are, in the overall picture, minor inducements, and they do not constitute the main course.

An evaluation of the success of ICRC mediation depends upon one's view of the ICRC's philosophy of operation. The ICRC tries to make progress in humanitarian matters only with the consent of public authorities and sometimes on the basis therefore of the lowest common denominator. This involves an incremental approach, requiring time for success. Although this mitigates criticism and thus preserves the role of the ICRC for the future, there are, of course, those who condemn it for not attempting more in a given situation. As in anything, judgments about success depend on prior expectations about how much the ICRC can and should try to accomplish.

Chapter 8: Notes

1.   For a more complete analysis see David P. Forsythe, Humanitarian Politics: The International Committee of the Red Cross (Baltimore: The Johns Hopkins Press, 1977). Statements of fact not otherwise attributed in the present essay are drawn from this source. That mediation can be accurately used in relation to the ICRC is seen in Jacques Freymond and Thierry Hentsch, On Mediating Violence: Armed Political Movements and Humanitarian Principles (Geneva: HEI, 1973).

2.   Max Huber, Croix-Rouge: Quelques Idees, Quelques Problemes (Geneva: Librairie Payot, 1941), 141-142.

3.   Jacques Freymond, "The International Committee of the Red Cross as a Neutral Intermediary," in Maureen R. Berman and Joseph E. Johnson, eds., Unofficial Diplomats (New York: Columbia University Press, 1977), 142.

4.   International Committee of the Red Cross, League of Red Cross Societies, International Red Cross Handbook (Geneva: Red Cross, 1971), 286.

5.   In addition to various Red Cross documents, see the informative memoir by Marcel Junod, Warrior Without Weapons (Geneva: International Committee of the Red Cross, 1982).

6.   ICRC, "Protection des prisonniers de guerre transportes par voie de mer," Revue Internationale de la Croix-Rouge 303 (March 1944): 199-213.

7.   Jean S. Pictet, ed., Commentary: Third Geneva Convention Relative To The Treatment Of Prisoners Of War (Geneva: ICRC, 1960), 602-13.

8.   See further David P. Forsythe, "Who Guards the Guardians: Third Parties and the Law of Armed Conflict," American Journal of International Law 70 (January 1976): 41-61.

9.   ICRC, "Attitude of the Red Cross on the Taking of Hostages," 24th International Red Cross Conference (Manila, November 1981), 1-9.

10.   The details can be found in ICRC, Bulletin 60 (January 1981): 6-7.

11.   The difficulties are especially evident in the ongoing situation in the Middle East, where the ICRC and the government of Israel differed over the applicability and requirements of the Fourth Geneva Convention of 1949 which pertains to occupied territories and the civilians therein.

12. In addition to n.8, see David P. Forsythe, "Legal Management of Internal War," American Journal of International Law 72 (April 1978): 272-95.

13. An important source on this subject is Jacques Moreillon, Le CICR et Detenus Politiques (Lausanne: L'age d'homme, 1973). Moreillon is an official of the ICRC.

14. See n.9.

15. ICRC, "Action by the ICRC in the Event of Breaches of International Humanitarian Law," International Review of the Red Cross 221 (March-April 1981): 76-83.

16. Forsythe, "The Red Cross as Transnational Movement," International Organization 30 (Autumn 1976): 607-30.

17. Especially useful for present purposes is Thierry Hentsch, Face au Blocus (Geneva, HEI, 1973). Hentsch was on the staff of an ICRC official.

18. I am thinking here of official histories of the ICRC, such as the one by Pierre Boissier, Histoire du Comite International de la Croix-Rouge (Paris: Plon, 1963).

19. An analytic example is that of the book by the former acting president of the ICRC, Jacques Freymond, Guerres, Revolutions, Croix-Rouge (Geneva, HEI, 1976). The ICRC will publish one of its prison reports when the detaining authority publishes only a part of a series of reports or misrepresents an ICRC report. This occurred, for example, when the Islamic Republic of Iran partially published ICRC reports about the shah's prisons. It is rare for a complete prison report or other document to be leaked to the press. This did happen recently, however, with regard to an ICRC prison report on Uruguay, apparently by an Uruguayan official.

20. Richard Magat, As Others See Us: Views on Red Cross, Background Paper 6, Joint Committee for the Reappraisal of the Role of the Red Cross (Geneva: Henri Dunant Institute, 1975).

21. David P. Forsythe, "Human Rights and Internal Conflicts: Trends and Recent Developments," California Western International Law Journal 12 (Spring 1982): 287-304.

22. Taylor, Nuremberg and Vietnam: An American Tragedy (Chicago: Quadrangle, 1970), 40.

CONCLUSION: MEDIATION IN THEORY AND PRACTICE

I. William Zartman and Saadia Touval

The common theme in this volume is the mediator's con-tribution to conflict resolution, especially to the successful conclusion of agreements between parties. The cases vary greatly, of course. There are different kinds and combinations of actors: the principals in the conflict are sometimes great powers, and sometimes medium or small states. The mediators can be super-powers, medium states, regional international organi-zations, or humanitarian international organizations. The issues also vary. Some involve a party's self-image, identity, or ideology, and thus concern "core values"; others have to do with vital interests related to national or regional security. Other issues, less vital, are nevertheless important enough to be hotly contested and not given up easily. Political contexts also vary; some take place within a compatible ideolo-gical and cultural environment, while in others, the disputing parties hail from rival or even inimical ideological persuasions and political groupings. Such variety holds promise for fruitful lessons for students of international affairs, particularly regarding struc-tural factors (actors, issues, motives), its qualities (impartiality, prestige, power), and the dynamics involved in mediation interaction.

Motives and Interests

Why do third parties take it upon themselves to mediate? When--under what circumstances--do they choose to do so? How do their interests affect their accepta-bility in a mediating role and their ability to persuade the principal parties to assent to a compromise agreement?

The cases discussed in this book illustrate both
categories of motives (defensive and expansionist). The
international organizations--the OAU, OAS, and ICRC--
mediated basically because it was their raison d'être.
But the regional organizations (OAU and OAS) also become
involved for defensive purposes: Their own involvement
reduced opportunities for external intervention and
interference within their regions. The OAS has traditionally been jealous of its nearly exclusive role in
Latin America, and the OAU's interest in mediation is
inspired, in part, by the desire to reduce superpower
involvement, which would intensify the cold war struggle
in Africa.

The interest of superpowers in mediation appears
inspired by the mixture of defensive and expansionist
motives.   United States mediation in the Rhodesia/
Zimbabwe conflict and Soviet mediation in the conflict
between India and Pakistan are good examples of this.
The United States feared that the newly independent
Zimbabwe provided opportunities for the Soviet Union to
gain influence by supporting the African nationalists.
But because the African groups concerned were already
politically close to the Soviet Union and China, one can
interpret American mediation as an attempt to win over,
or at least improve, relations with these groups,
instead of abandoning them to the exclusive influence of
its political rivals. Soviet mediation between India
and Pakistan was inspired, in part, by the USSR's desire
to improve its relations with Pakistan, which hitherto
had been on far better terms with the United States and
China than with the Soviet Union.   It also sought to
build up its prestige and to establish a precedent that
might help it to justify future involvement in the
affairs of the region. At the same time, the Soviets
had important defensive reasons to intervene: The
Indo-Pakistan conflict provided an opportunity for China
to extend its influence in Pakistan, and thus to establish its presence on the USSR's southern borders.   If
the Soviets could diminish the likelihood of conflict,
China's influence there would be curtailed.

Mediation by the medium-sized states appears to
have been motivated largely by the desire to enhance
their influence and prestige.   Egyptian and Algerian
mediation between Iran and Iraq appears to have been
motivated by their desire to prove their usefulness to
both belligerents, and by a feeling that each had a
role--a calling--of mediation among nations. Algerian
mediation for the United States and Iran seems to have
been inspired to a large extent by the hope that it
would generate goodwill toward Algeria among the
American public, and thus help to improve Algerian-
American relations.   Although we do not have direct
evidence to this effect, it is probable that the
Algerian desire to improve relations with the United

States was related to American support for Algeria's adversary, Morocco, which was engaged in the Sahara against the Algerian-supported Polisario movement. The attempts of Egypt and Algeria to enhance their international standing by means of mediation are not unique. India attempted to mediate a conflict involving the United States, the Soviet Union, and China in the 1950s; President Nkrumah of Ghana tried to mediate in the Vietnam War in 1965-66; Romania also played an intermediary role in that conflict and in American-Soviet and Arab-Israeli relations. There should be little wonder that small and medium-sized states seek to enhance their international standing by assuming the role of mediator--they have few ways in which to do so. Moreover, mediating often saves them from having to take sides when pressed to do so in a conflict.

While many states may occasionally become mediators, the United States often finds itself "condemned" to play this role (Stephen Low's phrase in Chapter 3). Because it fears that conflicts give the Soviet Union opportunities to intervene and expand its influence, the United States often seeks to dampen conflicts; mediation is often a convenient instrument to that end. Regardless of the Soviet Union, the United States, because of its power and prestige, is often solicited for support by smaller states engaged in conflicts, and is challenged to prove the value of its friendship. Pressed by its friends for support, and always fearful that support for one side in a local conflict will throw the other into the Soviets' embrace, the United States apparently often finds that the least risky course is mediation. (A number of examples since 1946 come readily to mind: between the Arab states and Israel since 1949; between Britain and Iran in 1950; Holland and Indonesia; the various Lebanese factions in 1958 and again since 1982; Italy and Yugoslavia over Trieste; Greeks and Turks in Cyprus; white and black Africans in Rhodesia/Zimbabwe; South Africa and the black Africans over Namibia; and Britain and Argentina over the Falklands/Malvinas.)

Assuming, like the United States, that mediation is "the least risky course" does not mean that it is entirely devoid of risk. Like any other negotiation, mediation may entail friction and may fail. It could damage the mediator's relations with one or both disputing parties. Failure could also be damaging to the mediator's prestige generally with respect to other audiences. On occasion, it could harm the incumbent leader's standing in domestic politics. Had the Soviet Union failed at Tashkent, its prestige probably would have been hurt. Had President Carter failed to bring about an Egyptian-Israeli agreement at Camp David in 1978, American relations with both parties would have been damaged, and Carter's standing, both domestically and internationally, would have been harmed. Yet, compared to some other instruments of power politics, the risks and costs of mediation are relatively low.

A mediator's success in furthering its power-political interests does not necessarily translate into success in promoting agreement between the disputants. An example of a double success is the improvement of Zimbabwe's relations with the West following the successful mediation--despite its rulers' ideological sympathy with the Communist bloc. It is possible that Algerian relations with the United States would have seen a significant turn for the better as a consequence of its mediation in the hostage crisis. But, as Gary Sick observes in Chapter 1, "the Algerians were in some measure cheated out of their triumph by the arrival of the Reagan administration."

The Disputing Parties' Motives

The motives of the disputants in seeking or accepting mediation also vary. The most obvious motive is a disputant's desire for a face-saving way out of a conflict. In such situations, negotiations through an intermediary may help protect a party's prestige. The desire for a settlement implies the need to make concessions, and the party may feel that making concessions through a mediator is less harmful to its reputation and future bargaining position than conceding to the adversary in direct negotiations. This seems to have been the case in both the Iran-Iraq dispute, and in the U.S.-Iranian dispute over the hostages and the frozen Iranian assets.

An interesting question, of course, is what brings governments to change course in mid-conflict, and to replace a confrontational approach with accommodation. Such shifts may be explained by recalculations of costs and benefits on the part of a disputant. For instance, Iran's readiness to negotiate a compromise settlement with the United States over the hostages and Iranian assets, and its eagerness to negotiate a new boundary with Iraq while dropping the Kurdish cause came from such calculations. Decisions to arrive at compromises in Zimbabwe and Namibia are also good examples. Another possibility--compatible with the cost/benefit calculations--points to a policy crisis. The party is confronted by the difficult choice of having to either escalate its military effort or to make concessions with the view toward concluding an agreement. As explained by Diana Lieb, the 1975 mediation between Iran and Iraq was brought about by such a crisis. Israel faced a similar dilemma in 1970 when it decided to accept American mediation for a ceasefire to end the war of attrition. Would-be mediators presumably can generate awareness of such policy dilemmas among the parties.

But there is no evidence that the mediator played such a role in the cases discussed in this book.

The India-Pakistan case and the Zimbabwe case give more complex illustrations. The African Front-line states and the Zimbabwe nationalists were interested in mediation as a means of achieving their goal, not for seeking an accommodation with their adversary. The Rhodesian whites, for their part, concluded that it would be less harmful for them to accept American mediation than to reject it, and they believed the United States had sufficient influence with the Front-line States to change the Patriotic Front's positions. They may have realized that they were fighting for a lost cause, especially after South Africa's policy shift. So, it is reasonable to assume that they concluded it was better to negotiate for capitulation terms while they were still strong through the mediation of a Tory government in Britain and a Republican administration in Washington than to postpone negotiations on the terms to a time when circumstances might be less favorable.

In the Indo-Pakistan conflict, Pakistan apparently perceived an opportunity to improve relations with India's principal backer, and thus to weaken Soviet support for India. India probably recognized the risks that Soviet mediation entailed. But India's acceptance suggests it concluded that it would be more harmful for Indo-Soviet relations to reject the Soviet interventiony than to accept it. (A similar pattern can be discerned in Arab interest in U.S. mediation of its conflict with Israel, and Israel's acceptance of such mediation.)

The parties acceptance of mediation by international organizations occurs for somewhat different reasons. Disputing parties often look to international organizations for their ability to bestow normative approval rather than for their ability to influence the adversary or to arrange for a satisfactory compromise. This is most pronounced in the case of the ICRC. As pointed out in Chapter 7 by David Forsythe, the ICRC's ability to offer an improved image to a fighting or detaining country can be a powerful incentive for the parties to accept its presence and services and to accede to its proposals.

Impartiality

As is already evident from the introduction, mediators do not have to be perceived as impartial in order to be acceptable or influential. Instead, acceptability is determined by power-political considerations--by the expected consequences of acceptance or rejection--not by perceptions of impartiality. Successful mediation is achieved not so much by the mediator's objectivity but,

rather, by the interests and capabilities of all participants, the mediator included.

Thus, Pakistan accepted the Soviet Union as a
mediator despite the Soviets' close relationship with
India. What probably influenced Pakistan's attitude was
its perception that the Soviets were concerned about the
growing cooperation between Pakistan and China and were
therefore motivated to improve their own relations with
Pakistan. Within the context of bargaining on such
implicit terms, Soviet mediation seemed acceptable, if
not entirely promising. Algeria was accepted by the
United States to mediate in its dispute with Iran not
because it was considered impartial. On the contrary,
Algeria's access to people close to Khomeini is what
rendered its success more likely in negotiating the
release of the hostages.

Even in the case of the international organiza-
tions--whose acceptability is the subject of a precom-
mitment by member states--mediation of disputes is not
automatic. Wolfers notes in Chapter 6 that when the OAU
establishes a commission to mediate a dispute, the consultation procedures provide the parties an implicit say
in the commission's makeup. The outcome may be a balanced slate. This is not the same as an impartial commission, because members are likely to seek to protect
the interests of their friends, rather than to compose
an impartial commission.

The ICRC, however, considers impartiality to be a
condition for effective mediation. Nevertheless, the
acceptability of ICRC mediation is another matter. To
quote Forsythe: "In principle, the ICRC is almost universally regarded as having some role to play in wars,"
however, "in any particular war, the ICRC may be unwelcome" (p. 238). What sometimes concerns states is not
whether the ICRC will perform its humanitarian functions
objectively, but whether the legal framework of its
involvement might not adversely affect the interests of
the parties. Thus, the legal aspects of ICRC involvement are sometimes subject to negotiation, and the terms
of its involvement are influenced more by their probable
effect on the parties' political interests than by
perceptions of the ICRC's impartiality.

By arguing that, as a rule, third parties need not
be perceived as impartial to be acceptable mediators, we
do not wish to suggest that a mediator can support one
party to a dispute without risking the loss of the
other's cooperation. Mediators must constantly be on
guard lest their behavior create suspicions that detract
from their effectiveness. But, depending on the circumstances, they do have some latitude in this regard.

This latitude may go so far as to enable them to
express their preference regarding the outcome of the
negotiation. A few of the cases discussed in this book
demonstrate that this is indeed possible, and that even

when such preferences are known, they do not preclude successful mediation. In the Zimbabwe and Namibia negotiations, the United States was not indifferent to the nature of the settlement. Its position was that the outcome must open the way for majority rule. Yet, although this meant that the United States basically supported the African position and, by implication, sought to eliminate the white Rhodesians as political actors, U.S. mediation was nevertheless accepted by the whites when it was seen as getting them out of a no-win situation and as securing certain lesser advantages.

The mediator may have two different "partialities" that balance each other only in the aggregate. Often a mediator, motivated by concern for its own position in the area, seeks to intervene only to maintain close ties with one side while improving ties with the other. We are told that Kosygin was neutral at Tashkent. But, in the negotiations between Pakistan and India, the USSR and India had good relations which neither wanted to jeopardize, and (if we accept the assumption that one Soviet motive was to inhibit the growth of Chinese-Pakistan relations), in addition to which the Soviets sought an outcome wherein Pakistan would lose interest in China. Thus we see that Kosygin had two apparently partial motives, yet was able to conclude negotiations successfully. If one of Egypt's motives in mediating the Iran-Iraq dispute was to improve relations with the shah, then clearly the fulfillment of its goals depended on how much it supported the Iranian position. If, by mediating for Iran and the United States in 1980 Algeria hoped to improve relations with the United States, then Algeria had to work for an outcome that would be satisfactory enough to the U.S. to win American goodwill for Algeria.

An interest in specific outcomes occurs quite often in mediations sponsored by international organizations. The ICRC, OAU, and OAS all seek specific solutions to disputes, not just agreements. They try to promote solutions that can be interpreted as compatible with the standards of the Geneva Conventions and of their charters, respectively, and that protect their image as a guardian of these standards. Indeed, they can condemn a member state's deviation from these standards in order to enforce them.

As for the mediator's influence, it, too, is not derived from its perceived impartiality. On the contrary, the Algerian mediation for Iran and the United States suggests that a bias in favor of one party--implying an ability to influence that party--does not necessarily detract from its influence upon the other. On the contrary, the closeness that implies a possibility to "deliver" its friend may stimulate the other party's cooperativeness. The Africans' suspicions about British and American relations and sympathies with the

white Rhodesians made the prospect of British and
American mediation more promising for them, and
stimulated their cooperation.

Timing and Synchronization

From our premise that mediators are motivated by
self-interest, it follows that they will not intervene
automatically but only when they think a conflict
threatens their interests, or when they perceive an
opportunity to advance them.

International organizations initiate mediation
somewhat differently than states. International organizations are required to intervene whenever certain situ-
ations--defined in their charters--occur. In theory,
their mediating services are permanently available.
States, on the other hand, are not permanently on-call
as mediators. But neither, as it turns out, are international organizations. Their charters and rules
require someone to take the initiative; and, by definition, mediation requires the consent and cooperation of
the parties involved.

In the instances examined in this volume, the ICRC
provides the closest thing to automatic intervention.
However, its effectiveness still depends upon the
cooperation of the parties. That was obtained for the
most part through the bargaining power of the ICRC
itself--its ability to confer upon the parties "the seal
of Good Housekeeping" (Forsythe's phrase). Since the
activities of the ICRC seldom touch upon the actors'
vital interests and core values, the promise of moral
approval seems in most cases sufficient to induce
cooperation and concessions.

Because the OAU and OAS are intergovernmental
organizations, their activation requires the involvement
of governmental representatives. Governments are stimulated to join mediation committees, in part, because a
conflict threatens regional solidarity, a value they
consider useful and worth defending. Yet, we often find
neighbors of the principal parties in mediating bodies,
suggesting that the conflict threatened the mediator's
security, or that the special relationship which neighbors have with each other required intervention. It is
also possible that a third party may wish to take advantage of the neighbor's difficulty and seek a mediating
role in order to alter its relationship with that neighbor in some favorable way. On at least one occasion,
for instance, the Algerian-Moroccan conflict, mediation
was induced by the mediator's vital interest in the
principle at issue--the legitimacy of inherited boun-
daries--and the precedent that the outcome of the conflict might create. Regional organizations, it must be
remembered, are groups of states, each with its inter-

ests, and are not autonomous, corporate actors in their
own right.

Looking at the stimuli for mediation by states, it
is noteworthy that for the seventeen years during which
the Indo-Pakistani conflict festered prior to 1965, the
Soviet Union was not moved to mediate. Specific conditions in 1965--American and British inactivity, and the
developing relationship between Pakistan and China--are
what induced Soviet mediation and made it possible. The
United States was not moved to mediate in the Rhodesian
conflict for eleven years--since the Unilateral Declaration of Independence in 1965 until 1976. What probably stimulated the United States in 1976 was the collapse of Portuguese rule in two neighboring states and
the Soviet success in Angola, which heightened awareness
of the threat to U.S. interests posed by the continued
conflict over Rhodesia. Recent developments in the Middle East, where American mediation from 1973 to 1975
succeeded in reducing tensions and weaking Soviet influence, may also have encouraged Secretary Kissinger to
embark on this initiative. Egyptian and Algerian mediation in the Iran-Iraq conflict was induced by the recognition that both Iran and Iraq were considering the
desirability of a settlement, and that this presented an
opportunity to the mediators, as already described
above. The Algerian mediation between Iran and the
United States was apparently also stimulated by
Algeria's impression that Iran was willing to consider
some compromise, and that this presented certain opportunities for Algerian diplomacy.

Thus, the mediator's initial action is stimulated
by two different developments: the mediator's perception of possible flexibility in the parties' attitudes,
and by a threatened turn of events inimical to the
interests of the mediator. In other words, a mediator
can be compelled to act when it perceives that the
moment is propitious for an agreed outcome or that only
such action will preserve its own interests. Thus,
mediation is sometimes induced solely by an evaluation
that the intervention is desirable or necessary for the
would-be mediator, without there being reasons to
believe that the moment is propitious for a negotiated
settlement. Together, however, the two provide the
optimal conditions for mediation.

It is advantageous to get the mediation process
started, even if the ripe moment for settlement is not
yet evident. During the initial period (which may last
a while), mediators should position themselves so as to
cultivate access, generate alternatives, and explore
positions. These moves comprise the diagnostic phase of
negotiations coupled with the mediator's efforts to
ensure its own future position. In both Namibia and
Zimbabwe, mediators kept on mediating until the ripe
moment appeared.

Thus, the synchronization of a mediator's efforts with the parties' readiness to compromise is sometimes self-regulated. The perception that the parties are moving toward greater flexibility may stimulate mediation efforts or, alternatively, mediation initiatives may induce flexibility. But such synchronization is by no means assured. Although a third party's expression of its desire to mediate a conflict confronts the parties concerned with new threats and opportunities, it does not follow that it always induces greater flexibility on their part.

When the parties do not become more flexible, or do not become flexible enough, the mediator will either give up, or it may persevere until such time that the parties become more flexible (success), or until he abandons its efforts (failure).

There remains the question of what, apart from the mediator, may induce the parties toward greater flexibility. The cases suggest two situations especially conducive to accommodation: "hurting stalemates," and the dilemma of having to choose between escalation or compromise.

Concepts of Mediation

The experiences reported in the previous chapters bear important lessons for theory and practice. Both areas are at once separate and interrelated--a crucial point, because much of the debate about theory and practice of conflict resolution is wasted in tripping over its own two feet. Theoretical issues are basic to a deeper understanding of the nature of the process, although they may not always directly address the busy practitioner's foremost concerns. Conversely, the major problems of the practitioner may be unimportant or even nonexistent in theory--of little consolation in the heat of the fray or the frustrations of the stalemate. Yet a better theoretical understanding is necessary to provide a sound basis and sharper insights and not in the more abstract process of deriving the proof. And the actions of the practitioner are all that there is to test the propositions of theory, even though the experiments are neither controlled nor replicable and the results are scarcely noise-free.

Two lessons of theoretical or conceptual interest stand out in these case studies; they relate to the nature and to the function of mediation. Conflicting parties, the case studies relate, call on or allow in mediators because they are seeking a better solution to their conflict than they are able to achieve alone. One positive aspect of the exercise is that each party is willing to entertain proposals that appear to have a net benefit greater than its current unilateral attempts can achieve. The mediator's role is to invent such out-

comes, to promote them if they have already been identified, or to make them possible if the two "halves" of
the negotiating front (as then perceived) do not yet
overlap to permit a jointly agreeable outcome. The limitation on the exercise is that neither party wants the
mediator to side with the other in bringing about an
opposing solution, nor does it want a third solution
imposed on it by the mediator. There is no need to go
further to fathom the nature of the mediator's role; all
of its ramifications are elaborations on this basic
theme, and the rest of the debate on mediation has
nothing to do with the mediator, but with what he does.

The ambivalence for the theorists and the trap for
the practitioners come from the fact that a great deal
of power for the mediator comes precisely from the two
areas where he is forbidden to tread. That is, the
mediator's power comes first from his ability to invent,
convey, and facilitate a jointly agreeable outcome preferable to either party's current unilateral solutions,
and second from his ability to threaten a worse outcome
either by siding with the other party or by imposing his
own solution. Yet by threatening to become a party if
his role as a mediator is not accepted, the mediator
weakens his primary role. In more conceptual terms, the
mediator's role is to enhance the process of negotiation
as a decision-making mode. The limits on that role are
found in the other two modes of decision-making--coali-
tion and judication. The first is the process of making
a choice by aggregation, such as voting, alliances, auc-
tioning, etc., depending on whether the items aggregated
are the number of parties themselves or some other quality they possess such as armies or money. When the
mediator threatens to form a coalition and is perceived
as taking sides, it leaves its mediating role. The
other mode is the hierarchical process of authoritative
choice, as practiced by executives, judges, and gen-
erals. When the mediator attempts to impose its own
solution, it departs from the negotiating role and loses
its welcome and legitimacy, even though a source of its
power may be the threat of taking the solution into its
own hands. In sum, the practical limitations on the
mediator's power are mirrored by the theoretical
limitations on its role, but they also strengthen its
role to the extent that they are implicitly understood.

Similarly, the function of mediation can be
related to the major conceptual conundrum of the negotiation process, the "Toughness Dilemma." In choosing
his tactics, the negotiator is torn between toughness
and softness, the former allowing him to defend his
positions but reducing chances of agreement, the latter
improving the chances of agreement but at the cost of
his positions. Because the negotiator is interested in
gaining agreement as close to his own positions as
possible, the dilemma is patent and has given rise to a

large body of literature. Softness and toughness can be thought of as referring to decisions whether to negotiate or not, to conciliatory vs. hardline positions, or to rates of concession, or even more broadly to personality types; the dilemma remains the same. A great advance provided by the theoretical literature comes with the notion that the answer to the dilemma is not an absolute or even a mix of the two stances, but rather a reactive response. Toughness and softness are appropriate responses at particular times in the negotiating process, reactions to particular moves. Yet some of this understanding, important as it is in grasping the nature of the negotiation process, only reinforces the Toughness Dilemma. Toughness is appropriate at the outset of negotiations, as the parties outline their positions, and at the end, to hold on to or improve an agreement, but softness is appropriate in the middle. Toughness is appropriate to demand and softness to reward; toughness is the appropriate response to an opponent's tough strategy and softness to a soft strategy. The heart of the dilemma remains, restated: not when to be tough, but when to shift from toughness to softness.

Mediation provides an answer to this dilemma. The mediator can convey changes in position as a third party without showing weakness, he can "hold" concessions until matched by the other side, he can be the repository of concession-producing trust by the parties in the absence of trust between them, he can be the provisional initiator of the search for new positions and formulas for agreement while the parties are ostensibly reaffirming their original positions. In all of the cases studied, the mediator provided the break in the hardline confrontation between the parties and explored its implications, before the parties actually began their own movement.

The mediator in fact carries on two sets of negotiations more or less simultaneously. He negotiates with himself to find appropriate solutions, and he negotiates with the two parties to get their adherence. The first he is able to do efficiently because he does not share the inhibitions provided by the parties' allegiance to their individual positions, and he is motivated by his own interest in a solution. A mediator can see past inhibitions and through to solutions more easily than parties for this reason, although it is important for him to spend a lot of time with the parties to make sure that he understands fully the parties' positions, both apparent and underlying. The second he is able to do largely by warning the parties about the unpleasant consequences inherent in the pursuit of unilateral solutions, as the testimony of Henry Kissinger, Mario Cuomo, and many other mediators shows. Mediators can bring out the implications of the parties'

courses more effectively than anyone else, since they
are arguing less for a particular solution than for
participation in a collective search for a joint
solution, but at the same time they can offer a way out
of the unpleasant consequences they are depicting.

Practitioners' Problems of Leverage

Although these issues have practical significance,
they are not the issues that most preoccupy mediators.
As these cases show, the most disturbing and even annoy-
ing problem for mediators is the matter of leverage.
The problem is understandable. Without leverage, the
mediator is left not merely to his own wits, but, worse,
to the mercy of the pressures of the conflict (which
eventually could make mediation unnecessary, in one way
or another), and of the parties' perceived need for his
services.
      As already seen, parties accept the services of a
mediator to the extent that they find him likely to
provide a favorable way out of the conflict, but if he
pushes that function too far, he loses his leverage by
becoming a would-be arbitrator. Thus, contrary to the
common image of mediation, the mediator is rarely
"hired" by the parties; if he were, he would at least
have a contract to perform the job of finding a solution
to the conflict. Instead, he is usually more interested
than the parties in ending the conflict, because he
fears the alternative for his own interests more than
they do for theirs. Parties have a stake in winning.
As a result, the mediator is frequently more interested
in mediation than are the parties, leaving him little
leverage. They criticize him for meddling in their
conflict and for not producing results that they find
attractive; they welcome him into the fray only to the
extent that he has leverage over the other party, and
each berates him for trying to exert it.
      There are only three sources of leverage, although
each category may cover a number of different manifestations. Leverage comes, first, from the parties' need
for a solution that the mediator can provide; second,
from the parties' susceptibility to shifting weight that
the mediator can apply; and third, from the parties'
interest in side-payments that the mediator can offer.
The first, the parties' need for a solution, is
extremely fragile and depends purely on the mediator's
persuasive skill in cutting through the noise of the
situation and changing the perceptions of the parties
about the costs and benefits of other situations and
outcomes. It is here that the mediator's role as a
communicator and formulator comes into play; he must
transmit and create information that will help change
the parties' views.

The second, shifting weight, is even more delicate, since the mediator must help balance the parties
in the conflict in such a way as to produce the hurting
stalemate that leads them to see a mediated solution as
the best way out, but do so in such a way that the
parties do not perceive the mediator as actually taking
sides. Shifting weight can be categorized in many ways:
on a spectrum from tangible to intangible actions, such
as arms supplies or U.N. votes; as negative or positive
actions, such as statements or deliveries favorable or
unfavorable to one side; or as present or future
actions, such as condemnation of a present attempt to
change reality during the conflict or condemnation of an
incident or announced policy as an indication of a
future attitude if the conflict were to continue. There
does not seem to be any significant theoretical distinction to be made within these various typologies. Russia
threatened to shift weight away from India in the U.N.
Security Council debate, and Britain threatened to shift
weight toward the internal settlement in Rhodesia.

The third, side-payments, is perhaps less delicate
but can be costly and can imply an ongoing commitment to
the area that the mediator might want to avoid. Side-
payments, of course, should not have the appearance of
buying adherence (which is what they do) but must be
presented as a facilitating aspect of the general settlement. Side-payments are also shifted weight, but in
areas unrelated to conflict itself. Kissinger offered
economic aid to the white Rhodesian settlers. Reagan
offered economic aid to an Angola free of Cubans, and
the OAS and IDB have told conflicting American states
that no development funds would be available until their
conflict was settled.

There are two major practical problems with
leverage not addressed by these distinctions: How to
maximize it, and how to avoid counterproductive reactions. On these subjects, the cases give only limited
insights. If anything, they reflect the anguish of
mediators over the elusiveness of leverage and the
unreasonable expectations of greater power with which
the parties burden them. Leverage, the cases indicate,
comes above all from the need of the parties for a solution they cannot get without the mediator's help. The
perception of that need can be enhanced by the mediator,
but it cannot be created out of nothing. Side-payments
can be useful when the mediation gets stuck, but they
are not a major source of leverage throughout the process, and even at the end, their use is limited. The
first lesson, then, is that the mediator's challenge is
above all one of persuasion, to bring out the parties'
sense of a need for his help. The second lesson is that
the mediator's work is nonetheless at the mercy of the
evolution of the conflict, on a particular conjuncture
of forces that makes his efforts appear like an opportu-

nity for the parties rather than a meddlesome distraction. Yet this lesson leads back to the first, for the mediator cannot merely sit by until the moment ripens and the need is felt with proper force. He must develop that need, arouse it, even anticipate it, so that as the moment ripens the parties will be ready to feel it and seize it.

The second source of leverage, shifting weight, is more delicate to use and more difficult to conceptualize. All that can be given are the limits within which it operates. On one hand, it is a necessary adjunct to mediation that the mediator be willing and expected to use his own country's weight to keep the parties on the mediated or multilateral track. This shift, it must be remembered, has its negative and positive exercises, involving direct pressure on one side or direct support for another. The negative exercise can indeed be counterproductive, if used crudely or as an irritant without direct effect on the conflict. Because the purpose of shifting weight is really designed to increase the first source of leverage--perception of need--pressure that shows the party that it can do without the mediator is pressure without leverage. Negative pressure is designed to block the party's efforts to arrive at its own solution, but not to weaken the party per se; positive shifting of weight is designed to strengthen a party but not to enable it to achieve its own solution at the expense of the mediator and of the other party. This reasoning is based on the notion, which the cases support, that parties come to agreement best when their own, preferred solution is blocked but they themselves are strong. This enables them to make a compromise decision and defend it against internal opposition. This condition, of course, makes mediation even more delicate, because strong opponents are difficult to deal with and are perhaps slower to see that their unilateral solutions are blocked.

There are not many examples of such carrots and sticks in the cases presented herein, and not many more outside. The conventional wisdom on Namibia--that Carter showed that there are no sticks and Reagan showed that there are no carrots--is only half true. The Carter initiative never got to using sticks, but the strategy during the Reagan administration was indeed based on the use of positive inducements toward South Africa--constitutional guarantees, improved relations, and Cuban withdrawal from Angola. It tripped over the third for a long while because it was able to deliver agreement from an Angolan government that was not internally strong enough to make the move. Kosygin in Tashkent, like Kissinger in the Middle East, had the leverage of need, which he used by threatening to call off the mediation. Lord Carrington at Lancaster House threatened to shift weight to one side. The other cases

have little to say about leverage. Some rare examples
of leverage outside the cases studied here come from
Arab-Israeli negotiations, where the United States is
constantly criticized for not pressuring more. One was
the reassessment of U.S. policy in the Middle East in
the summer of 1975, after the breakdown of the second
Sinai disengagement talks; discussions of a possible
Geneva conference, delays in deliver of military mate-
riel, and postponed consideration of Israeli applications for new economic and military aid were all part of
effective leverage.

It is noteworthy that in the cases discussed in
this book, the presence of several mediators did not
detract from their leverage, and may indeed have
strengthened it. Had the mediators competed with each
other, the triangular structure would have been turned
into a polygram, with multiple possibilities for coali-
tions between parties and mediators, reducing, if not
canceling, the mediators' leverage. Yet, this did not
happen. On the contrary, the mediators coordinated
their efforts, thus compounding their leverage. Coordination by the mediators also reflected their ability
to accommodate the many parties and interests affected
by the conflict and by the diplomacy surrounding it.
Yet, competition between mediators and the effects of
such competition are a theoretical and empirical possibility that deserves further scholarly attention.

The Issues

We have observed already in the introductory chapter that "successful mediation" can have many meanings.
That is why we chose as a working definition of successful mediation "a contribution toward a formal agreement
promising the reduction of conflict." Obviously, success defined in this manner does not tell us whether, or
to what extent, the mediator or the parties attained
their power-political objectives.

Success is necessarily related to the issues that
were subject to negotiations. In two cases--Namibia and
Rhodesia/Zimbabwe--the agreement addressed issues that
involved "core values." In all other cases, either the
issues were not perceived as involving "core values" (in
the sense of affecting an actor's existence or identity)
or, when "core values" were involved, the negotiations
circumvented them. However important, the issues in
conflict between Iran and Iraq, the United States and
Iran, all the OAS cases, most of the OAU cases, and all
of the ICRC mediations did not touch upon "core values."
They concerned the normalization of relations after
conflict, support of opposition groups (and
complications arising therefrom), the treatment of
prisoners, or boundary disputes that did not directly
involve an actor's perception of its identity.

In the Indo-Pakistani conflict "core values" were affected, since the dispute over Kashmir concerned their conflicting images of the scope of their national sovereignty and, even more important, the legitimating principle of their nationhood. But these were not the subject of the conclusions at Tashkent. Instead, the agreement was on the question of how to restore normal relations in the aftermath of their recent war, without this being interpreted as if Pakistan had conceded the question of principle. The issue was the restoration of normal relations, not the future of Kashmir. "Core values" were also at issue in two of the OAU mediations. But one of these mediations, in the Nigerian civil war, failed. In the other, between Algeria and Morocco, in which the territorial conflict was related to the principles legitimating the scope of these two nations, this issue was circumvented. What was negotiated and agreed upon were measures for the restoration of normal relations, and procedures for further discussion of the basic issues in dispute.

What is true of negotiations in general--that it is easier to reach agreement on matters that are not considered of vital importance--is true also of mediation. Yet, a significant difference that mediators can make is to help the parties to define the subject of the negotiations in a manner that allows the circumvention of vital issues on which no compromise is possible. In such cases, mediation helps to <u>reduce</u> conflicts, or to "<u>manage</u>" them, even if it does not resolve or eliminate them.

Still, the mediation in the Namibian and Rhodesian/Zimbabwe conflicts raises the question whether, and if so how, mediation can help <u>resolve</u> conflicts in which "core values" are involved. In this latter conflict, the mediation addressed itself to the incompatible existential goals of the parties: whether the white minority's idea of Rhodesia would survive, or whether the black majority's aspiration to establish the black African state of Zimbabwe, governed by the black African population, would be realized. The eventual agreement actually <u>resolved</u> this conflict. It was not a compromise between these incompatible goals. Rather, it was an agreement by which the white minority abandoned its goal and agreed to redefine the issue as one concerning the protection of their basic democratic rights as citizens. The Namibian effort in its Reagan phase also tried to effect this specific redefinition. But these two mediations, in which the mediators helped resolve a conflict in which "core values" were at issue, seem to have been exceptions, attributable to particular circumstances.

Whether dealing with core or other values, the mediator can help the parties to arrive at a solution by leading them to see the conflict as merely a means to get something else rather than a direct zero-sum clash over the primary contested item. The hostages' fate would be mediated once they had served the Iranians' internal political purposes and could be bargained against the frozen assets. Lord Carrington understood that he could put together an agreement based on the Rhodesian Front's demands for a constitution and the Patriotic Front's demands for a free and fair election. Mediation between Iran and Iraq became possible when the shah was able to give up the Kurdish war for a settlement on the Shatt al-Arab. The Western Five mediators (mainly the United States) tried to turn the Namibian impasse into a means for South Africa to see the Cubans leave Angola, rather than a zero-sum encounter on Namibia alone. Redefining the issues and enlarging the field of concern to include items that can be traded against each other are often the keys to a mediator's success and they often require both persistence and imagination.

In the broadest sense, even where basic issues were resolved, the mediation provided the conditions in which the parties could learn to live together, but it did not effect any deep reconciliation of the parties or a restructuring of their perceptions of each other.

For this reason, the mediator should keep as firm a hand as possible on the procedures of settlement while helping the parties work out the substance of the solution. A mediator's physical presence in otherwise bilateral sessions between the conflicting parties, and his follow-through as an observer of any agreement's implementation are important adjuncts to his role as a communicator and builder of trust. Left to their own devices, the parties may fall out of an agreement just as it is being made or implemented.

But the mediator cannot chaperone forever, nor can he be expected to reorient all the perceptions underlying the conflict--often perceptions that have been building for years and even centuries. Successful though they were, the mediations did not change the basic distrust between Iran and Iraq, America and Iran, some blacks and whites in Zimbabwe, Indians and Pakistanis, Moroccans and Algerians, Somalis and Ethiopians, among others. But to belittle their accomplishments on this account would be to measure them by an inhuman standard. Mediations succeed on three attainable levels. They can manage a conflict by dampening or removing its violent means and manifestations. They can resolve a conflict by arranging tradeoffs among its immediate causes and issues. They can provide mechanisms for handling future outbreaks of conflict among still-suspicious and troubled parties. Any of these is praiseworthy and shows skill; any combination is impressive.

INDEX